THE MICROWAVE LIBRARY

THE COMPLETE ILLUSTRATED

MICROWAVE COOKBOOK

**ELIZABETH CORNISH
& VERONICA BULL**

THE MICROWAVE LIBRARY

THE COMPLETE ILLUSTRATED

MICROWAVE COOKBOOK

ELIZABETH CORNISH & VERONICA BULL

NEW BURLINGTON BOOKS

THE
MICROWAVE
LIBRARY

A QUINTET BOOK

This edition published in 1990
by New Burlington Books
6 Blundell Street
LONDON N7 9BH

ISBN 1 85348 226 9

This book was designed and produced by
Quintet Publishing Limited
6 Blundell Street
LONDON N7 9BH

Art Director: Peter Bridgewater
Editor: Judith Simons
Photographers: Trevor Wood, Michael Bull
Home Economist: Veronica Bull

Typeset in Great Britain by
Central Southern Typesetters, Eastbourne
Manufactured in Hong Kong by Regent
Publishing Services Limited
Printed in Italy by Fratelli Spada SpA ·

THE MICROWAVE LIBRARY

CONTENTS

*A selection of cookware, some of it specially
designed for the microwave oven, which is
suitable for microwaving.*

1 Thorpak cake dish **2** Thorpak casserole dish
3 Microware freezer dishes **4** Roasting dish
5 Thorpak jug **6** Browning dish **7** Minidishes
(ramekins) **8** Double microwave serving dish
9 Glass loaf pan **10** Glass casserole with lid
11 Cake or soufflé dish **12** Three-section
vegetable dish **13** Browning dish **14** Glass
ovenproof dish

ABOUT THE
MICROWAVE OVEN

IF YOU are new to cooking with
the microwave, the first thing to
do is to read the instruction booklet
supplied with your model. This will
tell you all you need to know about
how your cooker works and how to
operate it.

Microwave cookers work by
emitting concentrated infra red
radiation that penetrates and
therefore heats food much faster
than conventional cookers. They
consequently save considerably on
cooking time.

The microwave is like any other
kitchen appliance that makes life
easier for the cook. Once you are

used to it, which takes remarkably
little time for such a sophisticated
gadget, experience will tell you how
long it will take to cook or reheat a
given dish. If in doubt, always
undercook – you can easily add on
another minute or so.

To familiarize yourself with the
cooker try baking a potato. Scrub the
potato and prick the skin a few times
with a fork. Lay it on a piece of
absorbent kitchen paper and cook on
full power for about 6 minutes for a
175 g/6 oz potato. Stop cooking halfway through to turn the potato over.
A successfully baked potato will
demonstrate how easy microwave
cooking is.

Remember to stir or rearrange
items during cooking or the food
may not be evenly cooked, and

always cover a dish with a lid or cling film (plastic wrap) which you have pierced in two or three places with a knife to make vents through which the steam can escape.

Don't use anything metallic in the microwave, and this includes china decorated with silver or gold leaf. If you want to test if a dish is microwave-proof, put it in the oven next to a cup of water and cook on full for a minute. If the water is hot and the dish stays cool, it is safe to use. If the dish is hotter than the water, avoid using it.

Always prick the skins of vegetables and fish to prevent them from bursting. Eggs should always be pricked for the same reason. Never put an egg in its shell in the microwave – it will explode.

All the recipes in this book are timed for a 700-watt oven, and where the recipe times are not specific, this is to avoid errors. A microwave may be a scientific instrument, but even identical ovens may cook at slightly different rates, and neither cooks nor food can be standardized – no two carrots are the same shape and no two cooks cut them in the same way.

However, the following can be taken as a general guide for ovens with a different power rating from that of the model used in the book. For every minute of cooking time specified in these recipes, add 5 seconds for a 650-watt oven, 10 seconds for a 600-watt oven and 30 seconds for a 500-watt oven. But remember, it is *always* safer to undercook and test.

Crockery, cutlery (flatware, glassware and cookware such as this must NOT be used in a microwave oven.

1 Ceramics with metal decoration 2 Dishes with metal decoration and glazes containing metal 3 Cutlery (silverware or flatware) 4 Metal flan tin and disposable foil bakeware 5 Glassware with metal rim or bands 6 Metal pots and pans 7 Metal bakeware 8 Metal skewers or fondue forks

THE MICROWAVE LIBRARY

COOKING WITH

Soups

AND HORS D'OEUVRES

ELIZABETH CORNISH

SOUPS AND HORS D'OEUVRES

SOUPS and hors d'oeuvres can be prepared ahead of time
for reheating, which in a microwave will not spoil either
their good looks or taste. Some soups and starters can be
assembled and cooked at the last minute, others can be eaten
cold.

When you are cooking with a microwave, it is particularly easy
to plan a menu as much to please the eye as the palate, because
foods keep their natural shapes and colours. This is important
when you are entertaining, as there is nothing more pleasing to
guests than having something really appetizing placed before
them, and nothing more pleasing to a host than an expression
of delighted anticipation – and clean plates at the end of the
meal.

When you're not entertaining, a soup or a starter, or a soup *and*
a starter, can make a whole meal, especially when served with
bread and salad.

Home-made soups, like home-made bread, are a simple luxury
that until recently many cooks could not spare the time to
make. With a microwave, you can enjoy the satisfying flavour
and natural goodness of a soup made from fresh ingredients in
only a little more time than it takes to heat up a tin, or
reconstitute a packet.

There is a soup in this book to suit every occasion and taste,
from delicate cool numbers for summer dinner parties to a
thick fish soup that will leave you wanting only a siesta to follow.

As for starters – there is a wide and interesting range of
appetizers both hot and cold, light and substantial, so that you
will have several choices to complement your main course. For
an elegant late-night supper you could opt simply to serve a
selection of starters, with perhaps fruit and coffee to follow.

CONTENTS

SPINACH AND RICOTTA PANCAKES

SERVES 4 / SET: FULL

Ingredients

1½ cups/175 g/6 oz flour

a pinch of salt

2 eggs

2 cups/425 ml/¾ pt milk

1 tbsp melted butter or oil

SPINACH AND RICOTTA FILLING

1 kg/2 lb fresh spinach

2 tbsp/25 g/1 oz butter

1¼ cups/225 g/8 oz ricotta cheese

salt and freshly ground black pepper

a pinch of nutmeg

Although pancakes can't themselves be made in the microwave, there is no better way of heating up stuffed pancakes so that each one tastes as if it had been freshly made and the edges aren't dry and leathery.

◆ First make the pancakes. Sift the flour with the salt into a bowl, make a well in the middle and break in the eggs. Add the milk slowly, beating to incorporate the flour.

◆ When half the milk has been added, stir in the melted butter or oil and beat until smooth. Add the remaining milk. The batter should be the consistency of thin cream. Leave it to stand for at least 30 minutes.

◆ For the filling, wash the spinach and discard any tough stalks and discoloured leaves.

◆ Put the butter in a large pot and cook for 1 minute until melted. Cram in the spinach, cover and cook for 6 minutes, turning the pot once, until the spinach is soft but still bright emerald green.

◆ Chop the spinach with the ricotta, mixing well, and season with salt, pepper and nutmeg.

◆ Make the pancakes on the hob. Pour a little oil into a heavy based pan and heat until very hot. Stir the batter well and spoon in enough to coat the bottom of the pan. Tilt and jiggle the pan over the heat until the pancake has set, then toss or turn it over with a spatula and cook the other side.

◆ Discard your first pancake as it will be too oily.

◆ Pile the pancakes on a plate as you make them, but don't attempt to keep them hot, or they will dry out.

◆ Divide the filling between the pancakes and roll up. Pack them into an oblong dish, cover with vented cling film (plastic wrap) and cook for 2–3 minutes until hot through.

◆ Serve with tomato sauce (see recipe for Stuffed Cabbage Leaves).

BORLOTTI BEAN SOUP

SERVES 4 / SET: FULL

Ingredients

2 cups/225 g/8 oz soup macaroni

oil

2½ cups/575 ml/1 pt boiling meat stock (broth)

30 ml/2 tbsp tomato pureé (paste)

2 cups/400 g/14 oz canned borlotti beans, drained

salt and freshly ground black pepper

◆ Put the macaroni in a large pot with a little oil and pour over half the stock. Cover and cook for 8 minutes.

◆ Add the tomato purée (paste), diluted in the rest of the stock, and the borlotti beans, cover and cook for 4 minutes.

◆ Season to taste and serve, with grated cheese if liked.

Borlotti Bean Soup

MUSSEL AND POTATO SOUP

SERVES 4 / SET: FULL

Ingredients

7 cups/850 ml/1½ pt mussels

45 ml/3 tbsp oil

1 small glass dry white wine

1 small onion, chopped

1 clove garlic, chopped

2 rashers (strips) bacon, chopped

2½ cups/575 ml/1 pt boiling fish stock (broth) (see recipe for Fish Soup).

1½ cups/225 g/8 oz cooked potato, diced

⅓ cup/75 g/3 oz rice

salt and freshly ground black pepper

◆ Scrub the mussels thoroughly under cold running water and scrape away their beards. Discard any that are broken or damaged.

◆ Put half the oil in a large pot with the wine and cook for 2 minutes, until very hot. Add the mussels. Cover and cook for about 3 minutes, stirring halfway through, until the shells open. Discard any mussels that remain closed.

◆ Remove the mussels from their shells, keeping some shells for decoration. Put mussels and cooking liquor to one side.

◆ Put the remaining oil in the pot with the onion, garlic and bacon, cover and cook for 3 minutes. Add half the fish stock (broth), stir in the cooked potato and rice. Cover and cook for 10 minutes, until the rice is tender.

◆ Stir in the remaining fish stock (broth), add the mussels and their cooking liquor and season to taste.

◆ Serve, decorated with a couple of mussels in their shells if liked.

FISH SOUP

SERVES 4 / SET: FULL

Ingredients

15 ml/1 tbsp olive oil

1 onion, chopped

1 clove garlic, crushed (minced)

½ fennel bulb, chopped

2 large or 4 small tomatoes, skinned and chopped

1 kg/2 lb mixed white fish, cleaned and skinned

10 ml/2 tsp turmeric

2½ cups/575 ml/1 pt boiling water or fish stock (broth), (see below)

salt and freshly ground black pepper

Parmesan cheese

NOTE *To make a fish stock (broth), put the fish trimmings in a large pot, add a bay leaf, a piece each of carrot, celery and onion and pour over 2½ cups/575 ml/1 pt boiling water. Cover and cook in the microwave for 7 minutes, then strain off the stock.*

◆ Put the oil in a large pot and cook for 30 seconds. Stir in the onion, garlic and fennel, cover and cook for 5 minutes.

◆ Add the tomatoes and fish, stir in the turmeric, then pour over the water or stock (broth). Cover and cook for 8–10 minutes, until the fish is done.

◆ Season to taste and serve with plenty of Parmesan cheese.

CHESTNUT SOUP

SERVES 4 / SET: FULL

Ingredients

2 tbsp/25 g/1 oz butter

1 large onion, chopped

1 carrot, chopped

1 stick (stack) celery, chopped

1¾ cups/400 g/14 oz canned chestnut purée (paste)

3¾ cups/850 ml/1½ pt very hot milk and stock (broth), mixed

salt and freshly ground black pepper

NOTE *If making this soup with fresh chestnuts, peel them according to the instructions in the recipe for Savoury Stuffed Vine Leaves and cook them in the stock (broth) and milk for 10–12 minutes until soft, then blend the soup in a liquidizer.*

◆ Put the butter in a large pot and cook for one minute until melted. Stir in the onion, carrot and celery. Cover and cook for 5 minutes.

◆ Stir in the chestnut purée (paste) and pour over the hot milk and stock (broth). Cover and cook for 6 minutes.

◆ Season and serve.

Chestnut Soup

MINESTRONE ALLA MILANESE

SERVES 6 / SET: FULL

Ingredients

4 rashers (strips) bacon
2 tbsp/25 g/1 oz butter
1 onion, chopped
1 clove garlic, chopped
1 carrot, chopped
1 stick (stack) celery, chopped
2 courgettes (zucchini), sliced
⅓ cup/75 g/3 oz rice
3¾ cups/850 ml/1½ pt boiling chicken stock (broth)
¼ white cabbage, shredded
3 cups/450 g/1 lb peas
¾ cup/200 g/7 oz canned tomatoes, mashed, with juice
a small handful of parsley, chopped
a few leaves each of basil and sage
salt and freshly ground black pepper
Parmesan cheese

◆ Put the bacon on a plate or bacon rack covered with absorbent kitchen paper (paper towels) and microwave for 4 minutes, turning once. Cut into pieces and set aside.

◆ Put the butter in a large pot and cook for 1 minute until melted. Stir in the onion, garlic, carrot and celery, cover with vented cling film (plastic wrap) and cook for 4 minutes.

◆ Add the courgettes (zucchini) and rice, pour over half the stock (broth), cover and cook for 10 minutes.

◆ Add the cabbage, peas, tomatoes and herbs, pour on the rest of the stock (broth), cover and cook for 5 minutes.

◆ Season to taste and serve with Parmesan cheese.

PASTA AND PEA SOUP

SERVES 4 / SET: FULL

Ingredients

2 tbsp/25 g/1 oz butter

1 onion, chopped

1 clove garlic, crushed (minced)

1 stick (stack) celery, finely chopped

1 carrot, finely chopped

1 tbsp tomato purée (paste)

2½ cups/575 ml/1 pt boiling beef stock (broth)

1 cup/100 g/4 oz pasta shapes

1 cup/200 g/7 oz peas

salt and freshly ground black pepper

a handful of parsley, chopped (optional)

Parmesan cheese (optional)

◆ Put the butter in a large pot and cook for 1 minute until melted. Stir in the onion, garlic, celery and carrot. Cover with vented cling film (plastic wrap) and cook for 4 minutes.

◆ Stir in the tomato purée (paste), pour over the boiling stock (broth) and add the pasta. Cover and cook for 8 minutes.

◆ Add the peas 6 minutes before the end of cooking time if fresh, 4 minutes if canned or defrosted.

◆ Season to taste and serve sprinkled with parsley or Parmesan cheese if liked.

GARLIC MUSHROOMS

SERVES 4 / SET: FULL

Ingredients

16 mushrooms, about 3 cm/1½ in across

15 ml/1 tbsp oil

2 cloves garlic, crushed (minced)

60 ml/4 tbsp chopped fresh herbs

2 slices wholemeal (whole-wheat) bread, soaked in milk and squeezed

salt and freshly ground black pepper

◆ Peel the mushrooms or wipe them. Cut off the stalks and chop finely.

◆ Put the oil in a small bowl and cook for 30 seconds. Add the garlic and cook for 1 minute.

◆ Mix the garlic with the mushroom stalks, herbs and bread, mashing it to a paste.

◆ Divide the filling between the mushroom caps, put them in a lightly oiled dish, covered with vented cling film (plastic wrap) and cook for 5 minutes, turning once.

◆ Serve hot.

CREAMED TOMATO SOUP

SERVES 4 / SET: FULL

Ingredients

2 kg/4 lb ripe tomatoes

1 onion

⅓ cup/50 g/2 oz chopped ham

½ cucumber, diced

5 ml/1 tsp Worcestershire sauce

a squeeze of lemon juice

⅔ cup/150 ml/5 fl oz cream

chopped basil or parsley

This is a luxurious soup to make if you have a glut of fresh tomatoes. The finished soup will be lukewarm – the ideal temperature at which to serve it.

◆ Plunge the tomatoes into boiling water for 1 minute until the skins split. Peel them and chop them, discarding the seeds and the cores.

◆ Put them in a large pot, cover with vented cling film (plastic wrap) and cook for 5 minutes, stirring once, until thick and pulpy. Blend in a food processor or blender until smooth.

◆ Put the onion in a cloth (cheesecloth) and squeeze it hard over the tomatoes to get as much juice out as you can.

◆ Stir all the ingredients together in a large bowl and serve, sprinkled with basil or parsley.

Creamed Tomato Soup

PRAWN (SHRIMP) STUFFED TOMATOES

SERVES 4 / SET: FULL

Ingredients

4 large (beef) tomatoes
salt
2 tbsp/25 g/1 oz butter
1 onion, finely chopped
1 clove garlic, finely chopped
1 generous cup/150 g/6 oz peeled prawns (shrimp)
¾ cup/75 g/3 oz fresh white breadcrumbs
30 ml/2 tbsp chopped parsley
30 ml/2 tbsp tomato purée (paste)
cayenne pepper
lemon wedges

◆ Cut the tops off the tomatoes, scoop out the pulp and reserve. Sprinkle the insides of the tomatoes with salt and leave upside down to drain.

◆ Meanwhile, make the filling. Put the butter in a bowl and cook for 1 minute. Stir in onion and garlic. Cover with vented cling film (plastic wrap) and cook for 2 minutes.

◆ Stir in tomato pulp and remaining ingredients, except lemon wedges. Mix well and season with cayenne pepper to taste.

◆ Stuff the tomatoes and put them upright in a dish they just fit. Cook, covered with vented cling film (plastic wrap), for 5 minutes, then allow to stand for 1–2 minutes.

◆ Serve hot with lemon wedges.

CHEESE AND ONION SOUP

SERVES 4 / SET: FULL

Ingredients

3 tbsp/40 g/1½ oz butter
2 medium onions, sliced
4 tbsp/25 g/1 oz flour
2½ cups/575 ml/1 pt boiling chicken stock (broth)
1½ cups/175 g/6 oz strong Cheddar cheese, finely grated
salt
Worcestershire sauce

A very tasty and nourishing thick soup to serve with wholemeal (whole-wheat) bread on a cold winter's day.

◆ Put the butter in a large pot and cook for 1 minute until melted. Add the onions, stirring to coat, cover and cook for 4 minutes. Stir in the flour and cook for 1 minute. Stir again.

◆ Pour on the stock (broth) and cook for 5 minutes, stirring every minute, until thickened.

◆ Stir in the cheese, a little at a time, until it has melted. Season with salt and Worcestershire sauce.

◆ Return to the microwave for a further 1½ minutes to reheat, then serve.

PIPERADE

SERVES 2—4
SET: FULL AND DEFROST

Ingredients

30 ml/2 tbsp olive oil
½ Spanish (Bermuda) onion, finely sliced
1 clove garlic, chopped
½ green pepper, cut into julienne strips
½ red pepper, cut into julienne strips
1 large tomato, peeled and finely sliced
5 eggs
15 ml/1 tbsp chopped fresh basil
salt and freshly ground black pepper
sprigs of watercress

This makes an interesting first course before plainly cooked fish or meat, rather like the French might eat an omelette (omelet) before a steak.

◆ Pour olive oil into a shallow oval dish and cook for 1 minute. Stir in onion, garlic and peppers and cook for 3 minutes. Add the tomatoes and cook for a further 2 minutes, or until vegetables are done.
◆ Beat the eggs with the chopped basil and season. Stir egg mixture into vegetables. Cook for about 3 minutes on defrost power, or until nearly cooked, stirring every minute to scramble the eggs.
◆ Allow to stand for 1 minute, then garnish with watercress and serve.

Piperade

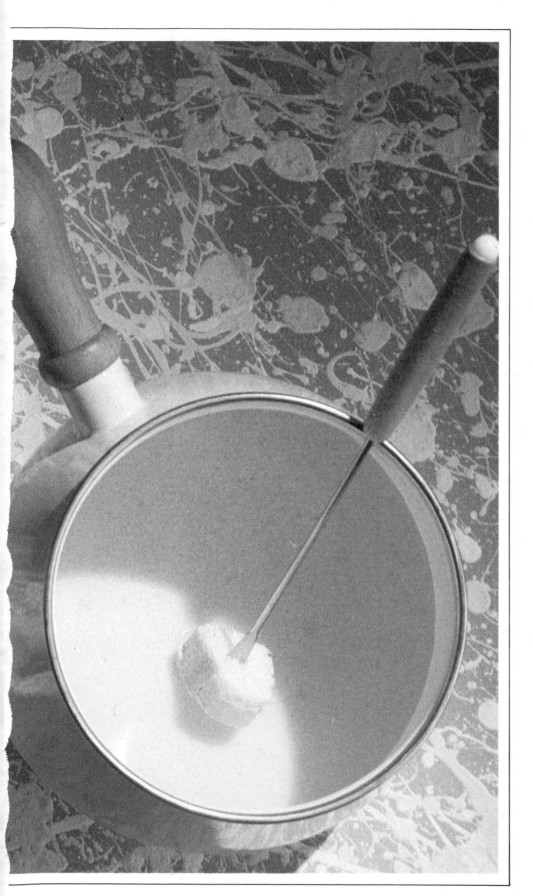

CHEESE FONDUE

SERVES 4 / SET: FULL

Ingredients

1 clove garlic, finely chopped

3/4 cup/200 ml/1/3 pt dry white wine

2 cups/225 g/8 oz Gruyère cheese, finely grated

10 ml/2 tsp cornflour (cornstarch)

30 ml/2 tbsp brandy

freshly ground black pepper

nutmeg

◆ Put garlic and wine in a bowl and cook for 2 minutes.

◆ Add cheese. Cook for 4 minutes, stirring 3 times, until cheese has melted.

◆ Mix together cornflour (cornstarch), brandy, pepper and nutmeg. Stir into cheese. Cook for 4 minutes.

◆ Serve with French bread cut into bite-sized pieces and accompany with a crisp salad. Provide each guest with a fondue fork or kebab stick for spearing the bread.

WELSH RAREBIT

SERVES 4
SET: FULL AND MEDIUM

Ingredients

4 slices wholemeal (whole-wheat) toast

4 slices ham

2 cups/225 g/8 oz grated Cheddar cheese

1 tbsp/15 g/½ oz butter

salt and freshly ground black pepper

2.5 ml/½ tsp Worcestershire sauce

2.5 ml/½ tsp paprika

45 ml/3 tbsp single (light) cream

tomato wedges

sprigs of watercress

This can also be served instead of a dessert, if you prefer to end your meal on a savoury note.

◆ Top each slice of toast with a slice of ham and keep warm.

◆ Put the cheese and butter in a bowl and cook on full, stirring every minute, for 3 minutes until cheese has melted.

◆ Season, stir in the Worcestershire sauce, paprika and cream and cook on medium for 8 minutes, stirring every minute, until smooth and creamy.

◆ Top the toast and ham with the cheese mixture and serve garnished with tomato wedges and sprigs of watercress.

Welsh Rarebit

CHICK PEA (GARBANZO) SOUP

SERVES 4 / SET: FULL

Ingredients

2 tbsp/25 g/1 oz butter

1 small onion, chopped

1 clove garlic, chopped

¾ cup/200 g/7 oz canned tomatoes, mashed, with juice

2 cups/400 g/14 oz canned chick peas (garbanzos), drained

a pinch of marjoram, or 5 ml/1 tsp chopped fresh marjoram

2½ cups/575 ml/1 pt boiling beef stock (broth)

salt and freshly ground black pepper

4 slices crusty white bread, toasted

Parmesan cheese

If using dried chick peas (garbanzos), soak them overnight, drain and boil vigorously in fresh water on the hob for 10 minutes. Turn down the heat and simmer until cooked. This may take up to 5 hours, depending on the age of the chick peas. How much simpler and cheaper to use the canned variety!

◆ Put the butter in a large pot and cook for 1 minute, until melted. Add the onion and garlic, cover and cook for 2 minutes.

◆ Add the tomatoes, chick peas (garbanzos) and marjoram. Pour on the beef stock (broth), cover and cook for 6 minutes. Season to taste.

◆ Lay a slice of toasted bread in each of 4 soup plates. Pour over the hot soup and serve with Parmesan cheese.

VEGETABLE SOUP WITH PESTO

SERVES 4 / SET: FULL

Ingredients

250 g/8 oz spinach

3 tbsp/40 g/1½ oz butter

2 cooked potatoes, diced

1 cup/100 g/4 oz green beans, cut into pieces

½ white cabbage, shredded

1 leek, sliced

1 onion, sliced

2½ cups/575 ml/1 pt boiling chicken stock (broth)

PESTO

4 cloves garlic

60 ml/4 tbsp grated Parmesan cheese

30 ml/2 tbsp pine nuts

a large bunch of basil

30–60 ml/2–4 tbsp olive oil

Stir a tablespoonful of pesto sauce into a tureen of soup for a lovely garlicky flavour. Make up a small jar of the sauce and keep it in the fridge for use on pasta too.

◆ First make the pesto by blending all the ingredients, except the oil, in a food processor or blender or, alternatively, pounding them in a mortar with a pestle.

◆ Add enough olive oil to make a thick, smooth paste. Store the sauce in a jar in the fridge and use as required.

◆ For the soup, wash the spinach and discard any tough stalks and discoloured leaves. Cram it into a big pot with half the butter, cover with vented cling film (plastic wrap) and cook for 6 minutes, turning once, until soft. Chop finely and set aside.

◆ Put the rest of the butter in the pot and cook for 30 seconds until melted. Add the remaining vegetables, stirring to coat them with the butter. Cover with vented cling film (plastic wrap) and cook for 5 minutes.

◆ Pour over the chicken stock (broth), stir in the spinach and cook for a further 6 minutes, stirring twice.

◆ Serve with pesto sauce.

MOULES A LA MARINIERE

SERVES 2 / SET: FULL

Ingredients

10 cups/1.25 l/2 pt mussels

4 tbsp/50 g/2 oz butter

1 onion, chopped

1 clove garlic, chopped

a handful of fresh parsley, chopped

freshly ground black pepper

1 glass dry white wine

◆ Scrub the mussels thoroughly under cold running water, scraping away the beards. Discard any mussels that are open or broken.

◆ Put the butter in a large bowl and cook for 1 minute. Add the onion, garlic, parsley, pepper and wine. Cover and cook for 2 minutes.

◆ Add the mussels, cover and cook for about 3 minutes until shells are open, giving the dish a good stir halfway through. Discard any mussels that remain closed.

◆ Serve in deep soup plates with French bread to mop up the juices and provide a dish for the discarded shells.

Moules à la Marinière

SMOKED SALMON SCRAMBLED EGGS

SERVES 2 / SET: FULL

Ingredients

6 medium eggs

15 ml/1 tbsp milk

freshly ground black pepper

⅔ cup/100 g/4 oz smoked salmon, cut into 1-cm/½-in squares

2 tbsp/25 g/1 oz butter

a pinch of cayenne pepper

This most luxurious starter makes a good prelude to a main dish of vegetables. Serve it with chilled champagne or Buck's Fizz. Have thin triangles of wholemeal (whole-wheat) toast buttered and kept hot on warmed plates so that all that remains to be done once the eggs are cooked is to pop the cork.

◆ Beat the eggs with the milk and season with black pepper. Stir in the salmon.

◆ Put the butter in a shallow oval dish and cook for 1 minute until melted.

◆ Stir in the eggs and smoked salmon. Cook for about 3 minutes, or until nearly done, stirring every minute.

◆ When the eggs are thick and creamy, pile them onto the hot toast. Add a sprinkling of cayenne pepper, allow to stand for 1 minute, then serve.

Risotto

RISOTTO

SERVES 4 / SET: FULL

Ingredients

¹/₂ cup/100 g/4 oz butter
1 large onion, chopped
2 small courgettes (zucchini), diced
1 carrot, diced
1 large tomato, peeled and chopped
³/₄ cup/50 g/2 oz mushrooms, wiped and sliced
2 cups/400 g/14 oz long-grain rice
4¹/₂ cups/1 l/1³/₄ pt boiling chicken stock (broth)
15 ml/1 tbsp tomato purée (paste)
salt and freshly ground black pepper
Parmesan cheese

This makes a substantial starter when there is plainly cooked meat or fish to follow. A risotto should be moist and succulent, not dry and fluffy.

◆ Put half the butter in a large bowl and cook for 1 minute. Stir in the vegetables, cover and cook for 8 minutes, stirring once.

◆ Stir in the rice, pour over the stock (broth) and add the tomato purée (paste). Season with a little salt, cover and cook for 15 minutes, stirring once.

◆ Allow to stand, covered, for 7 minutes. Stir in the remaining butter, plenty of black pepper and some Parmesan cheese.

◆ Serve, with more Parmesan cheese separately.

SMOKED FISH PATE

SERVES 4 / SET: MEDIUM

Ingredients

4 frozen smoked-fish fillets
1 onion, finely chopped
2 tbsp/25 g/1 oz butter
15 ml/1 tbsp lemon juice
good 5 tbsp/75 g/3 oz full fat cream cheese
15 ml/1 tbsp sherry
salt and freshly ground black pepper
parsley
lemon twists

◆ Put the smoked fish, onion, butter and lemon juice in a dish, cover and cook on medium for 8–10 minutes, turning once.

◆ Purée the smoked fish and onions with the sherry and cream cheese in a blender or food processor, or mash with a fork, and season to taste.

◆ Fill 4 individual ramekin dishes with the pâté and garnish with sprigs of parsley and lemon twists.

◆ Chill and serve with hot toast.

CHICKEN LIVER PATE

SERVES 4 / SET: FULL

Ingredients
1 cup/225 g/8 oz chicken livers
1 small onion, finely chopped
2 cloves garlic, crushed (minced)
²/₃ cup/150 g/5 oz butter
the leaves from 2 sprigs of fresh thyme, chopped
15 ml/1 tbsp port
15 ml/1 tbsp cream
salt and freshly ground black pepper
sprigs of fresh thyme
juniper berries

◆ Put the livers, onion, garlic, half the butter and the thyme in a bowl. Cover with vented cling film (plastic wrap) and cook for 5 minutes, stirring once.
◆ Put the mixture in a blender or food processor, with the port and cream and blend until smooth. Season and divide between 4 individual ramekin dishes.
◆ Put the remaining butter in a bowl and cook for 30 seconds, or until melted. Pour over the pâté and chill.
◆ Garnish with fresh thyme and juniper berries and serve with crusty bread or triangles of wholemeal (whole-wheat) toast.

Chicken Liver Pâté

THICK TOMATO SOUP

SERVES 4 / SET: FULL

Ingredients
30 ml/2 tbsp olive oil
1 or 2 cloves garlic, crushed (minced)
1 kg/2 lb ripe tomatoes, skinned and chopped
2½ cups/575 ml/1 pt boiling meat stock (broth)
salt and freshly ground black pepper
4 slices stale, crusty, white bread
a few leaves of sage and basil, chopped

This is a favourite supper time soup with children in Italy.

◆ Put the olive oil in a large pot and cook for 2 minutes. Add the garlic, stirring well to coat. Cook for 1 minute. Stir in the tomatoes, cover and cook for 8 minutes, stirring once or twice.
◆ Pour on the meat stock (broth), stir well and cook for a further 3 minutes. Season to taste.
◆ Lay a slice of bread in each of 4 soup plates. Pour the soup over and sprinkle sage and basil leaves on top.
◆ Serve with grated cheese if liked.

CABBAGE SOUP

SERVES 4 / SET: FULL

Ingredients

1 savoy cabbage
2½ cups/575 ml/1 pt boiling chicken stock (broth)
salt and freshly ground black pepper
4 slices crusty white bread
Parmesan cheese

◆ Wash the cabbage, discard any discoloured or tough leaves, quarter it and cut out the stalk.

◆ Put the leaves in a roasting or boiling bag with a generous spoonful of water and tie the top loosely. Microwave for 6 minutes. Remove and chop the cabbage.

◆ Put the cabbage in a large pot, pour over the boiling stock (broth) and cook, covered, for 3 minutes. Season to taste.

◆ Lay a slice of bread in the bottom of each of 4 soup plates. Pour over the soup and serve with plenty of Parmesan cheese.

MUSHROOM SOUP

SERVES 4 / SET: FULL

Ingredients

3 tbsp/40 g/1½ oz butter

1 small onion, chopped

1 clove garlic

10 cups/750 g/1½ lb mushrooms, peeled or wiped, and sliced

2½ cups/575 ml/1 pt boiling chicken stock (broth)

½ cup/100 g/4 oz tomatoes, peeled and chopped

salt and freshly ground black pepper

a pinch of nutmeg

◆ Put the butter in a large pot and cook for 1 minute. Add the onion and garlic, whole, cover with vented cling film (plastic wrap) and cook for 1 minute.

◆ Stir in the mushrooms, add a few spoonfuls of the chicken stock (broth), cover and cook for 4 minutes, stirring once.

◆ Remove the garlic, add the tomatoes and pour on the rest of the chicken stock (broth). Cover and cook for 4 minutes.

◆ Season to taste, add the nutmeg and serve.

BROAD (LIMA) BEAN AND HAM SOUP

SERVES 4 / SET: FULL

Ingredients

2 tbsp/25 g/1 oz butter
1 onion, chopped
1 clove garlic, crushed (minced)
1/3 cup/50 g/2 oz diced ham, off the bone
1.25 kg/2 1/2 lb broad (lima) beans (2 1/2 cups/450 g/1 lb beans shelled weight)
5 cups/1.25 l/2 pt boiling chicken stock (broth)
salt and freshly ground black pepper
30 ml/2 tbsp cream

This soup is best made with the first young broad (lima) beans of the season. Later in the summer, as the beans get tougher, remove the inner skins by lifting the beans from the soup with a slotted ladle when they are cooked, and pressing them out of the skins between your thumb and forefinger. Out of season, use canned or frozen beans.

◆ Put the butter in a large pot and cook for 1 minute until melted. Stir in the onion and garlic and cook, covered, for 2 minutes.

◆ Add the ham and beans and pour over the stock (broth). Cover and cook for 6 minutes, or until the beans are tender. Season to taste.

◆ Pour into soup plates and add a swirl of cream.

Broad (Lima) Bean and Ham Soup

CURRIED PARSNIP SOUP

SERVES 4 / SET: FULL

Ingredients

1 tbsp/15 g/½ oz butter

2.5 ml/½ tsp fennel seeds

1 slice fresh root (green) ginger

1 very large parsnip, finely sliced, weighing about 500 g/1¼ lb

1¼ cups/300 ml/½ pt boiling chicken stock (broth)

1¼ cups/300 ml/½ pt hot milk (approx.)

salt and freshly ground black pepper

a pinch of garam masala

The curry spices bring out the delicious natural sweetness of the parsnip. Parsnips are even sweeter after the first frost, which causes their sugar content to rise.

◆ Put the butter in a pot and cook for 1 minute until very hot. Add the fennel seeds and ginger, cover and cook for 45 seconds. Add the parsnip and 1–2 tbsp water.

◆ Cover and cook for 8 minutes, turning once, until the parsnip is really tender.

◆ Add the boiling chicken stock (broth) and cook for 3 minutes. Remove the ginger and purée the soup in a blender or food processor.

◆ Add enough hot milk to reach the desired consistency, season to taste with salt and pepper and stir in a pinch of garam masala.

◆ Heat through in the microwave for a couple of minutes if necessary and serve.

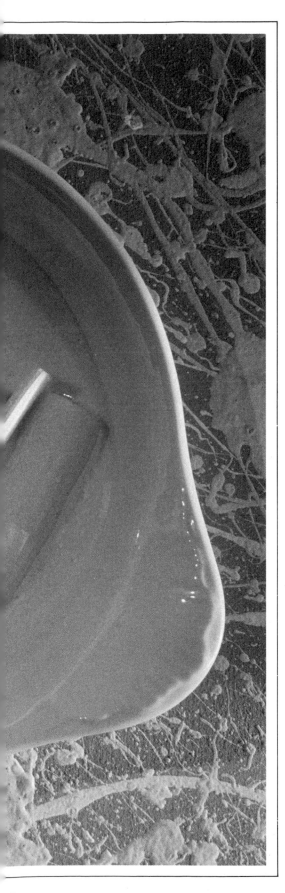

YOUNG LEEKS WITH HOLLANDAISE SAUCE

SERVES 4 / SET: FULL AND MEDIUM OR DEFROST

Ingredients

450 g/1 lb young leeks
45 ml/3 tbsp water
HOLLANDAISE SAUCE
½ cup/100 g/4 oz butter, diced
30 ml/2 tbsp lemon juice
3 egg yolks
salt and white pepper

◆ Trim the leeks, slit them and wash thoroughly. Lay them in a dish, add the water, cover and cook on full power for 6–8 minutes, rearranging once, until tender.

◆ Let the dish stand for a few minutes, then drain and arrange the leeks on a heated serving dish or individual plates.

◆ Meanwhile, make the sauce. Put the butter in a bowl and cook for 2 minutes on medium or defrost until melted. Add the lemon juice and the egg yolks and whisk lightly.

◆ Cook on medium or defrost for 1 minute, whisk again and season with salt and white pepper (black pepper would spoil the appearance of the sauce).

◆ Transfer the sauce to a heated jug and serve with the leeks.

STUFFED COURGETTES (ZUCCHINI)

*SERVES 4
SET: FULL AND DEFROST*

Ingredients

15 ml/1 tbsp oil
1 small onion, chopped
1 clove of garlic, chopped
30 ml/2 tbsp chopped parsley
30 ml/2 tbsp Parmesan cheese, grated
2 slices of bread, soaked in milk, squeezed out and crumbled
salt and freshly ground black pepper
4 fat courgettes (zucchini)
⅔ cup/150 ml/¼ pt Tomato Sauce
(see recipe for Stuffed Cabbage Leaves)

◆ Put the oil in a small bowl and cook for 30 seconds. Stir in the onion and garlic, cover with vented cling film (plastic wrap) and cook for 2 minutes.

◆ Mix in the parsley, Parmesan cheese and crumbled bread and season to taste.

◆ Cut the ends off the courgettes (zucchini) and hollow out the centres with an apple corer. Stuff the courgettes with the onion and bread mixture and arrange them in an oblong dish.

◆ Cover with vented cling film (plastic wrap) and cook on defrost power for 6 minutes, until tender, rearranging once.

◆ Serve the courgettes with the hot Tomato Sauce.

Young Leeks with Hollandaise Sauce

COUNTRY PATE

SERVES 6—8 / SET: FULL

Ingredients

½ cup/100 g/4 oz butter
2 onions, chopped
2 cloves garlic, chopped
1¼ cups/300 g/10 oz pigs' liver, chopped
1⅔ cups/300 g/10 oz belly pork, trimmed and chopped
15 ml/1 tbsp chopped fresh sage leaves
60 ml/4 tbsp sherry
60 ml/4 tbsp double (heavy) cream
salt and freshly ground black pepper
bay leaves
juniper berries

◆ Put half the butter in a large bowl and cook for 1 minute. Stir in the onion and garlic, cover with vented cling film (plastic wrap) and cook for 4 minutes, until soft.

◆ Stir in the pigs' liver and belly pork, cover and cook for 8–10 minutes, stirring once or twice, until cooked through.

◆ Put the mixture in a blender or food processor with the sage, sherry, cream and seasoning and blend until smooth. Fill a terrine with the pâté and smooth over the top.

◆ Dice the remaining butter and put it in a bowl and cook for 4 minutes until melted but not brown. Strain through a piece of muslin (cheese-cloth) and pour over the top of the pâté. Decorate with bay leaves and juniper berries and chill.

◆ Serve with hot toast.

HOT PASTA AND EGG SALAD

S E R V E S   4   /   S E T :   F U L L

Ingredients

2 cups/225 g/8 oz pasta shells

1¼ cups/300 ml/½ pt boiling water

30 ml/2 tbsp olive oil

⅓ cup/100 g/4 oz cooked or canned green beans

1 red pepper, cut into julienne strips

50 g/2 oz black olives

2 hardboiled (hard-cooked) eggs, quartered

salt and freshly ground black pepper

◆ Put the pasta shells in a pot with the boiling water, a little salt and a few drops of the oil. Cover and cook for 10 minutes.

◆ Leave to stand for 3 minutes, then drain and toss in the remaining oil.

◆ Mix in the beans, pepper and olives, season and divide the mixture between 4 individual dishes. Arrange the eggs on top.

◆ Serve and eat while the pasta is still warm – it makes an interesting contrast with the cold salad.

Hot Pasta and Egg Salad

LENTIL SOUP

SERVES 4 / SET: FULL

Ingredients

2 tbsp/25 g/1 oz butter
a squeeze of lemon juice
1 onion, finely sliced
1 clove garlic, crushed (minced)
½ fresh green chilli (chili), minced
1 carrot, chopped
1 stick (stack) celery, finely sliced
⅔ cup/175 g/6 oz lentils
2½ cups/575 ml/1 pt boiling chicken stock (broth)
salt and freshly ground black pepper
a handful of fresh parsley, roughly chopped

Brown and green lentils should be soaked overnight before use. The small red lentils can be used immediately.

◆ Put the butter in a large pot and cook for 1 minute until melted. Add the lemon juice, onion, garlic, chilli (chili), carrot and celery, cover with vented cling film (plastic wrap) and cook for 3 minutes.

◆ Stir in the lentils and pour over the boiling stock (broth). Cover with vented cling film (plastic wrap) and cook until the lentils are soft: 15 minutes if using red lentils and 20 minutes if using green or brown.

◆ Blend half the soup, return to the pot and season to taste.

◆ Serve strewn with parsley.

CORN ON THE COB WITH HERB BUTTER

SERVES 4 / SET: FULL

Ingredients

½ cup/100 g/4 oz butter
4 corn on the cob, fresh or frozen
45 ml/3 tbsp chopped mixed fresh herbs

The herb butter can be made in advance, allowed to cool, then chilled and served in pats if required.

◆ Cut up the butter and place in a small dish. Cook for 1 minute.

◆ Brush the corn with some of the melted butter and wrap individually in waxed paper. Pack into a shallow dish.

◆ Cover and cook until grains are tender when pierced: 10 minutes if fresh or 12 if frozen.

◆ Transfer corn to serving dishes.

◆ Stir herbs into remaining butter and cook for 30 seconds.

◆ Pour herb butter over corn to serve.

Corn on the Cob with Herb Butter

TOMATO, CARROT AND ORANGE SOUP

SERVES 4 / SET: FULL

Ingredients

good 3 cups/2 × 400 g/14 oz canned tomatoes, mashed, with juice

2 cups/225 g/8 oz carrots, chopped

juice of 1 orange

1 bayleaf

2½ cups/575 ml/1 pt hot chicken stock (broth)

rind of half an orange, finely grated

salt and freshly ground black pepper

single (light) cream

Carrots cook more quickly and evenly if they are chopped or chipped than they do when thickly sliced.

◆ Put tomatoes, carrots, orange juice and bayleaf in a bowl. Cover with vented cling film (plastic wrap) and cook for 10–15 minutes, stirring once or twice, until carrots are cooked.

◆ Remove the bayleaf and purée the mixture in a blender or food processor. Return to the bowl and add the stock (broth) and orange rind. Season to taste.

◆ Cook for 4 minutes and serve hot or cold with a swirl of cream.

VARIATION You can make this soup with lemon instead of orange, using the juice of only half the fruit.

Tomato, Carrot and Orange Soup

RICE AND TURNIP SOUP

SERVES 4 / SET: FULL

Ingredients

2 tbsp/25 g/1 oz butter

1 onion, chopped

2 turnips, peeled and diced

⅓ cup/75 g/3 oz rice

2½ cups/575 ml/1 pt boiling chicken stock (broth)

⅓ cup/50 g/2 oz ham, chopped

salt and freshly ground black pepper

a handful of parsley, chopped

Parmesan cheese

◆ Put the butter in a large pot and cook for 1 minute until melted. Stir in the onion and cook for 2 minutes.

◆ Stir in the turnips and rice, pour over enough chicken stock (broth) to cover, add the ham and cook, covered, for 12 minutes.

◆ Add the rest of the chicken stock (broth), season to taste and add the parsley.

◆ Serve with plenty of Parmesan cheese.

CHERRY SOUP

SERVES 4 / SET: FULL

Ingredients

approx. 8 cups/1 kg/2 lb ripe black cherries
juice of half a lemon
ground cinnamon
honey to taste
water
sour cream
mint leaves (optional)

This is a lovely fruit soup from Hungary, where it might be eaten to sharpen the palate before a rich main course of duck or game. Serve it with black bread if you have a hearty appetite.

◆ Wash and pick over the cherries. Take out the stones. Put the cherries in a bowl with the lemon juice, cover with vented cling film (plastic wrap) and cook for 3–5 minutes until the fruit is very soft.

◆ Transfer the cherries to a blender of food processor and blend with a little honey and a small pinch of cinnamon to taste. Add enough water to thin the soup to the desired consistency.

◆ Allow to cool, then chill in the fridge.

◆ Serve with a swirl of sour cream and decorate with mint leaves if liked.

TUSCAN VEGETABLE SOUP

SERVES 4 / SET: FULL

Ingredients

2 tbsp/25 g/1 oz butter

scant cup/100 g/4 oz potatoes, peeled and diced

scant cup/100 g/4 oz carrots, scraped and thinly sliced

scant cup/100 g/4 oz onions, sliced

1–2 cloves garlic, chopped

1½ cups/100 g/4 oz cabbage, roughly shredded

2 cups/400 g/14 oz canned butter beans, drained

1½ cups/400 g/14 oz canned tomatoes, mashed, with juice

2½ cups/575 ml/1 pt hot beef stock (broth)

salt and freshly ground black pepper

4 slices crusty bread

Parmesan cheese

In Tuscany soup is often poured over a thick slice of bread in the bottom of the soup plate. It is a good way of using up the last slices of the loaf. You can toast the bread and rub it with a cut clove of garlic.

◆ Put the butter in a large pot and cook for 1 minute. Add the potatoes, carrots, onion and garlic, cover with vented cling film (plastic wrap) and cook for 8 minutes, stirring once.

◆ Add the remaining vegetables and pour on the beef stock (broth). Cover and cook for 6 minutes, stirring once, until the potato and carrot are cooked. Season to taste.

◆ Lay a slice of crusty bread in each of 4 soup bowls. Pour on the soup and serve sprinkled liberally with Parmesan cheese.

VICHYSSOISE

SERVES 4 / SET: FULL

Ingredients

2½ cups/350 g/12 oz potatoes, peeled and diced

1 onion, sliced

¾ cucumber

3 leeks, trimmed, washed and sliced

4 tbsp/50 g/2 oz butter

60 ml/4 tbsp water

2½ cups/575 ml/1 pt boiling chicken stock (broth)

salt and freshly ground black pepper

⅔ cup/150 ml/¼ pt single (light) cream

This soup is best served chilled on a hot summer's day.

◆ Put the potatoes in a bowl with the onion, two thirds of the cucumber, peeled and diced, the leeks, butter and water. Cover and cook for 10 minutes, stirring once.

◆ Pour on the boiling stock (broth), cover and cook for 7 minutes, until the potatoes are soft, then purée in a blender or food processor. Season, allow to cool and chill well.

◆ Serve cold with a swirl of cream and decorated with the remaining cucumber, thinly sliced.

Vichyssoise

POACHED EGGS ON SPINACH WITH HOLLANDAISE SAUCE

SERVES 4
SET: FULL AND DEFROST

Ingredients

225 g/8 oz frozen spinach, thawed
and thoroughly drained

salt and freshly ground black pepper

4 eggs

Hollandaise Sauce (see recipe for Young
Leeks with Hollandaise Sauce)

◆ Divide the spinach between 4
individual buttered ramekin dishes
and cook on full power for
1½ minutes. Stir and season with salt
and pepper.

◆ Break the eggs onto the spinach
and prick the yolks gently with a
cocktail stick to prevent them
bursting. Cover the dishes with cling
film (plastic wrap) and cook for
3 minutes on defrost power.

◆ Serve the Hollandaise sauce
separately or pour over the eggs to
serve.

THANKSGIVING SOUP

SERVES 4 / SET: FULL

Ingredients

15 ml/1 tbsp oil

1 onion, chopped

scant 3 cups/350 g/12 oz squash (pumpkin), peeled, pips removed and diced

2 cups/225 g/8 oz carrots, chopped

2 potatoes, peeled and chopped

2½ cups/575 ml/1 pt boiling chicken stock (broth)

2 small courgettes (zucchini), thinly sliced

salt and freshly ground black pepper

parsley

◆ Put the oil in a pot and cook for 30 seconds. Add the onion, cover with vented cling film (plastic wrap) and cook for 2 minutes.

◆ Add the squash (pumpkin), carrots and potatoes and pour over the boiling stock (broth). Cover and cook for 15 minutes, until the vegetables are soft, adding the courgettes (zucchini) 5 minutes before the end of cooking time.

◆ Keeping back most of the courgettes (zucchini) blend or partially blend the soup. Season to taste.

◆ Float the reserved courgettes (zucchini) on top and serve sprinkled with parsley.

STUFFED CABBAGE LEAVES

SERVES 4
SET: FULL AND DEFROST

Ingredients

8 Savoy cabbage leaves

30 ml/2 tbsp water

2 tbsp/25 g/1 oz butter

1 onion, chopped

1 cup/175 g/6 oz cooked chicken or veal, chopped

1 cup/175 g/6 oz salami, derinded and chopped

30 ml/2 tbsp chopped fresh herbs

4 slices bread, crusts removed, soaked in milk, squeezed out and crumbled

salt and freshly ground black pepper

a little olive oil

TOMATO SAUCE

7.5 ml/½ tbsp oil

½ large onion, chopped

½ clove garlic, chopped

1 small carrot, chopped

½ stick (stack) celery, chopped

1½ cups/200 g/7 oz canned tomatoes, with juice

7.5 ml/½ tbsp tomato purée (paste)

a few sprigs of basil

salt and freshly ground black pepper

◆ Choose even-sized cabbage leaves. Wash them well and trim off each stalk at its base. Put them in a boiling or roasting bag with the water, fasten the top loosely and cook for 4 minutes. Lay the leaves flat on a kitchen towel to absorb the excess water.

◆ Meanwhile make the sauce. Put the oil in a pot and cook for 30 seconds. Add the onion, garlic, carrot and celery and cook, covered with vented cling film (plastic wrap) for 4 minutes.

◆ Stir in the tomatoes and their juice, tomato purée (paste) and basil. Cover and cook for 8 minutes, stirring twice.

◆ Put the sauce in a blender or food processor and blend until smooth, then season to taste.

◆ To make the filling for the cabbage leaves, put the butter in a pot and cook for 1 minute until melted. Stir in the onion, cover and cook for 3 minutes, until soft.

◆ Stir in the cooked chicken or veal, salami, herbs and breadcrumbs and season well, then divide the mixture between the cabbage leaves and roll up into parcels.

◆ Pack the cabbage parcels, join down, into a dish they just fit. Brush the tops with a little olive oil, cover the dish with vented cling film (plastic wrap) and cook on defrost setting for 8 minutes until hot through.

◆ Serve with the reheated tomato sauce.

CELERY SOUP

SERVES 4 / SET: FULL

Ingredients

3 tbsp/40 g/1 1/2 oz butter
1 onion, chopped
1/2 head (bunch) celery, finely chopped
6 tbsp/40 g/1 1/2 oz flour
1 1/4 cups/300 ml/1/2 pt milk
1 1/4 cups/300 ml/1/2 pt boiling chicken stock (broth)
salt and freshly ground black pepper
30 ml/2 tbsp cream
crispy bacon pieces

◆ Put the butter in a large pot and cook for 1 minute. Stir in the onion and celery, cover and cook for 4 minutes, until soft.

◆ Stir in the flour and cook for 1 minute. Stir in the milk and cook for 3 minutes, stirring every minute, until thick. Stir in the chicken stock (broth) and cook for a further 3 minutes. Season to taste.

◆ Pour into individual soup bowls, add a swirl of cream and sprinkle with crispy bacon pieces to serve.

SPINACH SOUP

SERVES 4 / SET: FULL

Ingredients

1 kg/2 lb spinach
6 tbsp/80 g/3 oz butter
1 small onion, chopped
6 tbsp/40 g/1 1/2 oz flour
1 1/4 cups/300 ml/1/2 pt milk
1 1/4 cups/300 ml/1/2 pt chicken stock (broth)
salt and freshly ground black pepper
2 egg yolks
30 ml/2 tbsp cream
2 slices white bread, cut into 1-cm/ 1/3-in dice

◆ Wash the spinach, discarding discoloured leaves and tough stalks. Pack it into a large pot, cover and cook for 6 minutes, turning once, until tender. Purée the spinach in a blender or food processor.

◆ Put half the butter in the pot and cook for 1 minute until melted. Add the onion and cook for 1 minute. Stir in the flour and cook for 1 minute.

◆ Whisk in the milk and cook for 3 minutes, whisking every minute. Whisk again until the sauce is smooth.

◆ Stir in the spinach, pour on the chicken stock (broth) and stir well. Cook to heat through for 4 minutes. Season to taste.

◆ Whisk the egg yolks with the cream, stir into the soup and heat for 30 seconds.

◆ Ladle the soup into individual soup bowls and serve garnished with croûtons made by frying the diced bread on the hob in the remaining butter until golden.

VARIATION This soup can also be made with sorrel or young nettles, picked before the plants flower.

Spinach Soup

THE MICROWAVE LIBRARY

COOKING WITH

Pasta

ELIZABETH CORNISH

PASTA

THE Italians claim to have as many types of pasta as there are days of the year, and when it comes to sauces their imagination never flags. Apart from the meat ragù traditionally served in Bologna, there are sauces of prawns, spinach, clams, chicken livers, herbs, tuna, beans, asparagus, cheese, squid, garlic, cream, mushrooms and even chillies (chilis), nuts and raisins.

Cooking with a microwave brings all these delicious flavours of Italy to your table with less fuss than ever before. If you have had problems with overcooked pasta sticking together in a lump, a kitchen full of steam and a saucepan that needs soaking for a week, relax: your microwave will come to the rescue. You can cook and serve pasta in the same dish, heating up the sauce while the pasta rests until it is just perfectly *al dente*.

Pasta is traditionally served in Italy as a starter, which is probably why it has unfairly been called fattening. A pasta dish from this book followed by a meat or fish dish with vegetables, then cheese and fruit would certainly be a very calorific meal. But the same pasta dish with a crisp salad and a glass of wine is a healthy balanced meal, and won't make you fat. Many of the sauces in this book are low-calorie anyway, because microwave cooking needs little or no fat.

Pasta should always have a little bit of a bite left in it (*al dente* = 'to the tooth') and it should always be served very hot in hot soup plates; offer extra black pepper and Parmesan cheese at the table. Cheese is not served on fish dishes in Italy.

When you are making an olive oil dressing for pasta (or for a salad too, for that matter), use the best olive oil you can afford. *Extra vergine* is the golden green oil from the first cold pressing, and it is both pungent and delicious.

CONTENTS

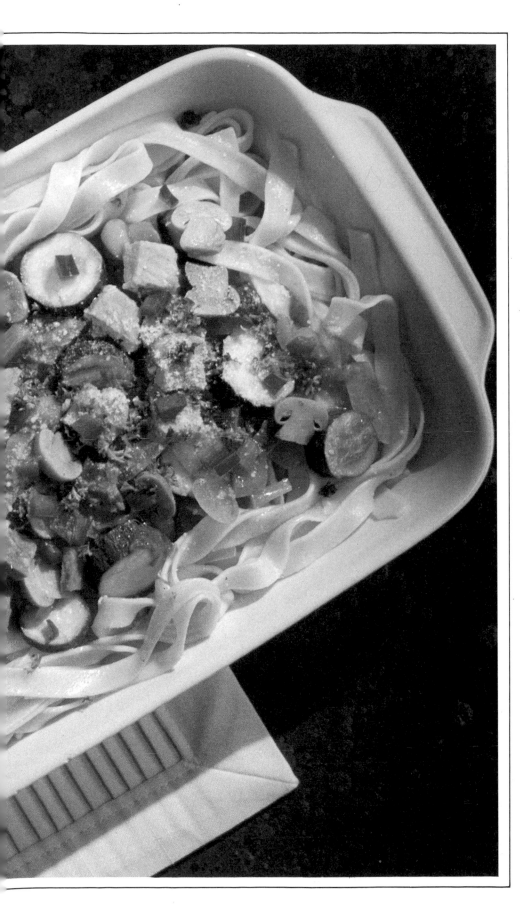

TAGLIATELLE WITH VEGETABLES AND HAM

SERVES 4 / SET: FULL

Ingredients

15 ml/1 tbsp olive oil

1 clove garlic, crushed (minced)

1 small onion, chopped

2 courgettes (zucchini), chopped

1 small red pepper, diced

1½ cups/100 g/4 oz mushrooms, wiped and sliced

⅓ cup/50 g/2 oz ham, chopped

¾ cup/200 g/7 oz canned tomatoes, drained and mashed

salt and freshly ground black pepper

400 g/14 oz tagliatelle

boiling water

chopped parsley

Parmesan cheese

◆ Put the oil in a bowl and cook for 30 seconds. Add the garlic and onion and cook for 2 minutes. Add the courgettes (zucchini), red pepper and mushrooms, cover with vented cling film (plastic wrap) and cook for 3 minutes. Add the ham and tomatoes, cover and cook for 2 minutes. Season to taste. Keep warm.

◆ Put the tagliatelle in a deep pot, just cover with boiling water and add a pinch of salt and a few drops of oil. Cover and cook for 6 minutes. Let the pot stand, covered, while you reheat the sauce if necessary.

◆ Drain the pasta, pour on the sauce, sprinkle with parsley and serve with plenty of Parmesan cheese.

PASTA WITH EARLY SUMMER VEGETABLES

SERVES 4 / SET: FULL

Ingredients

400 g/14 oz tagliatelle
boiling water
salt
oil
²/₃ cup/100 g/4 oz broad (lima) beans (shelled weight)
1 cup/100 g/4 oz peas
1 cup/100 g/4 oz green beans, topped and tailed (trimmed) and cut into pieces
²/₃ cup/150 ml/¼ pt single (light) cream
chopped fresh herbs
Parmesan cheese
freshly ground black pepper

◆ Put the tagliatelle in a deep pot and just cover with boiling water. Add a pinch of salt and a few drops of oil, cover and cook for 6 minutes. Set aside, covered.

◆ Put the broad (lima) beans, peas and green beans in a bowl with the cream. Cover with vented cling film (plastic wrap) and cook for 3 minutes.

◆ Drain the pasta, pour over the vegetable mixture and sprinkle with chopped fresh herbs.

◆ Serve hot with Parmesan cheese and offer black pepper at the table.

PENNE WITH SULTANAS (GOLDEN RAISINS) AND PINE NUTS

SERVES 4 / SET: FULL

Ingredients

3½ cups/400 g/14 oz penne (pasta quills)
boiling water
salt
45 ml/3 tbsp olive oil
1 clove garlic, chopped
3 tbsp/40 g/1½ oz sultanas (golden raisins), plumped up in a little marsala
¼ cup/40 g/1½ oz pine nuts
45 ml/3 tbsp finely chopped fennel leaves
grated Parmesan cheese
freshly ground black pepper

◆ Put the penne in a bowl and pour on enough boiling water to cover. Add a pinch of salt and a few drops of oil, cover and cook for 9 minutes. Set aside, covered, while you prepare the sauce.

◆ Put the olive oil in a dish and cook for 30 seconds. Add the garlic and cook for 1 minute. Stir in the sultanas (golden raisins) and pine nuts and cook for 2 minutes, stirring once.

◆ Drain the pasta, pour on the sauce, add the fennel and toss well.

◆ Serve with plenty of freshly grated Parmesan cheese and offer black pepper at the table.

RIGATONI WITH BORLOTTI BEANS

S E R V E S   4   /   S E T :   F U L L

Ingredients

3½ cups/400 g/14 oz rigatoni (or macaroni)
boiling water
salt
30 ml/2 tbsp olive oil
2 tbsp/25 g/1 oz butter
1 clove garlic, crushed (minced)
2 cups/400 g/14 oz canned borlotti beans, drained
1½ cups/175 g/6 oz mozzarella cheese, diced
chopped parsley
freshly ground black pepper

◆ Put the pasta in a deep pot and pour over enough boiling water to just cover. Add a pinch of salt and a few drops of the oil, cover and cook for 10 minutes. Leave covered.

◆ Put the remaining oil in a bowl with the butter and cook for 1 minute. Add the garlic and cook for 1 minute. Stir in the borlotti beans and cook for 2 minutes.

◆ Drain the pasta and stir in the bean mixture and cheese. Cover and cook for 1½ minutes, until the mozzarella begins to melt.

◆ Sprinkle with chopped parsley and serve. Offer black pepper at the table.

Rigatoni with Borlotti Beans

SPAGHETTI WITH RICOTTA AND ALMONDS

SERVES 4 / SET: FULL AND MEDIUM

Ingredients

400 g/14 oz spaghetti

4½ cups/1 l/1¾ pt boiling water (approx.)

salt

oil

¾ cup/75 g/3 oz ground almonds

⅔ cup/100 g/4 oz ricotta cheese

⅔ cup/150 ml/¼ pt single (light) cream

a pinch of mixed (sweet baking) spice

flaked (slivered) toasted almonds

Parmesan cheese

A delicious and very unusual combination of tastes.

◆ Hold the spaghetti in a deep pot and pour the water over it. As it softens, push the spaghetti under the water. Add a pinch of salt and a few drops of oil, cover and cook on full power for 12 minutes. Let the pot stand, covered, while you make the sauce.

◆ Blend together the ground almonds, ricotta cheese and cream. Stir in the mixed (sweet baking) spice to taste. Cover and heat through on medium power for 3 minutes.

◆ Drain the pasta and stir in the sauce.

◆ Sprinkle with flaked (slivered) toasted almonds and serve hot with plenty of Parmesan cheese.

PENNE WITH COURGETTES (ZUCCHINI) AND PISTACHIO NUTS

SERVES 4 / SET: FULL

Ingredients

3½ cups/400 g/14 oz penne (pasta quills)
salt
30–45 ml/2–3 tbsp olive oil
2½ cups/275 g/10 oz baby courgettes (zucchini), sliced
30 ml/2 tbsp water
1 clove garlic, crushed (minced)
⅓ cup/50 g/2 oz pistachio nuts, shelled
freshly ground black pepper
Parmesan cheese (optional)

◆ Put the penne in a deep pot and just cover with boiling water. Add a pinch of salt and a few drops of the oil, cover and cook for 9 minutes. Set aside, covered.

◆ Put the courgettes (zucchini) in a dish with the water, cover with vented cling film (plastic wrap) and cook for 3 minutes.

◆ Put the olive oil in a dish and cook for 30 seconds. Add the garlic and cook for 1 minute. Drain the courgettes (zucchini) and add them with the pistachio nuts. Stir well to coat in the oil. Cover and cook for 1–2 minutes.

◆ Drain the pasta, pour over the sauce and season with black pepper. Offer Parmesan cheese at the table, if liked.

Penne with Courgettes (Zucchini) and Pistachio Nuts

THE
MICROWAVE
LIBRARY

PASTA

SPAGHETTI WITH AUBERGINES (EGGPLANT) AND GARLIC

SERVES 4 / SET: FULL

Ingredients

400 g/14 oz spaghetti
4½ cups/1 l/1¾ pt boiling water
1 large aubergine (eggplant)
30–45 ml/2–3 tbsp olive oil
1–2 cloves garlic, crushed (minced)
Parmesan cheese (optional)

◆ Hold the spaghetti in a pot and pour on the boiling water. Push the spaghetti into it, add a few drops of oil and a little salt. Cover and cook for 12 minutes.

◆ Meanwhile, top and tail (trim) the aubergine (eggplant) and cut into thick matchsticks.

◆ Remove the spaghetti from the microwave when it is ready and leave to stand, covered.

◆ Put the olive oil in a dish and add the garlic and aubergine (eggplant). Cover and cook for 5 minutes, stirring once.

◆ Drain the spaghetti and toss in the aubergine (eggplant) and garlic.

◆ Serve with Parmesan cheese if liked.

SPAGHETTI WITH GARLIC AND OIL

SERVES 4 / SET: FULL

Ingredients

400 g/14 oz spaghetti
4½ cups/1 l/1¾ pt boiling water
salt
45 ml/3 tbsp olive oil
2 cloves of garlic, crushed (minced)
freshly ground black pepper

◆ Hold the spaghetti in a pot and pour on the boiling water. Push the spaghetti down into the water, add a pinch of salt and a few drops of oil, cover and cook for 12 minutes. Leave to stand, covered, while you prepare the sauce.

◆ Put the oil in a bowl and cook for 45 seconds. Add the garlic and cook for 2–3 minutes.

◆ Drain the spaghetti, pour over the hot garlic oil, add pepper, toss well and serve immediately.

MACARONI WITH TUNA FISH

SERVES 4 / SET: FULL

Ingredients

3 tbsp/40 g/1½ oz butter
6 tbsp/40 g/1½ oz flour
1¼ cups/300 ml/½ pt milk
½ cup/40 g/1½ oz Parmesan cheese
salt and pepper
3½ cups/400 g/14 oz macaroni
boiling water
oil
1 scant cup/200 g/7 oz canned tuna in brine, drained and flaked
pepper slices to garnish

◆ First make the sauce. Put the butter in a bowl and cook for 1 minute. Stir in the flour and cook for 1 minute. Stir in the milk and cook for 3 minutes, whisking after each minute. Stir in the cheese and cook for 1 minute. Whisk again and season to taste. Keep warm.

◆ Put the macaroni in a deep pot and just cover with boiling water. Add a pinch of salt and a few drops of oil. Cover and cook for 10 minutes. Let the pot stand, covered, for 3 minutes.

◆ Drain the pasta, stir in the sauce and tuna fish and heat through for 2–3 minutes. Garnish with pepper slices and serve hot.

Macaroni with Tuna Fish

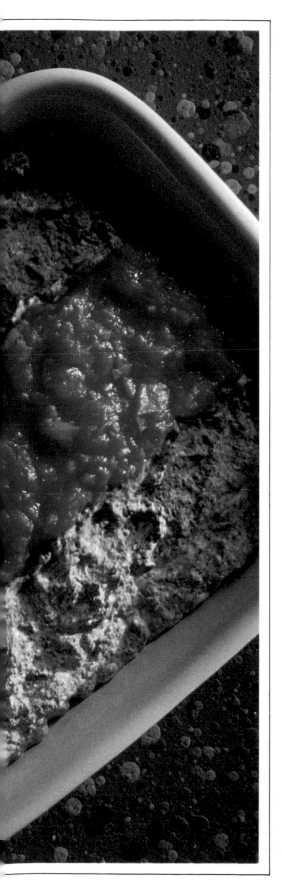

LASAGNE WITH SPINACH

SERVES 4 / SET: FULL AND MEDIUM

Ingredients

10–12 sheets lasagne
boiling water
salt
1 kg/2 lb fresh spinach
¾ cup/200 ml/⅓ pt cream
1⅓ cups/225 g/8 oz ricotta cheese
freshly ground black pepper
nutmeg
15 ml/1 tbsp oil
1 clove garlic, crushed (minced)
1 small onion, finely chopped
¾ cup/200 g/7 oz canned tomatoes, sieved (strained)

◆ Put the lasagne sheets in a deep oblong dish and cover with boiling water. Add a pinch of salt and a few drops of oil, cover and cook on full power for 10 minutes. Allow to stand, covered, while you make the sauces.

◆ Wash the spinach and discard any tough stalks and discoloured leaves. Put it in a boiling or roasting bag, with only the water clinging to it, tie loosely and cook on full power for 6 minutes. Drain and chop roughly.

◆ Mix together the cream and ricotta cheese until well blended. Stir in the spinach and season with salt, pepper and nutmeg to taste.

◆ Assemble the lasagne in an oiled oblong dish. Layer the pasta and the spinach sauce until all are used up. Begin with a layer of pasta and end with a layer of sauce.

◆ Make the tomato sauce. Put the oil in a bowl, add the onion and garlic and cook on full power for 2 minutes. Add the sieved (strained) tomatoes and cook on full power for 2 minutes. Season to taste.

◆ Pour the tomato sauce over the lasagne and heat through on medium power for 4– minutes. Serve hot.

Lasagne with Spinach

PAPPARDELLE WITH CHICKEN LIVERS

SERVES 4 / SET: FULL

Ingredients

3½ cups/400 g/14 oz pappardelle
boiling water
salt
a few drops of oil
15 ml/1 tbsp olive oil
30 ml/2 tbsp marsala
2 shallots, finely chopped
1 clove garlic, finely chopped
1 cup/225 g/8 oz chicken livers, trimmed and chopped
chopped parsley
lemon wedges

◆ Put the pappardelle in a deep pot and pour over enough boiling water to cover. Add a pinch of salt and a few drops of oil, cover and cook for 9 minutes. Leave to stand, covered, while you prepare the sauce.

◆ Put the oil and marsala in a dish with the shallots and garlic. Cover and cook for 2 minutes. Stir in the chicken livers, and cook for 2–3 minutes, stirring once, until just done.

◆ Drain the pasta and top with the sauce. Sprinkle with chopped parsley and serve with lemon wedges.

TAGLIATELLE WITH ASPARAGUS SPEARS

SERVES 4 / SET: FULL

Ingredients

400 g/14 oz tagliatelle
boiling water
salt
oil
²/₃ cup/150 ml/¼ pt single (light) cream
3 cups/400 g/14 oz freshly cooked or canned asparagus spears
Parmesan cheese

◆ Put the tagliatelle in a deep pot and just cover with boiling water. Add a pinch of salt and a few drops of oil, cover and cook for 6 minutes. Set aside, covered.

◆ Put the cream in a bowl and stir in the asparagus spears. Cook for 2 minutes.

◆ Drain the pasta, pour over the sauce and serve with plenty of Parmesan cheese.

Tagliatelle with Asparagus

LINGUINE WITH BACON AND CHICKEN

SERVES 4 / SET: FULL

Ingredients

400 g/14 oz linguine
boiling water
salt
a few drops of oil
3 tbsp/40 g/1½ oz butter
1 shallot, chopped
2 large tomatoes, peeled, seeded and chopped
¾ cup/150 g/5 oz cooked chicken, chopped
2 rashers (strips) bacon, cooked and chopped
freshly ground black pepper

◆ Put the linguine in a dish and pour over enough boiling water to cover. Add a pinch of salt and a few drops of oil, cover and cook for 9 minutes. Leave to stand, covered, while you prepare the sauce.

◆ Put the butter in a dish and cook for 45 seconds. Add the shallot and cook for 2 minutes. Add the tomatoes, chicken and bacon and cook for 3 minutes, stirring once, until hot. Season to taste.

◆ Drain the linguine, top with the sauce and serve at once.

HAY AND STRAW

SERVES 4 / SET: FULL

Ingredients

200 g/7 oz yellow tagliatelle
200 g/7 oz green tagliatelle
boiling water
salt
oil
⅔ cup/100 g/4 oz Parma ham, chopped
⅔ cup/150 ml/¼ pt single (light) cream
freshly ground black pepper
Parmesan cheese

The Italian name of this dish is paglia e
fieno. *'Hay and straw' refers to the two
colours of tagliatelle used. It is very quick
to make.*

◆ Put the yellow and green
tagliatelle together in a deep pot and
pour on enough boiling water to just
cover. Add a pinch of salt and a few
drops of oil. Cover and cook for
6 minutes. Let the pot stand, covered,
while you make the sauce.
◆ Stir the ham and cream together
in a bowl and season with black
pepper. Cook for 2 minutes.
◆ Drain the pasta, stir in the sauce
and serve with plenty of Parmesan
cheese.

Hay and Straw

SPAGHETTI WITH FETA CHEESE AND BLACK OLIVES

S E R V E S   4   /   S E T :   F U L L

Ingredients

400 g/14 oz spaghetti
4½ cups/1 l/1¾ pt boiling water
salt
45 ml/3 tbsp olive oil
1 clove garlic, crushed (minced)
12 black olives, stoned (pitted) and chopped
1¼ cups/150 g/5 oz feta cheese, crumbled
4 sage leaves, chopped
freshly ground black pepper

◆ Hold the spaghetti in a pot and pour on the boiling water. Push the spaghetti down into the water and add a pinch of salt and a few drops of oil. Cover and cook for 12 minutes. Leave the pot to stand, covered, while you make the sauce.

◆ Put the oil in a dish and cook for 45 seconds. Add the garlic and cook for 1 minute. Add the olives and cook for 30 seconds.

◆ Add the feta cheese to the hot oil, with the chopped sage. Grind on a little black pepper and mix the sauce well.

◆ Drain the spaghetti and stir in the sauce.

◆ Serve at once.

PASTA BOWS WITH CHICKEN LIVERS

S E R V E S   4   /   S E T :   F U L L

Ingredients

3¹/₂ cups/400 g/14 oz farfalle (pasta bows)
boiling water
salt
oil
1 cup/225 g/8 oz chicken livers, chopped
30 ml/2 tbsp marsala
1 clove garlic, crushed (minced)
cayenne pepper
Parmesan cheese

◆ Put the pasta into a deep pot and just cover with boiling water. Add a pinch of salt and a few drops of oil and cook, covered, for 9 minutes. Let the pot stand, covered, while you make the sauce.

◆ Put the chicken livers, marsala and garlic in a bowl and cook, covered, for 3 minutes.

◆ Drain the pasta, pour on the sauce, sprinkle with cayenne pepper and serve with Parmesan cheese.

TAGLIATELLE WITH ANCHOVIES AND TUNA FISH

SERVES 4 / SET: FULL

Ingredients

30 ml/2 tbsp olive oil

1 clove garlic, crushed (minced)

4 anchovy fillets, drained, soaked in milk, rinsed and chopped

½ cup/100 g/4 oz canned tuna fish drained

30 ml/2 tbsp capers

50 g/2 oz black olives, stoned (pitted)

400 g/14 oz tagliatelle

boiling water

salt

chopped parsley

◆ Put the oil in a bowl and add the garlic. Cook for 1 minute. Stir in the anchovies, tuna, capers and olives, cover and cook for 3 minutes.

◆ Put the tagliatelle in a deep pot and just cover with boiling water. Add a pinch of salt and a few drops of oil, cover and cook for 6 minutes. Let the pot stand for 3 minutes and reheat the sauce for 2 minutes while it is waiting.

◆ Drain the pasta, pour over the sauce and garnish with chopped parsley.

Tagliatelle with Anchovies and Tuna

LASAGNE WITH LEEKS AND SAUSAGE

SERVES 4 / SET: FULL

Ingredients

2 large leeks, sliced

1 1/3 cups/225 g/8 oz spicy sausage, sliced

3/4 cup/200 g/7 oz sieved (strained) tomatoes (passata)

a pinch dried mixed herbs

6 sheets spinach lasagne

boiling water

a few drops of oil

3 tbsp/40 g/1 1/2 oz butter

6 tbsp/40 g/1 1/2 oz flour

1 1/4 cups/300 ml/1/2 pt milk

1/2 cup/50 g/2 oz grated cheese

freshly ground black pepper / salt

60 ml/4 tbsp fresh breadcrumbs

◆ Put the leeks and sausage in a deep oblong dish with 60 ml/4 tbsp of the sieved (strained) tomatoes. Cover with vented cling film (plastic wrap) and cook for 6 minutes, stirring once. Add the rest of the tomato and the herbs, season, and set aside.

◆ Put the lasagne in a deep pot and pour over enough boiling water to cover. Add a pinch of salt and a few drops of oil, cover and cook for 15 minutes. Drain and rinse thoroughly under cold running water. Lay the pasta on a tea (dish) towel to dry. (Do not use kitchen paper (paper towels) – it will stick.)

◆ Make the cheese sauce. Put the butter in a dish and cook for 1 minute. Stir in the flour. Pour on the milk. Cook for 3 minutes, whisking after each minute. Stir in the cheese. Cook for a further minute and whisk again. Season to taste.

◆ Assemble the dish in layers until all the ingredients are used up, finishing with a layer of cheese sauce.

◆ Top with breadcrumbs and heat through in the microwave or in a conventional oven or under the grill (broiler).

◆ Serve hot.

CHICKEN LASAGNE

SERVES 4 / SET: FULL AND MEDIUM

Ingredients

10–12 sheets lasagne

boiling water

salt

oil

3 tbsp/40 g/1 1/2 oz butter

1 onion, chopped

1 clove garlic, chopped

1 1/2 cups/100 g/4 oz mushrooms, sliced

5 ml/1 tsp dried oregano

6 tbsp/40 g/1 1/2 oz flour

scant 2 cups/425 ml/3/4 pt milk

1 chicken stock (bouillon) cube

1 2/3 cups/275 g/10 oz cooked chicken, chopped

1/2 cup/40 g/1 1/2 oz grated Parmesan cheese, plus extra for the topping

◆ Put the lasagne sheets in a deep oblong dish and cover with boiling water. Add a pinch of salt and a few drops of oil, cover and cook on full power for 10 minutes. Allow to stand, covered, while you make the sauce.

◆ Put the butter in a bowl and cook on full power for 1 minute. Stir in the onion and garlic and cook on full power for 2 minutes. Stir in the mushrooms and oregano and cook on full power for 2 minutes.

◆ Stir in the flour and gradually add the milk, stirring. Crumble on the stock (bouillon) cube. Cook on full power for 3 minutes, stirring after each minute. Stir in the chicken and cheese and cook on full power for 1 minute. Keep warm.

◆ Drain the lasagne and lay the sheets out on a tea (dish) towel.

◆ Assemble. In an oiled oblong dish, layer the pasta and sauce until both are used up. Start with a layer of pasta and end with a layer of sauce. Sprinkle more Parmesan cheese on the top and cook on medium power for 5 minutes, turning the dish once.

◆ Serve hot.

TAGLIATELLE WITH MUSSELS AND PRAWNS (SHRIMP)

SERVES 4 / SET: FULL

Ingredients

15 ml/1 tbsp olive oil

1 clove garlic, crushed (minced)

¾ cup/200 g/7 oz canned tomatoes, drained and mashed

2.5 ml/½ tsp dried basil, or fresh basil to taste, chopped

freshly ground black pepper

1 cup/225 g/8 oz peeled prawns (shrimp), plus a few unpeeled ones for garnish

400 g/14 oz tagliatelle

boiling water

salt

5 cups/575 ml/1 pt mussels, scrubbed clean

1 glass dry white wine

chopped parsley

◆ Put the oil in a bowl and cook for 30 seconds. Add the garlic and cook for 1 minute. Add the tomatoes, basil, pepper and peeled prawns (shrimp) and cook for 4 minutes. Season with salt to taste, set aside and keep warm.

◆ Put the tagliatelle in a deep pot and pour over enough boiling water to just cover. Add a pinch of salt and a few drops of oil, cover and cook for 6 minutes. Set aside, covered.

◆ Discard any broken or open mussels and put the rest in a deep pot. Pour over the white wine. Add parsley to taste. Cover and cook for 3 minutes, or until the mussels open.

◆ Remove some mussels from their shells and stir into the sauce. Drain the pasta, pour over the sauce and garnish with the remaining mussels and the unpeeled prawns.

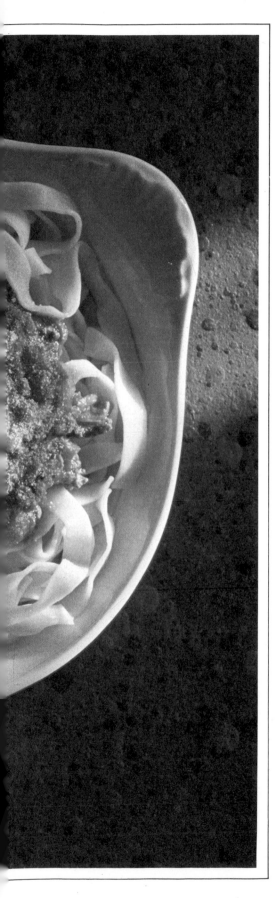

TAGLIATELLE BOLOGNESE

SERVES 4 / SET: FULL

Ingredients

15 ml/1 tbsp oil
1 clove garlic, crushed (minced)
1 onion, finely chopped
1 carrot, finely chopped
1 stick (stack) celery, finely chopped
¾ cup/200 g/7 oz canned tomatoes, drained and mashed
1 scant cup/200 g/7 oz minced (ground) beef
⅓ cup/50 g/2 oz ham
30 ml/2 tbsp red wine
1 bayleaf
3 chicken livers, chopped
salt and freshly ground black pepper
400 g/14 oz tagliatelle
boiling water
Parmesan cheese

◆ Put the oil in a bowl and cook for 30 seconds. Add the garlic, onion, carrot and celery and cook for 2 minutes. Stir in the tomatoes, beef and ham and add the red wine to moisten. Tuck the bayleaf into the mixture. Cook for 5 minutes, stirring once.

◆ Add the chicken livers and cook for 2 minutes. Season, set aside and keep warm.

◆ Put the tagliatelle in a deep pot and pour over enough boiling water to just cover. Add a pinch of salt and a few drops of oil, cover and cook for 6 minutes. Leave to stand, covered, for 3 minutes while you reheat the sauce if necessary.

◆ Drain the pasta, pour over the sauce and serve with plenty of Parmesan cheese.

Tagliatelle Bolognese

BUCATINI WITH RED LENTIL SAUCE

SERVES 4 / SET: FULL

Ingredients

15 ml/1 tbsp oil
1 onion, chopped
1 clove garlic, chopped
¾ cup/200 g/7 oz canned tomatoes, drained and mashed
salt and freshly ground black pepper
scant cup/150 g/5 oz red lentils
1¼ cups/300 ml/½ pt boiling water
3½ cups/400 g/14 oz bucatini
Parmesan cheese

◆ Put the oil in a dish and cook for 30 seconds. Add the onion and garlic, cover and cook for 2 minutes. Add the tomatoes and seasoning. Set aside.

◆ Put the lentils in a pot and pour over the boiling water. Cover and cook for 12 minutes. Stir in the tomato sauce and set aside.

◆ Put the bucatini in a deep pot. Cover with boiling water and add a few drops of oil. Cover and cook for 9 minutes. Set aside.

◆ Reheat the sauce.

◆ Drain the bucatini, stir in the sauce and serve topped with plenty of Parmesan cheese.

STUFFED CANNELLONI

SERVES 4 / SET: FULL

Ingredients

15 ml/1 tbsp oil
1 onion, finely chopped
1 carrot, finely chopped
1 stick (stack) celery, finely chopped
30 ml/2 tbsp red wine
15 ml/1 tbsp tomato purée (paste)
1 scant cup/200 g/7 oz lean minced (ground) beef
1 scant cup/200 g/7 oz lean minced (ground) veal
2/3 cup/100 g/4 oz ham, chopped
250 g/8 oz cannelloni
boiling water
3 tbsp/40 g/1 1/2 oz butter
6 tbsp/40 g/1 1/2 oz flour
1 1/4 cups/300 ml/1/2 pt milk
freshly ground black pepper
nutmeg
1/2 cup/40 g/1 1/2 oz Parmesan cheese, grated
1 egg yolk

◆ First make the stuffing. Put the oil in a bowl and cook for 30 seconds. Stir in the onion, carrot and celery and cook for 2 minutes. Stir in the wine mixed with the tomato purée (paste). Add the beef, veal and ham and combine well. Cover and cook for 5 minutes, until done. Season with salt and pepper.

◆ Put the cannelloni in a deep oblong dish and just cover with boiling water. Add a pinch of salt and a few drops of oil. Cover and cook for 9 minutes. Leave for 3 minutes, covered, then drain and stuff with the meat mixture.

◆ Meanwhile, make the sauce. Put the butter in a bowl and cook for 1 minute. Stir in the flour and cook for 1 minute. Pour on the milk and cook for 3 minutes, whisking after every minute. Add salt and pepper and a little nutmeg to taste. Stir in the Parmesan cheese and cook for a further minute. Whisk again, then stir in the egg yolk.

◆ Lay the stuffed cannelloni in a greased dish, in a single layer if possible. Pour over the sauce. Cover with vented cling film (plastic wrap) and cook for 1–2 minutes to heat through.

◆ Serve hot.

LINGUINE WITH MUSHROOM SAUCE

SERVES 4 / SET: FULL

Ingredients

3 cups/225 g/8 oz mushrooms, wiped
and sliced

30 ml/2 tbsp milk

400 g/14 oz green linguine

boiling water

salt

oil

⅔ cup/150 ml/5 fl oz single (light) cream

chopped parsley

◆ Put the mushrooms in a dish and
add the milk. Cover and cook for
3 minutes, stirring once. Set aside.
◆ Put the linguine in a deep pot and
pour over enough boiling water to
cover. Add a pinch of salt and a few
drops of oil. Cover and cook for
9 minutes. Set aside.
◆ Stir the cream into the
mushrooms. Reheat for 1 minute.
◆ Drain the pasta, pour on the
mushrooms, garnish with parsley and
serve.

TAGLIATELLE WITH PEAS AND CREAM

SERVES 4 / SET: FULL

Ingredients

400 g/14 oz tagliatelle

boiling water

salt

oil

⅔ cup/150 ml/¼ pt double (heavy) cream

good 2 cups/400 g/14 oz cooked peas (or
use canned peas)

½ cup/50 g/2 oz Emmenthal cheese,
grated

½ cup/50 g/2 oz Parmesan cheese, grated

strips of pepper

◆ Put the tagliatelle in a pot and
pour over enough boiling water to
just cover. Add a pinch of salt and a
few drops of oil, cover and cook for
6 minutes. Leave to stand, covered.
◆ Pour the cream into a bowl and
stir in the peas. Cook for 1½ minutes.
Stir in both cheeses and cook for
1½ minutes, stirring twice, until
melted.
◆ Drain the tagliatelle, stir in the
sauce and serve at once garnished
with strips of pepper.

Tagliatelle with Peas and Cream

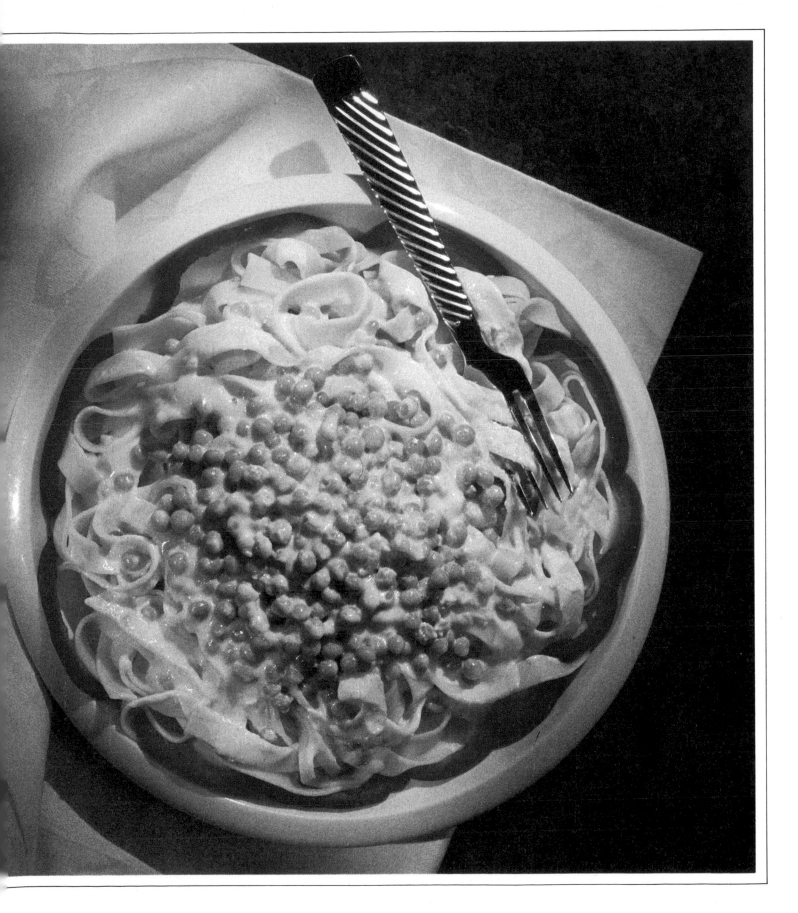

LINGUINE WITH GREEN BEANS, TOMATOES AND PUMPKIN SEEDS

SERVES 4 / SET: FULL

Ingredients

2 cups/225 g/8 oz green beans, topped and tailed (trimmed) and cut into bite size pieces
30 ml/2 tbsp water
¾ cup/225 g/8 oz tomatoes, peeled, seeded and cut into strips
⅓ cup/50 g/2 oz pumpkin seeds
400 g/14 oz green linguine
boiling water
salt
15–30 ml/1–2 tbsp oil
Parmesan cheese (optional)

◆ Put the beans in a dish with the water, cover with vented cling film (plastic wrap) and cook for 4 minutes.

◆ Add the tomatoes and cook for a further 4 minutes. Add the pumpkin seeds. Keep covered and keep warm.

◆ Put the linguine in a deep pot with enough boiling water to cover. Add a pinch of salt and a few drops of oil. Cover and cook for 8 minutes. Set aside, covered.

◆ Drain the vegetables and dress with the oil. Reheat, covered, for 1 minute.

◆ Drain the pasta and mix in the vegetables.

◆ Serve with Parmesan cheese if liked.

MACARONI WITH PRAWNS (SHRIMP)

SERVES 4 / SET: FULL

Ingredients

15 ml/1 tbsp oil

2 cloves garlic, crushed (minced)

1 red chilli (chili), seeded and chopped

1½ cups/400 g/14 oz canned tomatoes, drained and mashed

1½ cups/350 g/12 oz shelled prawns (shrimp)

15 ml/1 tbsp lemon juice

freshly ground black pepper

a sprig of thyme

1 bayleaf

a few sprigs of parsley

3½ cups/400 g/14 oz macaroni

boiling water

salt

cucumber slices

◆ Put the oil in a bowl and cook for 30 seconds. Add the garlic and chilli (chili) and cook for 1 minute. Stir in the tomatoes and cook for 3 minutes. Stir in the prawns (shrimp) and lemon juice, sprinkle with black pepper and add the herbs. Cover and cook for 2 minutes.

◆ Put the macaroni in a bowl and just cover with boiling water. Add a pinch of salt and a few drops of oil, cover and cook for 10 minutes. Leave to stand for 3 minutes. Reheat the sauce if necessary.

◆ Drain the pasta and mix in the sauce.

◆ Garnish with cucumber slices and serve hot.

Macaroni with Prawns (Shrimp)

BUCATINI ALL'AMATRICIANA

SERVES 4 / SET: FULL

Ingredients

½ cup/75 g/3 oz bacon, derinded (trimmed) and chopped
2 tbsp/25 g/1 oz butter
1 onion, finely chopped
good cup/400 g/14 oz canned tomatoes, drained and mashed
1¾ cups/200 g/7 oz canned peas, drained
salt
3½ cups/400 g/14 oz bucatini
boiling water
salt
oil
grated pecorino cheese

◆ Put the bacon on a plate covered with absorbent kitchen paper (paper towels). Cook for 2 minutes. Set aside.

◆ Put the butter in a bowl and cook for 1 minute. Add the onion and cook for 2 minutes. Stir in the tomatoes and cook for 2 minutes. Stir in the peas and bacon and cook for 2 minutes.

◆ Put the bucatini in a pot and just cover with boiling water. Add a pinch of salt and a few drops of oil, cover and cook for 10 minutes. Set aside, covered. Reheat the sauce if necessary during standing time.

◆ Drain the pasta, top with the sauce and serve with grated pecorino cheese.

SPAGHETTI WITH MANGETOUT (SNOW PEAS)

SERVES 4 / SET: FULL

Ingredients

15 ml/1 tbsp oil
2 tbsp/25 g/1 oz butter
1 clove garlic, crushed (minced)
¾ cup/100 g/4 oz mangetout (snow peas), stalks removed
1½ cups/100 g/4 oz button mushrooms, wiped and sliced
scant ½ cup/100 g/4 oz fresh tomatoes, skinned and chopped
salt, freshly ground black pepper
400 g/14 oz spaghetti
4½ cups/1 l/1¾ pt boiling water
chopped fresh herbs
Parmesan cheese

◆ Put the oil in a bowl with the butter and cook for 1 minute. Add the garlic and cook for 1 minute. Stir in the mangetout (snow peas), mushrooms and tomatoes. Cover with vented cling film (plastic wrap) and cook for 3 minutes. Season and set aside.

◆ Hold the spaghetti in a deep pot. Pour over the boiling water and push the spaghetti down into the pot. Add a pinch of salt and a few drops of oil, cover and cook for 12 minutes. Leave to stand, covered, for 5 minutes. Reheat the sauce during standing time if necessary.

◆ Drain the pasta and top with the sauce. Sprinkle with fresh herbs and offer Parmesan cheese at the table.

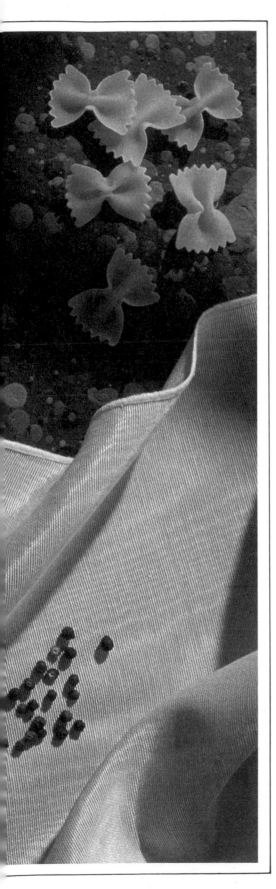

FARFALLE AL GORGONZOLA

S E R V E S   4   /   S E T :   F U L L

Ingredients

175–250 g/6–8 oz ripe gorgonzola cheese

²/₃ cup/150 ml/¼ pt double (heavy) or single (light) cream

3½ cups/400 g/14 oz farfalle (bow-shaped) pasta

boiling water

salt

oil

freshly ground black pepper

This is a luxurious dish that can be prepared very quickly.

◆ If necessary, soften the cheese by putting it, wrapped, in the microwave for a few seconds on defrost power. Cream the cheese with the cream in a blender or food processor. Put the mixture in a bowl and cook for 2 minutes to warm through.

◆ Put the pasta in a deep pot and just cover with boiling water. Add a pinch of salt and a few drops of oil, cover and cook for 10 minutes. Leave to stand for 3 minutes.

◆ Heat the sauce through again if necessary during the standing time. It should be warm, not hot.

◆ Drain the pasta and stir in the sauce. Offer black pepper at the table.

Farfalle al Gorgonzola

BEAN-STUFFED CANNELLONI

S E R V E S   4   /   S E T :   F U L L

Ingredients

2 cups/400 g/14 oz canned cannellini beans, drained

²/₃ cup/100 g/4 oz ricotta cheese

1 bunch parsley, chopped

1 onion, chopped

¾ cup/225 g/8 oz tomatoes, skinned, peeled and chopped

salt and freshly ground black pepper

8 cannelloni

boiling water

a few drops of oil

²/₃ cup/150 ml/¼ pt single (light) cream

When cooked like this, the onion and tomato in the stuffing will still be crisp and firm respectively, which makes a refreshing change.

◆ Make the stuffing by mixing together the beans, ricotta, parsley, onion and tomatoes, and season well with salt and pepper.

◆ Put the cannelloni in a deep oblong dish and cover with boiling water. Add a few drops of oil and a pinch of salt. Cover and cook for 12 minutes. Drain and rinse under cold running water.

◆ Stuff the cannelloni with the bean mixture and arrange in the dish. Pour the cream over and reheat for 2 minutes.

◆ Serve at once.

GREEN TAGLIATELLE WITH PEPPERS

SERVES 4 / SET: FULL

Ingredients

15 ml/1 tbsp olive oil
1 small onion, chopped
1 clove garlic, crushed (minced)
1½ cups/400 g/14 oz canned tomatoes, drained
salt and freshly ground black pepper
½ red pepper, cut into strips about 2.5 cm/ 1 in long
½ green pepper, cut into strips about 2.5 cm/1 in long
½ yellow pepper, cut into strips about 2.5 cm/1 in long
30 ml/2 tbsp water
400 g/14 oz spinach tagliatelle
boiling water
salt
Parmesan cheese

◆ Put the oil in a bowl and cook for 30 seconds. Add the onion and garlic and cook for 2 minutes. Add the tomatoes and cook for 2 minutes. Purée in a blender or food processor and season to taste.

◆ Put the pepper strips in a bowl and add the water. Cover with vented cling film (plastic wrap) and cook for 4 minutes, until tender. Set aside.

◆ Put the tagliatelle in a deep pot and just cover with boiling water. Add a pinch of salt and a few drops of oil, cover and cook for 6 minutes. Leave to stand for 3 minutes. Reheat the sauce if necessary during standing time.

◆ Drain the pasta, pour over the sauce and garnish with the strips of pepper.

◆ Serve with Parmesan cheese.

TAGLIATELLE WITH SPINACH AND WALNUT SAUCE

SERVES 4 / SET: FULL

Ingredients

450 g/1 lb fresh spinach

4 rashers (strips) bacon, derinded (trimmed) and chopped

1 tbsp/15 g/¹/₂ oz butter

1 clove garlic, crushed (minced)

²/₃ cup/150 ml/5 fl oz single (light) cream

¹/₃ cup/50 g/2 oz walnut pieces

400 g/14 oz tagliatelle

boiling water

salt

oil

Parmesan cheese

◆ Wash the spinach and discard any tough leaves and stalks. Put it into a roasting or boiling bag with only the water clinging to it, tie loosely and cook for 6 minutes, until the leaves have collapsed. Purée the spinach in a blender or food processor.

◆ Put the bacon on a plate covered with absorbent kitchen paper (paper towels) and cook for 2 minutes until done.

◆ Put the butter in a small bowl with the garlic, add the bacon and cook for 2 minutes.

◆ Stir the spinach into the cream, add the walnuts and cook for 4 minutes. Set aside, covered.

◆ Put the tagliatelle in a deep bowl and just cover with boiling water. Add a pinch of salt and a few drops of oil and cook for 6 minutes. Let the bowl stand, covered, while you reheat the spinach cream sauce if necessary.

◆ Drain the pasta and stir in the cream sauce. Top with the garlic and bacon.

◆ Serve hot with Parmesan cheese.

LASAGNE WITH FISH

SERVES 4 / SET: FULL

Ingredients

6 sheets lasagne
boiling water
salt
oil
1 cup/225 g/8 oz cooked white fish, flaked
1 good cup/200 g/7 oz canned sweetcorn kernels (corn), drained
¾ cup/200 g/7 oz canned tomatoes, sieved (strained)
chopped parsley
freshly ground black pepper
3 tbsp/40 g/1½ oz butter
6 tbsp/40 g/1½ oz flour
1¼ cups/300 ml/½ pt milk
½ cup/50 g/2 oz Edam cheese, grated
30 ml/2 tbsp Parmesan cheese

◆ Put the lasagne in a dish and pour over enough boiling water to cover. Add a pinch of salt and a few drops of oil. Cover and cook for 15 minutes. Drain and rinse well under cold running water. Lay the sheets on a tea (dish) towel to dry. (Do not use kitchen paper (paper towels) – it will stick.)

◆ Mix the fish, sweetcorn kernels (corn), tomatoes and parsley together and season with salt and pepper.

◆ Put the butter in a bowl and cook for 1 minute. Stir in the flour. Pour on the milk and cook for 3 minutes, whisking after each minute. Stir in the Edam cheese and cook for a further minute. Whisk again. Season with salt and pepper.

◆ Assemble. Begin with a layer of fish and tomato, then cover with lasagne and top with cheese sauce. Continue until all the ingredients have been used up, ending with the cheese sauce. Sprinkle with Parmesan cheese.

◆ Heat through in the microwave, or under the grill (broiler), or in a conventional oven if you want the top to brown.

PENNE AL PESTO

SERVES 4 / SET: FULL

Ingredients

1 large bunch fresh basil
15 ml/1 tbsp pine nuts
4 cloves garlic
30 ml/2 tbsp grated Parmesan cheese
virgin olive oil
salt and freshly ground black pepper
3½ cups/400 g/14 oz penne (pasta quills)
boiling water

This dish is a speciality of Genoa, on the Ligurian coast of Italy. Pesto sauce can be served equally well with rice.

◆ To make the pesto sauce chop the basil leaves into a mortar. Add the pine nuts and garlic and crush with the pestle. Add Parmesan cheese and olive oil, pounding all the while, until you have a thick paste. Season with salt and pepper. You can make the sauce by combining all the ingredients in a blender or food processor, but it is more satisfying by hand.

◆ Put the penne in a large pot and just cover with boiling water. Add a pinch of salt and a few drops of oil, cover and cook for 10 minutes. Leave to stand for a couple of minutes, then drain and stir in the sauce.

◆ Serve hot.

Penne al Pesto

RIGATONI COUNTRY-STYLE

SERVES 4 / SET: FULL

Ingredients

3½ cups/400 g/14 oz rigatoni (or macaroni)

boiling water

salt

oil

1 cup/175 g/6 oz spicy sausage, cut into chunks or sliced

1 cup/100 g/4 oz cauliflower florets

15 ml/1 tbsp water

1 cup/100 g/4 oz green beans, topped and tailed (trimmed) and cut into bite size pieces

15–30 ml/1–2 tbsp olive oil

cayenne pepper

1 whole mozzarella cheese, diced

Use the long spicy sausages sold in coils for this dish. If you can't find these, use diced salami.

◆ Put the rigatoni in a deep pot and just cover with boiling water. Add a pinch of salt and a few drops of oil. Cover and cook for 10 minutes. Leave to stand, covered, while you make the sauce.

◆ Put the sausage pieces on a plate covered with absorbent kitchen paper (paper towels) and cook for 1½ minutes. Cover and keep warm.

◆ Put the cauliflower in a bowl with the water. Cover and cook for 1 minute. Add the beans, cover and cook for 3 minutes.

◆ Drain the pasta and vegetables. Pour the olive oil over the pasta and season with cayenne pepper. Stir in the cauliflower, beans, sausage and diced mozzarella cheese, cover and heat through for 1 minute.

◆ Serve hot.

Rigatoni Country-Style

LASAGNE AND HAM ROLLS

SERVES 4 / SET: FULL

Ingredients

4 sheets spinach lasagne

boiling water

salt

oil

4 slices ham, the same size as the lasagne sheets

This makes a tasty and attractive appetizer and it is also an unusual accompaniment to drinks. It is simple to prepare, but looks elegant.

◆ Put the lasagne in a deep pot with enough boiling water to cover. Add a pinch of salt and a few drops of oil. Cover and cook for 10 minutes. Leave to stand for 3 minutes. Drain and rinse well under cold running water.

◆ Lay the lasagne sheets out on a tea towel to dry. Do not use kitchen paper (paper towels) – it will stick to the pasta.

◆ When the lasagne has cooled, lay a slice of ham on top of each sheet and roll up tightly.

◆ Cut each roll into slices and serve cold.

SPAGHETTI WITH CLAMS

S E R V E S   4   /   S E T :   F U L L

Ingredients

6 cups/750 g/1½ lb clams (or other small shellfish)
30 ml/2 tbsp olive oil
1 clove garlic, crushed (minced)
1¾ cups/450 g/1 lb ripe tomatoes, peeled and chopped
salt and freshly ground black pepper
400 g/14 oz spaghetti
4½ cups/1 l/1¾ pt boiling water
a small glass of dry white wine
chopped parsley

This dish is one of the specialities of Naples.

◆ Clean the clams thoroughly under running water.

◆ Put the olive oil in a bowl and cook for 30 seconds. Add the garlic and cook for 1 minute. Add the tomatoes, cover with vented cling film (plastic wrap) and cook for 4 minutes, until soft. Season with salt and pepper and keep warm.

◆ Hold the spaghetti in a large pot and pour the boiling water over it. Push the spaghetti down into the water, add a pinch of salt and a few drops of oil, cover and cook for 2 minutes. Set aside, covered.

◆ Put the clams in a pot with the white wine, cover and cook for 2–3 minutes, until the shells open. Set aside.

◆ Drain the spaghetti and stir in the tomato sauce. Drain the clams and pile on top of the pasta.

◆ Sprinkle with parsley and serve hot.

VARIATION The clams may be removed from their shells before serving if you prefer.

Spaghetti with Clams

MACARONI WITH BROCCOLI AND ALMONDS

SERVES 4 / SET: FULL

Ingredients

3½ cups/400 g/14 oz macaroni

boiling water

oil

salt

4 tbsp/50 g/2 oz butter

good 3 cups/225 g/8 oz broccoli florets

⅓ cup/50 g/2 oz flaked (slivered) toasted almonds

60 ml/4 tbsp grated pecorino cheese

◆ Put the macaroni in a deep pot and pour over enough boiling water to cover. Add a few drops of oil and a pinch of salt, cover and cook for 9 minutes. Allow to stand.

◆ Put half the butter in a dish and cook for 1 minute. Add the broccoli and almonds and cook for 6 minutes, stirring twice, until the broccoli is tender, but still crisp.

◆ Drain the pasta, add the rest of the butter and the broccoli and almonds, toss and sprinkle with grated cheese before serving.

SPAGHETTI ALLA PUTANESCA

SERVES 4 / SET: FULL

Ingredients

400 g/14 oz spaghetti

4½ cups/1 l/1¾ pt boiling water

salt

oil

2 cloves garlic, chopped

½ cup/50 g/2 oz black olives, stoned (pitted) and roughly chopped

15 ml/1 tbsp capers, roughly chopped

5 anchovies, soaked in milk, rinsed, dried and chopped

1 red chilli (chili), seeded and chopped

30 ml/2 tbsp olive oil

¾ cup/200 g/7 oz canned tomatoes, drained and chopped

chopped parsley

Legend has it that this dish was prepared by the whores of Rome. It is hot and fiery.

◆ Hold the spaghetti in a pot and pour the boiling water over it. Push the spaghetti down into the pot, add a pinch of salt and a few drops of oil, cover and cook for 12 minutes. Set aside, covered.

◆ Put the garlic, olives, capers, anchovies, chilli (chili) and olive oil in a bowl. Stir well, cover and cook for 2 minutes. Stir in the tomatoes, cover and cook for 3 minutes.

◆ Drain the spaghetti, stir in the sauce and top with chopped parsley to serve.

Spaghetti alla Putanesca

PASTA AND FISH SALAD

SERVES 4 / SET: FULL

Ingredients

3½ cups/400 g/14 oz farfalle

boiling water

salt

30 ml/2 tbsp oil

scant cup/200 g/7 oz canned tuna in brine, drained and flaked

2 pink onions, chopped

1 scant cup/200 g/7 oz canned kidney beans, drained

freshly ground black pepper

chopped parsley

lemon wedges

◆ Put the farfalle in a pot and pour on enough boiling water to cover. Add a pinch of salt and a few drops of oil, cover and cook for 9 minutes. Drain and rinse thoroughly under cold running water. Drain thoroughly.

◆ Toss the pasta in the oil, add the tuna, onions and kidney beans and mix well.

◆ Season with salt and pepper, sprinkle with parsley and serve with lemon wedges.

PASTA AND HAM SALAD

S E R V E S   4   /   S E T :   F U L L

Ingredients
3 1/2 cups/400 g/14 oz shell pasta
boiling water
salt
a few drops of oil
2/3 cup/100 g/4 oz diced ham
2 cups/200 g/7 oz cooked broad (lima) beans (or use canned beans, drained)
2/3 cup/150 ml/5 fl oz sour cream
freshly ground black pepper
mint leaves

◆ Put the pasta in a dish and pour over enough boiling water to cover. Add a pinch of salt and a few drops of oil, cover and cook for 9 minutes. Drain and rinse thoroughly under cold running water. Drain thoroughly.

◆ Toss the pasta with the ham and broad (lima) beans in sour cream. Season with salt and pepper and garnish with mint leaves.

PASTA WITH CHICK PEAS (GARBANZOS)

S E R V E S   4   /   S E T :   F U L L

Ingredients
3 1/2 cups/400 g/14 oz multi-coloured pasta
boiling water
salt
15 ml/1 tbsp oil
2 tbsp/25 g/1 oz butter
1 clove garlic, crushed (minced)
2 cups/400 g/14 oz canned chick peas (garbanzos), drained
1/3–1/2 cup/50–75 g/2–3 oz freshly grated Parmesan cheese
freshly ground black pepper

This is a very simple dish called "thunder and lightning" in Italy. Make it with canned chick peas (garbanzos) to save time.

◆ Put the pasta in a bowl and just cover with boiling water. Add a pinch of salt and a few drops of oil, cover and cook for 10 minutes. Allow to stand, covered.

◆ Put the butter in a bowl and cook for 1 minute. Stir in the garlic and chick peas (garbanzos), cover and cook for 2 minutes.

◆ Drain the pasta. Pour over the oil and the garlic chick peas (garbanzos) and add the Parmesan cheese.

◆ Stir and serve at once. Offer black pepper at the table.

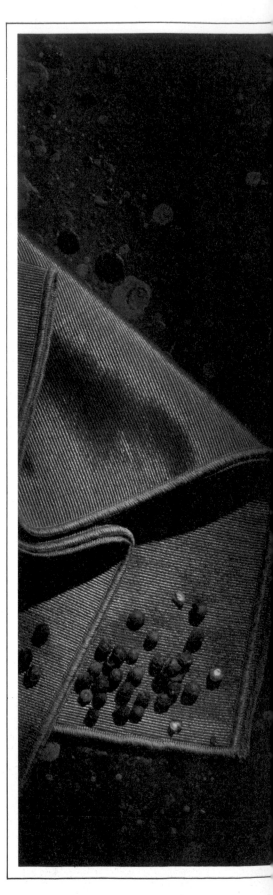

Pasta with Chick Peas (Garbanzos)

SPAGHETTI WITH SQUID

SERVES 4 / SET: FULL

Ingredients

1³/₄ cups/400 g/14 oz small squid
30 ml/2 tbsp olive oil
1 onion, finely chopped
1 clove garlic, crushed (minced)
1 stick (stack) celery, finely sliced
1 carrot, finely chopped
15 ml/1 tbsp lemon juice
chopped parsley
salt and freshly ground black pepper
400 g/14 oz spaghetti
4¹/₂ cups/1 l/1³/₄ pt boiling water (approx.)

◆ Remove the eyes and mouth of the squid, take out the cuttlefish bone and wash the squid thoroughly, peeling off the outer skin as you do so. Cut the body and tentacles into slices.

◆ Put the oil in a pot and cook for 30 seconds. Add the onion, garlic, celery, carrot and squid, sprinkle with lemon juice, cover and cook for 5 minutes. Stir in the parsley and season with salt and pepper.

◆ Hold the spaghetti in a pot and pour the water over it. As the spaghetti softens, push it down into the water. Add a pinch of salt and a few drops of oil, cover and cook for 12 minutes. Leave to stand for 5 minutes while you reheat the squid mixture.

◆ Drain the spaghetti and stir in the sauce. Serve at once.

Spaghetti with Squid

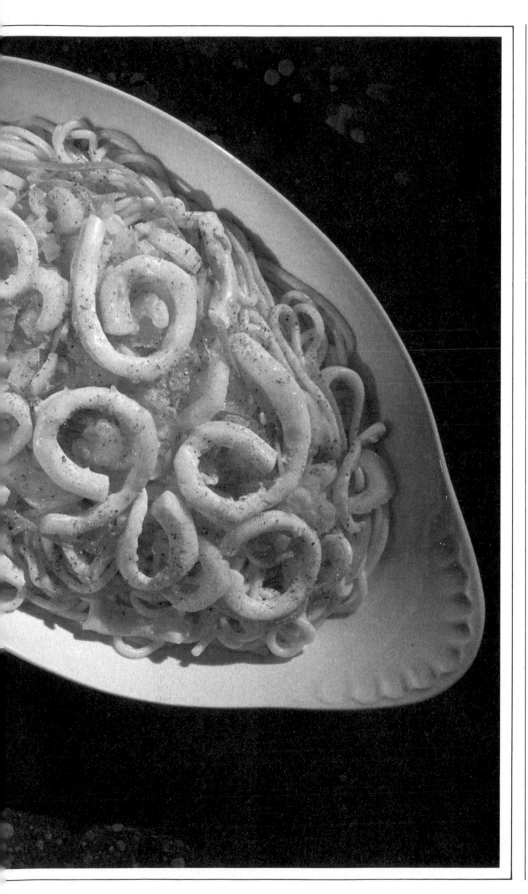

SPINACH AND RICOTTA ROLLS

SERVES 4 / SET: FULL

Ingredients

1 kg/2 lb fresh spinach

1¼ cups/225 g/8 oz ricotta cheese

salt and freshly ground black pepper

freshly grated nutmeg

8 sheets lasagne

boiling water

15 ml/1 tbsp oil

1 clove garlic, crushed (minced)

1 small onion, chopped

1½ cups/400 g/14 oz canned tomatoes, sieved (strained)

◆ Wash the spinach and remove tough stalks and discoloured leaves. Put it in a roasting or boiling bag, tie loosely and cook for 6 minutes, shaking the bag once. Allow to cool.

◆ Chop the spinach, draining away excess moisture. Mix it well with the ricotta and season with salt, pepper and nutmeg.

◆ Put the lasagne in a dish and pour over enough boiling water to cover. Add a pinch of salt and a few drops of oil. Cover and cook for 15 minutes. Drain and rinse thoroughly under cold running water. Lay the lasagne sheets out on a tea (dish) towel to dry.

◆ Meanwhile, make the sauce. Put the oil in a bowl and cook for 30 seconds. Add the garlic and onion and cook for 3 minutes. Stir in the sieved (strained) tomato and cook for 4 minutes. Season to taste with salt and pepper.

◆ To assemble, divide the spinach and ricotta mixture between the lasagne sheets. Spread it out to cover the lasagne and roll each sheet up. Pack them in a dish they just fit and pour over the hot tomato sauce.

◆ Heat through in the microwave for a couple of minutes and serve hot.

SPAGHETTI ALLA CARBONARA

SERVES 4 / SET: FULL AND MEDIUM

Ingredients

400 g/14 oz spaghetti
4½ cups/1 l/1¾ pt boiling water
salt
oil
⅔ cup/150 ml/5 fl oz double (heavy) cream
2 tbsp/25 g/1 oz butter
4 eggs
60 ml/4 tbsp grated Parmesan cheese
½ cup/75 g/3 oz diced ham (or gammon)
freshly ground black pepper

This favourite Roman dish is named after the charcoal burners who are said to have invented it.

◆ Put the spaghetti in a pot and pour on the boiling water. Push the spaghetti down into the pot. Add a pinch of salt and a few drops of oil. Cover the pot and cook on full for 12 minutes. Leave to stand, covered.

◆ Put the cream in a bowl with the butter and heat through on medium for 1½ minutes. Break in the eggs and beat well. Stir in the Parmesan and ham (or gammon) and season with black pepper. Cook on medium for 2–3 minutes, until the eggs are almost cooked and lightly scrambled in the cream, stirring twice.

◆ Drain the spaghetti, stir in the hot sauce and serve at once.

Spaghetti alla Carbonara

SPAGHETTI MASCARPONE

SERVES 4 / SET: FULL

Ingredients

400 g/14 oz spaghetti
4½ cups/1 l/1¾ pt boiling water
salt
a few drops of oil
2 egg yolks
approx. ⅔ cup/100 g/4 oz mascarpone cheese
freshly ground black pepper
60 ml/4 tbsp grated Parmesan cheese

Mascarpone is an Italian cheese sold in muslin (cheesecloth) bags. You can substitute cream cheese if you can't get the real thing.

◆ Hold the spaghetti in a deep pot and pour over the boiling water. Push the spaghetti down into the water. Add more to cover if necessary. Add a pinch of salt and a few drops of oil, cover and cook for 12 minutes. Leave to stand.

◆ Stir the egg yolks into the mascarpone.

◆ Drain the pasta, top with the mascarpone and sprinkle with black pepper and Parmesan.

◆ Heat through for 1 minute, then serve.

PASTA SHELLS WITH CRAB MEAT

SERVES 4 / SET: FULL

Ingredients

3½ cups/400 g/14 oz pasta shells

boiling water

salt

oil

1 scant cup/200 g/7 oz canned or fresh crab meat, flaked

⅔ cup/150 ml/¼ pt single (light) cream

15 ml/1 tbsp marsala

cayenne pepper

chopped parsley

◆ Put the pasta shells in a deep pot, just cover with boiling water, add a pinch of salt and a few drops of oil, cover and cook for 9 minutes. Allow to stand, covered, while you make the sauce.

◆ Stir the crab meat into the cream, add the marsala and cook for 3 minutes.

◆ Drain the pasta, stir in the sauce, sprinkle with cayenne pepper and garnish with chopped parsley.

Pasta Shells with Crab Meat

RIGATONI WITH SARDINES

SERVES 4 / SET: FULL

Ingredients

3½ cups/400 g/14 oz rigatoni

boiling water

salt

15 ml/1 tbsp oil

1 clove garlic, crushed (minced)

150 g/5 oz canned sardines in tomato sauce

4 leaves fresh sage, chopped

freshly ground black pepper

◆ Put the rigatoni in a dish and cover with boiling water. Add a pinch of salt and a few drops of the oil, cover and cook for 9 minutes. Leave to stand, covered, while you prepare the sauce.

◆ Put the remaining oil in a bowl and cook for 30 seconds. Add the garlic and cook for 1½ minutes.

◆ Mash the sardines in their tomato sauce and add to the bowl. Cover and cook for 2–3 minutes, stirring once, until hot through.

◆ Drain the pasta, pour the sauce over it, sprinkle with fresh sage and pepper and serve.

THE MICROWAVE LIBRARY

COOKING WITH

Fish

ELIZABETH CORNISH

FISH

ANYONE who has ever tasted fish cooked in a microwave will agree that there is no better way of retaining its succulence, freshness, delicacy of flavour and fineness of texture.
Fish is so moist that it can be cooked in little or no liquid or fat, so none of its flavour is lost or changed. It can also be cooked very fast, so it won't go dry or rubbery.
Fish is an excellent source of protein, vitamins and minerals and is becoming increasingly popular, particularly in comparison with meat, because it is less fat.

As people eat more and more fish, so the selection available grows and unusual varieties begin to appear. There are at least 50 types of edible fish, so most of us have many more to look forward to.
This book features a selection of fish, among them salmon, trout, sole (flounder), monkfish, and snapper, all types of seafood and molluscs, and even eel and squid. If you find a fish that you haven't tried before which isn't in the book, ask for advice on its preparation when you buy it. You will certainly be able to adapt several recipes to suit different fish because most of them, soft- or firm-fleshed are cooked in the same way.
Perhaps in the past the plainness of traditional fish cooking has put some people off eating it more than once a week. It's just as easy to be adventurous with fish as with any other food, and as the photographs in this book demonstrate, you can create something that looks spectacular and tastes exciting with very little effort.
Fish is such a clean and simple food and it lends itself perfectly to dishes that are bright and elegant with combinations of tastes that surprise and delight. As these dishes take such little time to prepare, you will be able to cook something good enough for a dinner party every night of the week.

CONTENTS

PAELLA

SERVES 4 / SET: FULL

Ingredients

15 ml/1 tbsp olive oil

1 onion, finely sliced

1 clove garlic, crushed (minced)

1 good cup/225 g/8 oz long-grain rice

a few strands of saffron

2½ cups/575 ml/1 pt boiling chicken stock (broth)

salt and freshly ground black pepper

1 good cup/200 g/7 oz peas

1 generous cup/175 g/6 oz peeled prawns (shrimp), plus a few in their shells for garnish

⅔ cup/100 g/4 oz cooked chicken, chopped

⅔ cup/100 g/4 oz cooked ham, chopped

5 cups/575 ml/1 pt mussels, scrubbed and rinsed

2½ cups/300 ml/½ pt clams (or other small shellfish), thoroughly rinsed

small glass of dry white wine

It is important to scrub the mussels thoroughly under running water to remove their beards and any grit. Discard any shells that are open or broken.

◆ Put the oil in a large pot and cook for 30 seconds. Stir in the onion and garlic and cook for 2 minutes. Stir in the rice and saffron, pour over the boiling stock (broth), add seasoning, cover and cook for 8 minutes.

◆ Stir in the peas, prawns (shrimp), chicken and ham, cover and cook for 4 minutes. Leave the pot to stand, covered, while you cook the mussels and clams.

◆ Put the mussels and clams in a large pot and pour over the wine. Cook for about 3 minutes, until the shells have opened. Discard any shells that remain closed.

◆ Arrange the paella on a heated serving plate. Take some of the mussels and clams out of their shells and add to the rice. Garnish the dish with the remaining mussels, clams and prawns (shrimp).

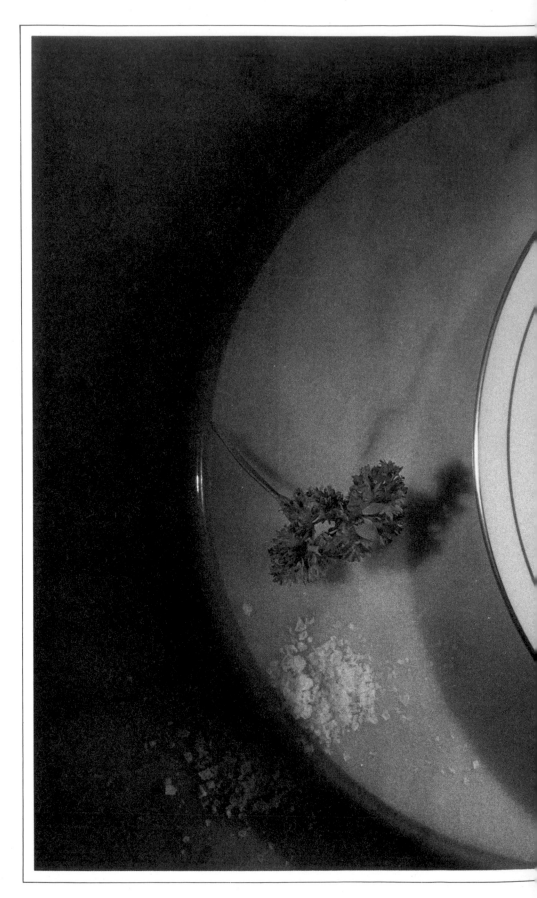

SALMON STEAKS WITH HOLLANDAISE SAUCE

SERVES 4 / SET: DEFROST AND FULL

Ingredients

½ cup/100 g/4 oz butter, diced

30 ml/2 tbsp lemon juice

3 egg yolks

salt and white pepper

4 salmon steaks, about 175 g/6 oz each

Serve this dish on a special occasion with new peas and new potatoes. Salmon is so succulent that it will cook perfectly without the addition of any water or fat.

◆ First make the sauce. Put the butter in a bowl and cook for 2 minutes on medium or defrost until melted. Add the lemon juice and the egg yolks and whisk lightly.

◆ Cook on medium or defrost for 1 minute, whisk again and season with salt and white pepper (black pepper would spoil the appearance of the sauce). Transfer the sauce to a heated jug and keep warm while you cook the salmon.

◆ Rinse the salmon steaks, pat dry and lay in a shallow dish. Cover with vented cling film (plastic wrap) and cook on full for 3½–4 minutes, turning the dish once.

◆ Serve the salmon steaks with the Hollandaise sauce.

◆ This dish is equally good served cold, but not chilled.

Fisherman's Pie

FISHERMAN'S PIE

S E R V E S   4   /   S E T :   F U L L

Ingredients

700 g/1¹/₂ lb smoked cod or haddock fillets, skinned

1¹/₂ cups/100 g/4 oz mushrooms

4 small leeks, sliced

1¹/₄ cups/300 ml/¹/₂ pt milk

3 tbsp/40 g/1¹/₂ oz butter

6 tbsp/40 g/1¹/₂ oz flour

6 tbsp/40 g/1¹/₂ oz Gruyère cheese, grated

¹/₂ cup/40 g/1¹/₂ oz Parmesan cheese, grated

salt and freshly ground black pepper

2 hardboiled (hard-cooked) eggs, sliced

1¹/₂ cups/225 g/8 oz prawns (shrimp), peeled

3 cups/700 g/1¹/₂ lb potatoes, cooked and mashed with plenty of butter and a little milk

◆ Put the fish fillets in a deep pic dish with the mushrooms and leeks and add about 60 ml/4 tbsp of the milk. Cover and cook for 3–4 minutes until fish is tender. Pour off the milk and reserve. Flake the fish with a fork.

◆ Put the butter in a jug or bowl and cook for 1 minute, until melted. Stir in the flour. Cook for 1 minute. Pour on the milk the fish was cooked in and the remaining milk. Cook for 3 minutes, whisking the sauce after each minute. Add the cheeses and season. Cook for a further minute and whisk again.

◆ Combine the fish, mushrooms, leeks, eggs and prawns (shrimp) in the pie dish and stir in the sauce. Top with the mashed potato and heat through for about 4 minutes.

◆ Brown the top under the grill (broiler) if liked before serving.

FRIED FISH ROE

S E R V E S   1   /   S E T :   F U L L

Ingredients

a little flour

1 fish roe

a little beaten egg

1¹/₂ cups/50 g/2 oz fresh breadcrumbs (approx.)

1 tbsp/15 g/¹/₂ oz butter

lemon wedges

The fish roe that you buy will have already been cooked. Fried fish roe makes a very nourishing lunch for one with a crisp salad.

◆ Sprinkle flour over the roe to coat it evenly. Dust off the excess. Roll it in egg, then in breadcrumbs, pushing them on with your fingers.

◆ Heat a browning dish to maximum according to the manufacturer's instructions. Put the butter on the dish and, wearing oven gloves, tilt it so that it is covered in hot fat.

◆ Put the roe on the dish and cook for 30–45 seconds on each side.

◆ Let it stand for 1 minute, then serve with lemon wedges.

HOMEMADE FISH CAKES IN TOMATO SAUCE

SERVES 4–6 / SET: FULL

Ingredients

450 g/1 lb firm, white fish fillets

45 ml/3 tbsp water

450 g/1 lb even size potatoes

3 tbsp/40 g/1½ oz butter

6 tbsp/40 g/1½ oz flour

1¼ cups/300 ml/½ pt milk

chopped parsley

salt and freshly ground black pepper

golden (packaged) breadcrumbs (breading mix)

TOMATO SAUCE

15 ml/1 tbsp oil

1 onion, chopped

1 clove garlic, crushed (minced)

1½ cups/400 g/14 oz canned tomatoes, drained

15 ml/1 tbsp tomato purée (paste)

◆ Put the fish fillets in a dish with the water. Cover with vented cling film (plastic wrap) and cook for 4 minutes, until done. Drain and flake the fish with a fork.

◆ Put the potatoes in the oven and cook for 4–7 minutes, depending on their size, rearranging once. When they are done, remove and allow them to cool. Remove the skins and mash the potato well.

◆ Put the butter in a bowl and cook for 1 minute. Stir in the flour and cook for 1 minute. Stir in the milk and cook for 3 minutes, whisking after each minute.

◆ Mix the fish and potatoes together and bind with the sauce. Add enough sauce so that you have a very stiff mixture. Mix in the parsley and seasoning.

◆ Form the mixture into cakes. Roll them in golden (packaged) breadcrumbs (breading mix) and set aside while you make the tomato sauce.

◆ Put the oil in a bowl and mix in the onion and garlic. Cook for 2 minutes. Add the tomatoes, tomato purée (paste) and seasoning. Cook for 3 minutes. Mix until smooth in a food processor or blender. Return to the oven to heat through for 2 minutes.

◆ Cook the fish cakes. Heat a browning dish to maximum, according to the manufacturer's instructions, and cook the cakes in batches of 3 for 3 minutes each, turning them over half-way through. If you have no browning dish, they can be cooked on a greased plate, but they won't be crisp.

◆ Spoon a pool of sauce onto each plate and lay the fish cakes in it. Serve at once.

VARIATION This is an excellent way of serving bought fish fingers (fish sticks).

FILLETS OF SOLE (FLOUNDER) WITH GRAPES, ALMONDS AND PRAWNS (SHRIMP)

SERVES 4 / SET: FULL

Ingredients

12 large green grapes

³⁄₄ cup/75 g/3 oz toasted flaked (slivered) almonds

8 large prawns (shrimp)

²⁄₃ cup/150 ml/¹⁄₄ pt canned consommé

15 ml/1 tbsp sherry

4 sole (flounder) fillets, skinned

a little butter

◆ Halve the grapes and remove the pips (seeds). Put them in a dish with the flaked (slivered) almonds, prawns (shrimp), consommé and sherry and cook for 2–3 minutes, until hot through. Keep warm.

◆ Lay the plaice (flounder) fillets in a buttered dish and dot with butter. Cover with vented cling film (plastic wrap) and cook for 2–3 minutes, turning once, until cooked through.

◆ Put the fillets on 4 heated plates and spoon the sauce around them. Serve at once.

Fillets of Sole (Flounder) with Grapes, Almonds and Prawns (Shrimp)

FISH IN VERMOUTH SAUCE

SERVES 4 / SET: FULL

Ingredients

15 ml/1 tbsp oil

1 shallot, chopped

1 good cup/75 g/3 oz mushrooms, wiped and sliced

30 ml/2 tbsp dry vermouth

²/₃ cup/150 ml/¹/₄ pt single (light) cream

salt

cayenne pepper

4 fillets white fish

a little butter

Use any white fish fillets for this recipe.

◆ First make the sauce. Put the oil in a dish and cook for 30 seconds. Add the shallot and cook for 2 minutes. Add the mushrooms and vermouth, cover with vented cling film (plastic wrap) and cook for 3 minutes, stirring once.

◆ Stir in the cream and season to taste with salt and cayenne pepper. Set aside.

◆ Put the fish fillets in a dish and dot with butter. Cover with vented cling film (plastic wrap) and cook for 3–4 minutes, until done, rearranging once.

◆ Heat the sauce through for 1 minute

◆ Lay the fish fillets on heated plates, pour over the sauce and serve.

FISH IN SWEET AND SOUR SAUCE

SERVES 2—4 / SET: FULL

Ingredients

15 ml/1 tbsp minced onion
1 clove garlic, crushed (minced)
2 hot chillies (chilis), seeded and finely sliced
1 slice root (green) ginger, grated
45 ml/3 tbsp sherry
4 firm, white fish fillets, weighing about 450 g/1 lb in total
¾ cup/200 g/7 oz canned tomatoes, drained and sieved (strained)
15 ml/1 tbsp tomato purée (paste)
a pinch of sugar
finely shredded spring onions (scallions)
tomato slices

Serve this dish with fluffy white rice.

◆ For the marinade, mix together in a dish the onion, garlic, chillies (chilis), ginger and sherry. Lay the fish in the marinade and leave for an hour, turning occasionally.

◆ Mix together the tomatoes, tomato purée (paste) and sugar and pour over the fish. Cover with vented cling film (plastic wrap) and cook for about 5 minutes, until done, turning once.

◆ Serve garnished with finely shredded spring onions (scallions) and tomato slices.

FILLETS OF FISH WITH CRANBERRY SAUCE

SERVES 4 / SET: FULL

Ingredients

2 medium-sized, dark-fleshed fish
2 cups/225 g/8 oz cranberries
30 ml/2 tbsp lemon juice
15 ml/1 tbsp port
salt and freshly ground black pepper
radicchio

A colourful and tasty winter dish.

◆ To fillet the fish, gut them, cut off the fins and carefully remove the bone from the head downwards. Cut off the heads. Remove the skin and the remaining bones.

◆ Make the sauce. Combine the cranberries, lemon juice and port in a bowl and season with salt and pepper. Cook for 4 minutes, until the berries are soft. Keep warm.

◆ Lay the fish in a shallow dish, cover with vented cling film (plastic wrap) and cook for 4 minutes, turning once.

◆ Arrange the fish fillets on heated plates, on a bed of radicchio, pour over the sauce and serve.

VARIATION Try using gooseberries instead of cranberries.

TROUT WITH CUCUMBER AND MUSHROOM

SERVES 4 / SET: FULL AND MEDIUM

Ingredients

¹⁄₄ cucumber, sliced
2 cups/100 g/4 oz mushrooms, sliced
²⁄₃ cup/150 ml/¹⁄₄ pt canned consommé
4 small trout of even size
60 ml/4 tbsp water
parsley
lemon wedges

◆ Put the cucumber and mushrooms in a dish and pour over the consommé. Cover with vented cling film (plastic wrap) and cook for 4 minutes. Set aside.

◆ Put the trout in a dish, add the water, cover with vented cling film (plastic wrap) and cook for 4 minutes, turning once, until cooked through.

◆ Put the trout on heated plates and pour the sauce over.

◆ Serve garnished with parsley and lemon wedges.

SOUSED FISH

SERVES 4 / SET: FULL

Ingredients

15 ml/1 tbsp oil
1 onion, cut into rings
1 large apple, peeled, cored and sliced
15 ml/1 tbsp pickling spices
1 bay leaf
2/3 cup/150 ml/1/4 pt cider vinegar
4 small, dark-fleshed fish, filleted

◆ Roll up the fish and secure with cocktail sticks (toothpicks).

◆ Put the oil in a dish and cook for 30 seconds. Add the onion and cook for 2 minutes.

◆ Mix the onion with the apple, add the pickling spices and bay leaf and pour over the cider vinegar. Lay the fish on top. Cover with vented cling film (plastic wrap). Cook until the vinegar boils and then for about 3 more minutes, until the fish are done. Leave to cool.

◆ Serve the fish cold with a spoonful of the cooking vinegar and apple and onion slices on top.

Soused Fish

FISH AND VEGETABLES ON A BED OF NOODLES

SERVES 4 / SET: FULL

Ingredients

3 tbsp/40 g/1½ oz butter
6 tbsp/40 g/1½ oz flour
⅔ cup/150 ml/¼ pt milk
⅔ cup/150 ml/¼ pt single (light) cream
½ cup/40 g/1½ oz Parmesan cheese
1 egg yolk
4 firm, white fish fillets, about 175 g/6 oz each, skinned
30–45 ml/2–3 tbsp milk
1½ cups/200 g/7 oz asparagus spears
1 cup/200 g/7 oz broad (lima) beans, cooked or canned
225 g/8 oz fresh spinach tagliatelle
boiling water
salt
5 ml/1 tsp oil
paprika

◆ First make the sauce. Put the butter in a bowl and cook for 1 minute. Stir in the flour and cook for 1 minute. Stir in the milk and cook for 2 minutes, whisking after each minute. Stir in the cream and cheese and cook for 2 minutes, whisking after each minute. Stir in the egg yolk. Keep the sauce warm.

◆ Put the fillets in a dish with the milk, asparagus spears and broad (lima) beans. Cover with vented cling film (plastic wrap) and cook for 4 minutes, turning once, until the fish is done. Keep warm.

◆ Put the tagliatelle in a pot and pour over boiling water to just cover. Add a pinch of salt and the oil, cover and cook for 3–4 minutes, until *al dente* (firm to the bite).

◆ Pour pools of sauce onto 4 heated serving plates. Drain the noodles well and divide between the plates of sauce.

◆ Flake the fish on top of the noodles, dust with paprika and serve with the broad (lima) beans and asparagus spears.

FISH WITH CARROTS AND CELERY

SERVES 4 / SET: FULL

Ingredients

1 bulb fennel, sliced
3 carrots, peeled and cut into strips lengthways
3 sticks (stacks) celery, sliced
45 ml/3 tbsp fish stock (broth) or milk
15 ml/1 tbsp lemon juice
4 small, whole fish, cleaned
salt and freshly ground black pepper
chopped parsley or fennel fronds
lemon wedges

◆ Put the sliced fennel, carrots and celery in a large oblong dish and add the fish stock (broth) or milk and lemon juice. Cover with vented cling film (plastic wrap) and cook for 8 minutes, stirring once, until the vegetables are tender.

◆ Lay the fish on top of the vegetables and cover again. Cook for 3 minutes, turning the dish once, until the fish are done.

◆ Lay the fish on warmed plates and spoon the vegetables beside them. Add a little of the cooking liquor, season and garnish with parsley or fennel fronds.

◆ Serve with lemon wedges.

FISH STEAKS WITH RED PEPPER SAUCE

SERVES 4 / SET: FULL

Ingredients

1 courgette (zucchini), chopped
4 small tomatoes, skinned, seeded and chopped
15 ml/1 tbsp water
1 large red pepper, seeded and chopped
½ clove of garlic, crushed (minced)
a little chopped onion
⅔ cup/150 ml/¼ pt canned consommé
15 ml/1 tbsp sherry
salt and white pepper
4 firm white fish steaks, about 175 g/6 oz each, skinned
a little butter
a lemon

◆ First make the garnish. Put the courgette (zucchini) and tomatoes in a dish with the water. Cook for 2 minutes. Set aside.

◆ Make the sauce. Combine the pepper, garlic, onion, consommé and sherry in a small bowl and cook for 5 minutes, until the pepper is very soft. Blend in a food processor or blender, season and keep warm.

◆ Lay the fish steaks in a buttered dish and dot with butter. Cover with vented cling film (plastic wrap) and cook for 3–4 minutes, turning once, until done.

◆ Put the fish on 4 heated plates. Add a spoonful of sauce and garnish with a little mound of the courgette (zucchini) and tomato mixture and the lemon.

Fish Steaks with Red Pepper Sauce

PRAWNS (SHRIMP) AND COURGETTES (ZUCCHINI) IN TOMATO SAUCE

SERVES 4 / SET: FULL

Ingredients
15 ml/1 tbsp oil

2 shallots, chopped

4 baby courgettes (zucchini), sliced

1½ cups/400 g/14 oz canned tomatoes, sieved (strained)

2½ cups/400 g/14 oz peeled prawns (shrimp)

freshly chopped basil

salt and freshly ground black pepper

◆ Put the oil in a bowl and cook for 30 seconds. Add the shallots and courgettes (zucchini) and cook for 3 minutes.

◆ Stir in the sieved (strained) tomatoes and the prawns (shrimp) and cook, covered with vented cling film (plastic wrap), for 5 minutes, until heated through.

◆ Sprinkle with plenty of basil and season to taste with salt and pepper.

◆ Serve with rice.

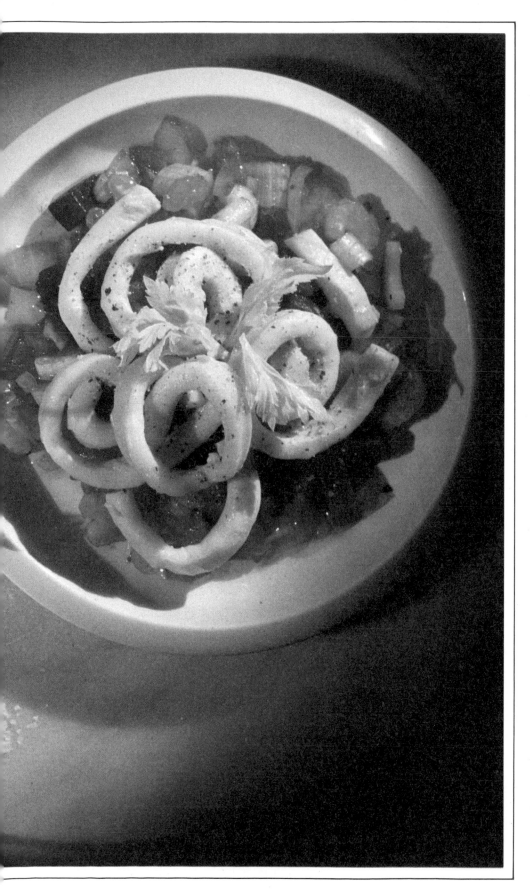

SQUID WITH BEETROOT (BEETS)

SERVES 4 / SET: FULL

Ingredients

approx. 3 cups/450 g/1 lb small squid
15 ml/1 tbsp olive oil
1 small onion, chopped
1 clove garlic, crushed (minced)
1 stalk (stack) celery, finely chopped
2 cooked beetroot (beets) chopped
1/2 glass dry white wine
15 ml/1 tbsp tomato purée (paste)
salt and freshly ground black pepper
celery tips

◆ First clean the squid. Remove the eyes, mouth, ink sac and outer membrane. Take out the cuttlefish bone. Wash the squid well, then slice body and tentacles.

◆ Put the olive oil in a pot and cook for 30 seconds. Stir in the onion and garlic and cook for 2 minutes.

◆ Add the celery, beetroot (beets) and squid. Mix the white wine and tomato purée (paste) and pour over the squid. Cover and cook for 8 minutes, or until the squid is tender.

◆ Season with salt and pepper and serve garnished with celery tips.

Squid with Beetroot (Beet)

FISH STEAKS IN ORANGE SAUCE WITH BROCCOLI AND ALMONDS

SERVES 4 / SET: FULL

Ingredients

2 tbsp/25 g/1 oz butter

3 tbsp/25 g/1 oz cornflour (cornstarch)

1¼ cups/300 ml/½ pt orange juice

grated rind of 1 orange

4 fish steaks, about 150 g/5 oz each

30 ml/2 tbsp water

8 spears broccoli

⅓ cup/50 g/2 oz flaked (slivered) almonds

◆ Put the butter in a bowl and cook for 1 minute. Stir in the cornflour (cornstarch) and cook for 1 minute. Stir in the orange juice and cook for 3 minutes, whisking after each minute. Stir in the orange rind. Keep the sauce warm.

◆ Put the fish steaks in a dish with the water. Add the broccoli and the almond slivers. Cover with vented cling film (plastic wrap) and cook for 4 minutes, rearranging once, until the fish is done and the broccoli is tender.

◆ Pour the orange sauce over 4 heated plates, add the fish and garnish with the broccoli and almonds.

Fish Steaks in Orange Sauce with Broccoli and Almonds

FILLETS OF FISH IN CRAB SAUCE WITH RED PEPPERS

SERVES 4 / SET: FULL

Ingredients

1 red pepper, seeded and cut into julienne strips

30 ml/2 tbsp water

⅔ cup/150 ml/¼ pt single (light) cream

50 g/2 oz canned dressed crab meat

salt and white pepper

4 firm fish fillets

2 tbsp/25 g/1 oz butter

◆ Put the strips of red pepper in a dish with the water. Cover with vented cling film (plastic wrap) and cook for 4–5 minutes, until tender, stirring once. Set aside.

◆ Mash the cream into the crab meat until smooth. Season to taste with salt and white pepper.

◆ Put the fish fillets in a dish, dot with butter, cover with vented cling film (plastic wrap) and cook for 4 minutes, rearranging once.

◆ Cook the crab sauce for 1–2 minutes to heat through.

◆ Spoon a pool of crab sauce onto 4 heated plates, put the fish on top and garnish with strips of red pepper.

FILLETS OF SOLE (FLOUNDER) WITH SPINACH SAUCE

SERVES 4 / SET: FULL

Ingredients

5 tbsp/65 g/2½ oz butter

6 tbsp/40 g/1½ oz flour

1¼ cups/300 ml/½ pt milk

1 egg yolk

100 g/4 oz frozen spinach, defrosted
and squeezed very thoroughly to drain

salt and freshly ground black pepper

4 sole (flounder) fillets

a squeeze of lemon juice

fine slices of carrot, cut into flower shapes

chives, chopped

*Serve this creamy dish with a crisp salad in
a contrasting colour – radicchio would go
very well.*

◆ First make the sauce. Put 3 tbsp/
40 g/1½ oz of the butter in a bowl and
cook for 1 minute. Stir in the flour
and cook for 1 minute. Pour on the
milk and cook for 3 minutes, whisking
after every minute. Stir in the egg yolk
and spinach and season to taste. Cook
for 1 minute, then keep warm.

◆ Lay the fillets in a dish, dot with
the remaining butter and sprinkle
with lemon juice. Cook for 3–4
minutes, rearranging once.

◆ Arrange the fish on heated plates,
pour the sauce over and garnish with
carrot slices and chives to look like
flowers and stalks.

◆ Serve at once.

Fillets of Sole (Flounder) with Spinach Sauce

FISH STEAKS WITH TOMATOES AND BASIL

SERVES 4 / SET: FULL

Ingredients

15 ml/1 tbsp olive oil
15 ml/1 tbsp chopped onion
1 clove garlic, crushed (minced)
1¼ cups/350 g/12 oz ripe tomatoes, peeled, seeded and chopped
a few leaves of basil or 5 ml/1 tsp dried basil
4 firm, white fish steaks
a little butter
30 ml/2 tbsp canned peas, drained
30 ml/2 tbsp canned yellow or white beans, drained

◆ First make the sauce. Put the oil in a bowl and cook for 30 seconds. Stir in the onion and garlic and cook for 2 minutes. Stir in the tomatoes and basil, cover and cook for 4 minutes, or until soft, stirring twice.

◆ Put the fish in a buttered dish, cover with vented cling film (plastic wrap) and cook for 4 minutes, until done, turning once.

◆ Put the peas and beans in a bowl and cook for 1 minute.

◆ Put a portion of mixed peas and beans onto 4 heated plates, lay the fish on top and pour the sauce over.

MUSSEL SALAD

SERVES 4 / SET: FULL

Ingredients

1 tbsp/15 g/½ oz butter
1 small onion, chopped
4 cups/450 g/1 lb mussels, well scrubbed
30 ml/2 tbsp lemon juice
30 ml/2 tbsp dry white wine
4 sticks (stacks) celery, sliced
1 cup/100 g/4 oz cooked green beans, cut into bite-size pieces
1 red pepper, cut into julienne strips
1½ cups/225g/8 oz cooked potatoes, sliced
30 ml/2 tbsp mayonnaise
chopped parsley
salt and freshly ground black pepper

◆ Put the butter in a deep pot and cook for 30 seconds. Add the onion and cook for 2 minutes.

◆ Put in the mussels (discarding any that are broken or open), pour in the lemon juice and white wine and cook, covered, for 3–4 minutes, until the mussels have opened.

◆ Discard any closed shells. Allow the mussels to cool, then remove them from their shells.

◆ Mix the mussels in a large bowl with the celery, green beans, red pepper and potatoes. Stir the mayonnaise into the cooking liquor and onion and pour over the salad.

◆ Add chopped parsley and seasoning, mix well and serve.

KEDGEREE

SERVES 4 / SET: FULL

Ingredients

1 cup/225 g/8 oz rice
2½ cups/575 ml/1 pt boiling fish or chicken stock (broth)
salt
4 smoked fish fillets
30 ml/2 tbsp water
2 tbsp/25 g/1 oz butter
2–4 hardboiled (hard-cooked) eggs, chopped or sliced
cayenne pepper
2 tomatoes, sliced or cut into wedges
sprigs of parsley
a few prawns (shrimp) (optional)

A traditional breakfast dish, kedgeree makes a good evening snack and can be put together easily from the storecupboard (pantry).

◆ Put the rice in a pot and pour over the boiling stock (broth). Season with a pinch of salt, cover and cook for 12 minutes. Remove from the oven and leave covered while you prepare the smoked fish fillets.

◆ Lay the fillets in a dish with the water, cover and cook for 2 minutes. Flake the fish with a fork, discarding any bits of skin.

◆ Stir the fish, butter and eggs into the rice and season with cayenne pepper to taste. Garnish with tomatoes, parsley and a few prawns (shrimp) if liked.

◆ Serve hot.

Kedgeree

KING PRAWNS (SHRIMP) WITH MALTAISE SAUCE

SERVES 4 / SET: FULL AND MEDIUM

Ingredients

½ cup/100 g/4 oz butter, diced
grated rind and juice of 1 orange
3 egg yolks
salt and white pepper
12 king prawns (shrimp)
curly endive

◆ Put the butter in a bowl and heat on full power for 1½ minutes until melted.
◆ Whisk the orange rind and juice with the egg yolks and whisk into the hot butter, blending well. Season to taste with salt and white pepper, then cook on medium power for 1 minute, watching to make sure that the sauce does not boil.
◆ Arrange the king prawns (shrimp) on curly endive on 4 plates and serve with the Maltaise sauce. Provide your guests with finger bowls and large napkins.

VARIATION This is an excellent way of serving crawfish (crayfish).

King Prawns (Shrimp) with Maltaise Sauce

RED SNAPPER WITH LEMON AND LIME

SERVES 4 / SET: FULL

Ingredients

2 tbsp/25 g/1 oz butter
½ fennel bulb, chopped
juice of ½ lemon
juice of 1 lime
4 small, red snapper, cleaned
slices of lemon
slices of lime
fronds of fennel

◆ Put the butter in a dish and cook for 30 seconds. Add the chopped fennel, cover with vented cling film (plastic wrap) and cook for 3 minutes, stirring once.
◆ Pour on the lemon and lime juice and lay the red snapper on top of the fennel. Cover with vented cling film (plastic wrap) and cook for 4 minutes, until done, turning the dish once.
◆ Arrange the fish and fennel on 4 heated plates and spoon over the juice. Garnish with slices of lemon and lime and fennel fronds.

MONKFISH, CAULIFLOWER AND MANGETOUT (SNOW PEAS)

SERVES 4 / SET: FULL

Ingredients

½ *cauliflower*
30 *ml/2 tbsp water*
2¼ *cups/350 g/12 oz mangetout (snow peas)*
1½ *cups/350 g/12 oz monkfish pieces (grouper, groper or other firm white fish)*
30 *ml/2 tbsp dry sherry*
30 *ml/2 tbsp soy sauce*
1 *clove garlic, crushed (minced)*

This is a very popular dish in Singapore, where it is served with a bowl of rice.

◆ Break the cauliflower into florets, discarding tough stalks and leaves. Put it in a bowl with the water, cover and cook for 3–4 minutes, until you can pierce the stalks with the point of a sharp knife. Stir once during cooking.

◆ Cut the stalks from the mangetout (snow peas). Put the cauliflower and peas in a bowl with the fish.

◆ Combine the sherry, soy sauce and garlic. Pour over the vegetables and fish, stirring well. Leave for 30 minutes to marinate, stirring occasionally.

◆ Cover the bowl with vented cling film (plastic wrap) and cook for 3 minutes, stirring once.

◆ Serve immediately.

PRAWNS (SHRIMP) ST JACQUES

SERVES 4 / SET: FULL

Ingredients

3 tbsp/40 g/1½ oz butter
6 tbsp/40 g/1½ oz flour
⅔ cup/150 ml/¼ pt milk
⅔ cup/150 ml/¼ pt single (light) cream
60 ml/4 tbsp grated Parmesan cheese
salt and freshly ground black pepper
3 cups/450 g/1 lb prawns (shrimp) shelled weight

TOPPING

2 cups/450 g/1 lb cooked mashed potato
3 tbsp/40 g/1½ oz butter
salt
30 ml/2 tbsp grated Parmesan cheese
15 ml/1 tbsp golden (packaged) breadcrumbs (breading mix)
chopped parsley

◆ Put the butter in a bowl and cook for 1½ minutes until melted. Stir in the flour and cook for 1 minute. Stir in the milk and cook for 1 minute. Stir or whisk in the cream and cook for 1 minute. Stir in the cheese and cook for 1 minute. Season the sauce to taste and whisk or stir until smooth.

◆ Reserve some prawns (shrimp) for the garnish. Stir the peeled prawns into the sauce.

◆ Mash the potato with the butter and season with salt.

◆ Divide the prawn mixture between 4 scallop shells, top with the mashed potato and sprinkle with Parmesan cheese, golden (packaged) breadcrumbs (breading mix) and parsley. Heat through in the microwave for 1 minute, decorate with the unshelled prawns and serve hot.

Prawns (Shrimp) St Jacques

MONKFISH AND BABY LEEKS IN CHEESE SAUCE

SERVES 4 / SET: FULL

Ingredients

1¾ cups/400 g/14 oz monkfish (grouper, groper or any other firm white fish), skinned and cut into pieces
8 baby leeks, washed and trimmed
30–45 ml/2–3 tbsp water
3 tbsp/40 g/1½ oz butter
6 tbsp/40 g/1½ oz flour
1¼ cups/300 ml/½ pt milk
½ cup/50 g/2 oz grated Parmesan cheese
salt and freshly ground black pepper

◆ Put the monkfish (or equivalent) and leeks in a large oblong dish and add the water. Cover with vented cling film (plastic wrap) and cook for 5 minutes, rearranging once, until the fish is done and the leeks are tender. Set aside while you make the sauce.

◆ Put the butter in a jug and cook for 45 seconds. Stir in the flour. Pour on the milk and cook for 3 minutes, whisking after each minute. Stir in the cheese and cook for a further minute. Whisk again. Season to taste.

◆ Pour the sauce over the leeks and fish and heat through before serving.

FISH STEAKS WITH TWO SAUCES

SERVES 4 / SET: FULL AND MEDIUM

Ingredients

1 ripe avocado pear
1¼ cups/300 ml/½ pt single (light) cream
salt and white pepper
black pepper
1½ cups/225 g/8 oz strawberries
a squeeze of lemon juice
4 firm, white fish steaks
30 ml/2 tbsp milk

Strawberries and avocados make a surprisingly good combination, and they look very pretty together too.

◆ First make the sauces. Cut the avocado in half with a sharp knife and remove the stone. Scoop out the flesh from one half and put in a blender or food processor with half the cream. Blend until smooth. Season with salt and white pepper and put in a jug.

◆ Hull the strawberries. Put about ¾ cup/150 g/5 oz in a blender or food processor with the remaining cream and liquidize until smooth. Season with salt and black pepper and put in a jug.

◆ Prepare the garnish. Carefully remove the other half of the avocado from its shell without spoiling the shape. Cut into slices. Sprinkle with lemon juice to stop it going brown. Slice the remaining strawberries. Set aside.

◆ Put the fish steaks in a dish, add the milk and cover with vented cling film (plastic wrap). Cook on full for 4 minutes, or until done, turning once.

◆ Put the jugs of sauce in the microwave and cook on medium for 1−2 minutes, until warmed through.

◆ Put the fish on 4 heated serving plates. Spoon the avocado sauce to one side of the fish and the strawberry sauce to the other.

◆ Garnish with the avocado and strawberry slices and serve at once.

SMOKED FISH
AND POACHED EGG

*SERVES 2 / SET: FULL AND
MEDIUM*

Ingredients

2 pieces smoked fish, about 175 g/6 oz each
3 tbsp/40 g/1½ oz butter
2 tbsp milk
salt and freshly ground black pepper
2 eggs
sprigs of fennel or parsley

*This dish of smoked fish and egg makes a
very good brunch or late breakfast.*

◆ Put the smoked fish in a buttered
dish, dot with two-thirds of the butter
and add the milk. Cover with vented
cling film (plastic wrap) and cook on
full for 3–4 minutes, turning once.
Season and keep warm.
◆ Break the eggs into 2 buttered
individual dishes and pierce the yolks
carefully with a cocktail stick
(toothpick) to prevent bursting. Cook
on medium for 1½–2 minutes.
◆ Put the fish on 2 heated plates, add
the remaining butter and the poached
eggs.
◆ Garnish with sprigs of fennel or
parsley and serve with wholemeal
(whole-wheat) bread and butter.

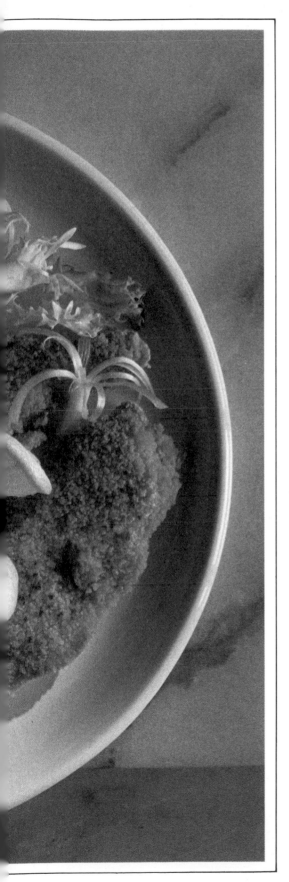

CRISPY FISH FILLETS

SERVES 4 / SET: FULL

Ingredients

8 white fish fillets

salt and freshly ground black pepper

2 eggs, beaten

golden (packaged) breadcrumbs (breading mix)

15 ml/1 tbsp oil

2 tbsp/25 g/1 oz butter

lemon slices

◆ Sprinkle the fish with salt and pepper. Dip in beaten egg and then in golden (packaged) breadcrumbs (breading mix), pressing them on well to cover the fish.

◆ Heat a browning dish to maximum, according to the manufacturer's instructions. Add the oil and butter. Cook for 30 seconds. Protecting your hands with oven gloves, tilt the dish so that it is well oiled.

◆ Lay the fish fillets in the dish (cook them in 2 batches if necessary) and cook for 4 minutes, turning once.

◆ Serve with lemon slices and wholemeal (whole-wheat) bread and butter and a salad if liked.

EELS WITH PEAS AND PARSLEY SAUCE

SERVES 4 / SET: FULL

Ingredients

3 cups/700 g/1½ lb eels, skinned, boned and cut into 5-cm/2-in pieces (try to buy it ready prepared)

⅔ cup/150 ml/¼ pt boiling fish stock (broth) (or see method)

2 slivers of lemon

3 tbsp/40 g/1½ oz butter

6 tbsp/40 g/1½ oz flour

⅔ cup/150 ml/¼ pt milk

salt and freshly ground black pepper

30 ml/2 tbsp chopped parsley

1¾ cups/200 g/7 oz canned marrowfat (large) peas, drained

◆ Put the eels in a deep oblong dish and add the boiling fish stock (broth). Alternatively, use the liquor from the canned peas. Add the lemon slivers, cover with vented cling film (plastic wrap) and cook for 5 minutes, until tender. Discard the lemon.

◆ Put the butter in a jug and cook for 45 seconds. Stir in the flour. Pour on the milk and the cooking liquor from the eels and cook for 3 minutes, whisking after each minute. Season and stir in the parsley.

◆ Add the peas to the dish of eels and pour over the sauce. Reheat for 1 minute, then serve with mashed potatoes.

Crispy Fish Fillets

FLATFISH FILLETS IN BEETROOT (BEET) SAUCE

SERVES 4 / SET: DEFROST AND FULL

Ingredients

1 beetroot (beet), cooked
⅔ cup/150 ml/5 fl oz single (light) cream
salt and white pepper
4 flatfish fillets, about 175 g/6 oz each, skinned
a little butter
spring onion (scallion) tassels

Spring onion (scallion) tassels are made by cutting 2 slits through the top of each trimmed and washed onion, at right angles to one another, and leaving them in ice water until the tops curl back.

◆ Peel and chop the beetroot (beet). Put it in a blender or food processor, with the cream and reduce to a smooth sauce. Season to taste with salt and pepper. Cook for 1–2 minutes on defrost to heat through. Keep warm.
◆ Trim the fillets to an even size, lay in a buttered dish and dot with butter. Cover with vented cling film (plastic wrap) and cook for 3–4 minutes, turning once, until cooked through.
◆ Spoon the sauce onto 4 heated plates, lay the fish on top and garnish with spring onion (scallion) tassels.

Flatfish Fillets in Beetroot (Beet) Sauce

FISH KORMA

*SERVES 4 / SET: FULL
AND MEDIUM*

Ingredients

3 cups/700 g/1½ lb firm, white fish, skinned and cubed
⅔ cup/150 ml/¼ pt yoghurt (yogurt)
5 ml/1 tsp turmeric
1 clove garlic, crushed (minced)
3 tbsp/40 g/1½ oz butter
1 large onion, finely sliced
5 cardamoms
3 cloves

◆ Put the fish pieces in a dish. Mix together the yoghurt (yogurt), turmeric and garlic and stir into the fish. Leave to marinate for an hour.
◆ Put the butter in a large dish and cook on full power for 45 seconds. Add the onions and spices, cover and cook on full power for 3 minutes.
◆ Stir in the fish and marinade, cover and cook on medium power for 10 minutes, stirring once.
◆ Serve with rice.

SPICY FISH CASSEROLE WITH RICE

SERVES 4 / SET: FULL

Ingredients

approx. 3 cups/700 g/1½ lb white fish fillets, skinned and cut into chunks
salt and freshly ground black pepper
15 ml/1 tbsp turmeric (approx.)
30 ml/2 tbsp olive oil
1 large onion, finely sliced
2 cloves garlic, crushed (minced)
1 green pepper, cut into julienne strips
1 red pepper, cut into julienne strips
1 good cup/225 g/8 oz long-grain rice
1½ cups/400 g/14 oz canned tomatoes, drained and juice reserved
boiling water or fish stock (broth)

◆ Sprinkle the fish with salt and dust with turmeric. Set aside.

◆ Put the olive oil into a large pot and cook for 30 seconds. Add the onion, garlic and peppers. Cover and cook for 3 minutes.

◆ Stir in the rice. Make the reserved tomato juice up to 2½ cups/575 ml/ 1 pt with boiling water or fish stock (broth), pour over the rice, cover and cook for 8 minutes.

◆ Stir in the drained tomatoes and the fish. Cover and cook for 4–6 minutes, until the fish and rice are done.

◆ Let the pot stand for 5 minutes, check the seasoning and serve.

ANCHOVY AND POTATO BAKE

SERVES 4 / SET: FULL AND MEDIUM

Ingredients
3 tbsp/40 g/1½ oz butter

1 large onion, finely sliced

8 cups/1 kg/2 lb potatoes, peeled and coarsely grated

50 g/2 oz canned anchovies, drained, soaked in milk for 30 minutes, then dried and chopped

30 ml/2 tbsp capers

cayenne pepper

⅔ cup/150 ml/¼ pt single (light) cream

45 ml/3 tbsp grated Parmesan cheese

◆ Put the butter in a dish and cook on full for 45 seconds. Add the onion, cover and cook on full for 3 minutes.

◆ Mix in the potatoes, cover and cook on full for 8 minutes, until soft.

◆ Stir in the anchovies and capers and season with cayenne pepper. Pour on the cream and top with grated Parmesan.

◆ Cook on medium power for 4 minutes, until hot through.

FISH FILLETS IN MUSTARD SAUCE

SERVES 4 / SET: FULL AND DEFROST

Ingredients
diamonds of red and green pepper

15 ml/1 tbsp water

4 firm, white fish fillets, weighing about 175 g/6 oz each

a squeeze of lemon juice

⅔ cup/150 ml/5 fl oz single (light) cream

5 ml/1 tsp English mustard powder

◆ First make the garnish. Cut out the pepper diamonds and put them in a dish with the water. Cook, covered with vented cling film (plastic wrap), on full for 2 minutes.

◆ Trim the fillets so that they are of even size and square in shape. Lay them in a dish, sprinkle with lemon juice and cover with vented cling film (plastic wrap). Cook on full for 4 minutes, turning once, until cooked.

◆ Mix the cream with the mustard powder to give it a delicate yellow hue and a pleasantly pungent taste. Heat through on defrost power for 1–2 minutes.

◆ Pour a pool of sauce onto each of 4 heated plates.

◆ Lay the fish fillets on the sauce and garnish with the pepper shapes.

Fish Fillets in Mustard Sauce

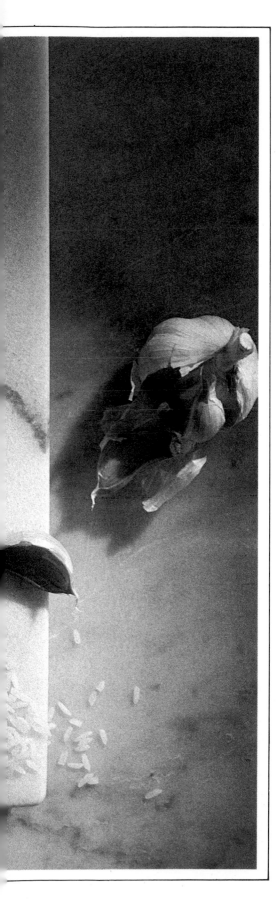

CHINESE PRAWNS (SHRIMP) WITH VEGETABLES

SERVES 4 / SET: FULL

Ingredients

2 good cups/450 g/1 lb unpeeled prawns (shrimp)

45 ml/3 tbsp soy sauce

15 ml/1 tbsp sherry

1 clove garlic, crushed (minced)

15 ml/1 tbsp chopped onion

1 scant cup/200 g/7 oz canned water chestnuts, drained

3 cups/200 g/7 oz button mushrooms

1 cup/200 g/7 oz canned whole baby sweetcorn (corn), drained

1 cup/100 g/4 oz canned green beans, drained

1 cup/100 g/4 oz mung bean sprouts

strips of red and yellow pepper

Serve this dish with rice. The prawns (shrimp) look much nicer unpeeled, but peel them if you wish.

◆ Slit the prawns (shrimp) down the back and remove the blackish veins. Put them in a bowl and stir in the soy sauce, sherry, garlic and onion. Leave to marinate for an hour, stirring occasionally.

◆ Stir in the remaining ingredients, cover with vented cling film (plastic wrap) and cook for 3–4 minutes, stirring once.

◆ Garnish with pepper strips and serve hot with rice.

Chinese Prawns (Shrimp) with Vegetables

SQUID IN TOMATO AND WINE SAUCE

SERVES 4 / SET: FULL

Ingredients

4 small squid

15 ml/1 tbsp olive oil

2 shallots, chopped

1 clove garlic, chopped

1½ cups/400 g/14 oz canned tomatoes, drained and sieved (strained)

1 glass dry white wine

chopped fresh herbs (thyme, parsley and basil)

salt and freshly ground black pepper

◆ Clean the squid. Cut away the eyes and mouth and discard, together with the ink sac and the "nib". Wash the squid thoroughly and pull off the outer membrane. Cut the body and tentacles into rings.

◆ Put the oil in a dish and cook for 30 seconds. Add the shallots and garlic and cook for 2 minutes.

◆ Stir in the sieved (strained) tomatoes, wine and squid. Sprinkle on the herbs. Cover with vented cling film (plastic wrap) and cook for 6–8 minutes, until the squid is tender. Season to taste with salt and pepper.

◆ Serve with rice.

THE MICROWAVE LIBRARY

COOKING WITH

Meat

VERONICA BULL

MEAT

MEAT forms a major part of the household budget. By using the correct cooking methods your microwave oven will enable you to produce moist, tender dishes representing good value for money.

For the housewife who is concerned with healthy eating, the microwave cooking method both preserves nutrients and helps to cut down the use of fats.

As with conventional cooking, prime quality meat will produce the best result. However, the less tender cuts of meat can also be cooked successfully. You will achieve excellent results with curries, casseroles and stews cooked at low temperatures over a longer period. These dishes reheat in minutes, losing none of the original freshness, they remain moist and succulent with a flavour that develops and improves. For this reason they are an excellent choice when entertaining, allowing you to spend more time with your guests while producing the perfect meal.

Large roasts of meat brown naturally in a microwave cooker; smaller cuts can be browned in a special browning dish, or by conventional means, in the oven or under the grill (broiler); before or after the cooking period. If a crisp finish is not essential, a sauce or glaze will make the dish appear even more appetizing.

The recipes featured in this book include exotic dishes such as Chinese Pancakes and Tandoori Chicken, together with a selection of more traditional fare. Microwaved meat offers a tasty and attractive selection of dishes that will make every meal a special occasion.

CONTENTS

SAVOURY HAMBURGER MIXTURE

SERVES 4 / SET: HIGH

Ingredients

2 cups/450 g/1 lb minced (ground) beef

30 ml/2 tbsp tomato ketchup (catsup)

60 ml/4 tbsp soy sauce

30 ml/2 tbsp chopped fresh herbs

2.5 ml/1/2 tbsp celery salt

15 ml/1 tbsp horseradish sauce

15 ml/1 tbsp French mustard

◆ Combine all the ingredients in a large bowl and mix well. Place 1 tbsp on a plate and cook on high for 2 minutes. Taste to test for flavour.

◆ This is the basic, uncooked recipe to which sauces and liquids may be added for 'wet' dishes or eggs and breadcrumbs for 'dry' dishes such as hamburgers, meatballs etc.

◆ To cook this dish on its own, place the mixture in a casserole dish, cover and cook for 7–9 minutes, stirring twice during the cooking time. Add sauce or gravy as required.

HAMBURGERS

S E R V E S   4 – 6 / S E T :   H I G H

Ingredients

1 onion, finely chopped

¼ cup/50 g/2 oz fresh breadcrumbs

1 egg, beaten

2¼ cups/500 g/1 lb 2 oz Savoury Hamburger Mixture (see recipe)

4–6 hamburger buns

G A R N I S H

sliced tomatoes

onion

lettuce leaves

relish of your choice

◆ Add the onions, breadcrumbs and egg to the Savoury Hamburger Mixture and combine well.

◆ Divide into 4 or 6 even portions and shape into patties.

◆ Heat a browning dish to the maximum recommended by the manufacturer and press the hamburgers onto the bottom. Cook for 7½–9 minutes, turning the hamburgers over after 4 minutes.

◆ If you prefer, cook for only half the above time and finish off under the grill (broiler) or on a barbecue.

◆ Serve with onion, tomato, lettuce and relish in a hot or cold bun.

Hamburgers

LEEKS AU GRATIN

*SERVES 2—4 / SET: HIGH
AND MEDIUM*

Ingredients

1¾ cups/350 g/12 oz Savoury Hamburger Mixture (see recipe)
6 tbsp/75 ml/3 fl oz hot, thick gravy
4 large leeks
¼ cup/50 ml/2 fl oz water
1 cup/100 g/4 oz grated cheese

◆ Place the Savoury Hamburger Mixture in a dish, cover and cook on high for 6–7 minutes. Stir after 3 minutes. Drain off any fat, then add the gravy and stir well. Keep to one side.

◆ Trim the leeks, and with a sharp knife slice down the length, cutting only as deep as the centre. Spread the leaves apart and wash. Select the widest leaves and place in a dish with the water, cover and cook on high for 1½–2 minutes until softened. Pour over cold water, drain and pat dry with absorbent kitchen paper (paper towels).

◆ Lay the leeks flat and place approx 15 ml/1 tbsp of mince mixture at the narrow end of each leaf. Roll up to enclose the meat. Place in a dish, cover and cook on high for 4–5 minutes or until heated through. Sprinkle over the grated cheese and cook, uncovered, on high for 2 minutes.

STUFFED CANNELLONI IN TOMATO SAUCE

SERVES 2 / SET: HIGH

Ingredients

8 cannelloni tubes

5 ml/1 tsp dried oregano

1 clove of garlic, crushed (minced)

30 ml/2 tbsp tomato purée (paste)

2 cups/450 g/1 lb Savoury Hamburger Mixture (see recipe)

SAUCE

1 small onion, finely chopped

1 clove garlic, crushed (minced)

5 ml/1 tsp dried oregano

2 tbsp/25 g/1 oz butter, diced

4 tbsp/25 g/1 oz plain flour

1½ cups/400 g/14 oz canned of tomatoes, chopped

60 ml/4 tbsp tomato purée (paste)

45 ml/3 tbsp garlic vinegar

15 ml/1 tbsp sugar

salt and pepper

4 slices of mozzarella cheese

◆ Stir the garlic, oregano and 2 tbsp of tomato purée (paste) into the meat mixture. Place in a shallow dish and cook for 3 minutes, stirring halfway through the cooking time. At this stage the meat will not be completely cooked.

◆ For the sauce, place the onion, garlic, oregano and butter in a bowl, cover and cook for 3 minutes. Stir in the flour, tomatoes, vinegar, sugar and remaining tomato purée (paste) with the salt and pepper (to taste). Cook uncovered for 4–5 minutes. Dilute with a little water or red wine if the sauce is too thick.

◆ Stuff the cannelloni tubes with the meat mixture. Place them in an oblong dish, pour on the sauce, cover and cook for 12–15 minutes. Place the cheese slices on top of the cannelloni and melt for 2 minutes or brown under a conventional grill (broiler).

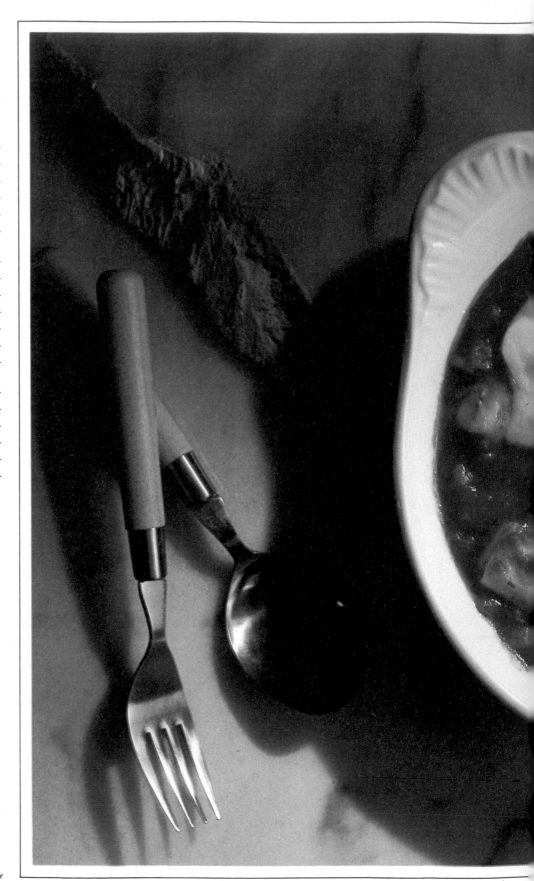

Stuffed Cannelloni in Tomato Sauce

LASAGNE

S E R V E S   4 — 6 / S E T :   H I G H

Ingredients

175 g/6 oz lasagne
7 ml/½ tbsp oil
3¾ cups/850 ml/1½ pts boiling water
salt to taste
2¼ cups/500 g/1 lb 2 oz Savoury Hamburger Mixture (see recipe)
1½ cups/400 g/14 oz canned tomatoes, chopped
3 cups/225 g/8 oz button mushrooms, sliced
1 clove garlic, crushed (minced)
175 g/6 oz blue cheese
⅔cup/150 ml/5 fl oz single (light) cream
mushroom slices to garnish

◆ Place the lasagne in a deep dish, cover with the boiling water, add oil and salt. Cover and cook for 9–11 minutes. Set aside covered. Alternatively cook on a conventional hob (burner) according to the instructions on the package while you prepare the remainder of the dish.

◆ Place the beef mixture in a large shallow dish, cover and cook for 5 minutes. Drain, add the tomatoes, garlic and mushrooms, stir well and cook for 5 minutes, stirring occasionally.

◆ Drain the pasta and, in a shallow oblong dish, place alternative layers of meat and lasagne, finishing with a layer of lasagne.

◆ Place the blue cheese in a bowl and cook for 1 minute. Mash it and blend in the cream. Replace in the oven and cook for a further minute. Blend to a smooth sauce and add it to the dish. Brown under a conventional grill (broiler).

◆ Cook the mushroom slices with a little butter for 1 minute and use as a garnish.

MEAT LOAF

SERVES 4—6 / SET: HIGH

Ingredients

1 cup/225 g/8 oz Savoury Hamburger Mixture (see recipe)
1 cup/225 g/8 oz pork sausage meat (ground pork)
1 medium onion, finely chopped
1 clove garlic, crushed (minced)
2 cups/100 g/4 oz fresh breadcrumbs
1 egg, beaten
salt and pepper to taste

◆ Place the butter, onion and garlic in a bowl. Cover and cook for 2 minutes.

◆ Mix together the beef, pork, breadcrumbs and seasoning to taste. Stir in the onion, garlic and beaten egg. Combine well and cook uncovered for 5 minutes. Stir and break up with a fork.

◆ Transfer to a microwave loaf dish or any other suitable container, press down and smooth the top. Cook for 5–7 minutes.

◆ Chill and turn out. Slice and serve with salad.

BRAISED BEEF

SERVES 4 / SET: HIGH & LOW

Ingredients

675 g/1½ lb braising steak (chuck, skirt, flank), cubed
1 large onion, chopped
3 medium sized carrots, sliced
3 cups/225 g/8 oz button mushrooms
1 celery stick (stack), sliced
30 ml/2 tbsp tomato purée (paste)
5 ml/1 tsp mixed dried herbs
2 tbsp/25 g/1 oz butter, diced
4 tbsp/25 g/1 oz plain flour
2 cups/425 ml/¾ pint hot beef stock (broth)

◆ Place the onions, carrots and celery in a large dish with 2 tbsp of stock (broth). Cover and cook on high for 5–6 minutes.

◆ Stir in the meat and butter, cover and cook on high for 4 minutes. Add the flour, mushrooms, herbs, tomato purée (paste) and the rest of the beef stock (broth). Stir, cover and cook on high for 6–7 minutes.

◆ Cook for a further 40 minutes on low. Stir several times during the cooking period.

◆ Let it stand covered for 10 minutes. Garnish with parsley and serve.

Braised Beef

CREOLE STEAK

SERVES 4 / SET: HIGH

Ingredients

4 fillet steaks, approx 200 g/6–7 oz each
¼ cup/50 g/2 oz butter, diced
2 onions, finely chopped
4 celery sticks (stacks), sliced
1½ cups/100 g/4 oz button mushrooms, chopped
1½ cups/400 g/14 oz canned tomatoes, finely chopped
30 ml/2 tbsp tomato purée (paste)
15 ml/1 tbsp soy sauce
salt and pepper to taste

◆ Place the steaks in a casserole dish. Cook uncovered for 3–4 minutes, depending on how rare you like your steak. Turn over and rearrange halfway through the cooking time.

◆ Place the butter, onions, celery and mushrooms in a dish, cover and cook for 6 minutes, stirring after 3 minutes.

◆ Stir in the remaining ingredients, season to taste, cover and cook for 4 minutes.

◆ Arrange the steaks on a serving dish, pour over the sauce and sprinkle with parsley.

Creole Steak

BEEF GOULASH

SERVES 4 / SET: FULL AND MEDIUM

Ingredients

1 kg/2 lb lean braising steak
1/2 cup/50 g/2 oz flour
7 ml/1/2 tbsp paprika
30 ml/2 tbsp oil
2 cloves garlic, crushed (minced)
15 ml/1 tbsp tomato purée (paste)
2 onions sliced
2 1/2 cups/575 ml/1 pint hot beef stock (broth)
1 bayleaf
3/4 cup/200 g/7 oz canned tomatoes, mashed
60 ml/4 tbsp yoghurt (yogurt)
30 ml/2 tbsp parsley, chopped

◆ Cut the meat into bite-sized cubes. Mix the flour and paprika together and toss the meat in the mixture.

◆ Heat a browning dish on full power according to manufacturer's instructions. Pour the oil into the dish and cook on full for 1 minute. Add the beef and cook for 5 minutes on full, turning frequently to brown all sides.

◆ Place the meat in a casserole with garlic, tomato purée (paste), onion, stock (broth), bayleaf and tomatoes. Cover and cook on full for 45 minutes until beef is tender. Leave to stand for 5 minutes.

◆ Spoon the yoghurt over the casserole and serve garnished with parsley. The dish goes well with noodles or mashed potatoes.

SAUSAGE CASSEROLE WITH DUMPLINGS

SERVES 4 / SET: HIGH AND MEDIUM

Ingredients

15 ml/1 tbsp cooking oil

1 medium onion, chopped

2 rashers (strips) lean bacon, diced

8 sausages (links)

2½ cups/575 ml/1 pt hot gravy

1½ cups/100 g/4 oz button mushrooms

1 cup/100 g/4 oz mixed frozen vegetables, defrosted

DUMPLINGS

½ cup/50 g/2 oz self-raising (self-rising) flour

2 tbsp/25 g/1 oz beef suet or shortening

pinch dried sage

salt and pepper to taste

water

◆ For the dumplings, mix together all the ingredients, add enough water to make a soft dough, then on a floured board form the dough into four dumplings. Set to one side.

◆ Preheat a browning dish to maximum as recommended by the manufacturer. Add the butter, onions, sausages and bacon. Cover and cook on high for 7 minutes, stirring once. Add the gravy, mushrooms and vegetables, cover and cook on medium for 6–7 minutes.

◆ Then add the dumplings, cook on high for 2 minutes and serve.

Sausage Casserole with Dumplings

BRAISED TOPSIDE (TOP ROUND)

SERVES 6—8 / SET: MEDIUM AND LOW

Ingredients

1.4–1.8 kg/3–4 lb topside (top round) of beef
1 beef stock (bouillon) cube
½ cup/125 ml/4 fl oz hot water
15 ml/1 tbsp Worcestershire sauce
2 bay leaves
1 large carrot, sliced
2 celery sticks (stacks), sliced
1 onion, quartered

◆ Trim off excess fat, pierce the meat all over with a skewer and place in a casserole dish.

◆ Dissolve the stock (bouillon) cube in the hot water and Worcestershire sauce and add to the dish. Cover and cook on medium for 35 minutes.

◆ Turn the meat and add the vegetables and bay leaves, cover and cook on low for 70 minutes. Leave it standing, covered, for 10 minutes. If using a microwave thermometer, remove it from the oven when the temperature reaches 65°C/150°F.

BEEF AND BACON CASSEROLE

SERVES 4 / SET: HIGH AND MEDIUM

Ingredients

1 tbsp/25 g/1 oz butter
300 g/12 oz beef, cut into strips
3 rashers (strips) of bacon, chopped
1 large onion, quartered and finely sliced
3 medium carrots, thinly sliced
2 cups/425 ml/15 fl oz hot chicken stock (broth)
2.5 ml/½ tsp dried basil
4 tbsp/25 g/1 oz flour for coating

◆ Toss the beef in flour to coat. Preheat a browning dish to maximum, according to the manufacturer's instructions. Add the butter, beef, bacon, onions and carrots. Cover and cook on high for 8 minutes, stirring once.

◆ Add the stock (broth) and herbs. Cook on medium for 8–10 minutes.

LAMB HOTPOT

SERVES 4 / SET: HIGH AND LOW

Ingredients

570 g/1¼ lb lamb steaks, cut from the leg
4 tbsp/25 g/1 oz flour
¼ cup/50 g/2 oz butter, diced
1 onion, finely sliced
1 clove garlic, crushed (minced)
1 leek, trimmed and sliced
2 large carrots, finely sliced
4 celery sticks (stacks), sliced
1 bay leaf
1 chicken stock (bouillon) cube, crumbled
30 ml/2 tbsp tomato purée (paste)
1½ cups/400 g/14 oz canned tomatoes
1½ cups/100 g/4 oz button mushrooms
salt and pepper to taste
2 large cooked potatoes, sliced

◆ Place 2 tbsp/25 g/1 oz butter in a large deep casserole dish. Cook on high for 1 minute then add the onion, garlic and leek. Cover and cook on high for 3 minutes. Add the carrots, celery and 30 ml/2 tbsp of juice from the tomatoes. Cover and cook on high for 6 minutes.

◆ Trim the fat from the lamb and cut it into cubes. Toss the cubes in the flour and add to the vegetables together with the tomatoes, stock (bouillon) cube, tomato purée (paste) and bay leaf. Cover and cook on high for 6 minutes, stirring halfway through the cooking time.

◆ Add the mushrooms, reduce to low and cook for a further 30 minutes, stirring every 5 minutes.

◆ Taste and season the stew, then layer the potatoes over the meat, dot with butter and brown in a conventional oven.

Lamb Hotpot

GUARD OF HONOUR

SERVES 4 / SET: HIGH AND MEDIUM

Ingredients

2 pieces best end of neck (rib chops left in 1 piece), 5–6 cutlets (chops) (approx 1 kg/ 2 lb) each

30 ml/2 tbsp cranberry sauce

15 ml/1 tbsp mint jelly

cutlet frills (optional)

◆ Weigh the meat and calculate cooking time at 2 minutes per 450 g/ 1 lb on high initially, plus 7–9 minutes per 450 g/1 lb on medium.

◆ Score the fatty side of each piece of meat, interlock the trimmed bone ends to form a 'guard of honour', meaty side inwards. Wrap a piece of foil around each bone end to prevent burning.

◆ Place the cranberry and mint jelly in a bowl and melt them for 1–2 minutes on high. Paint the fatty sides of the lamb mixture. Place the lamb on a roasting rack, cover and cook on high for 4 minutes. Reduce to medium and cook for 15–16 minutes. Remove the lid for the last 8 minutes. Paint on more cranberry mixture. Loosely wrap with foil and leave it to stand for 10 minutes.

◆ Replace the foil on the bone ends with the paper frills (if used) and set on a serving dish with vegetables.

◆ Variation: Stuff the lamb with your favourite stuffing (dressing) mix (as you would a crown roast) and allow an extra 3 minutes on the cooking time.

Guard of Honour

SAGE AND MOZZARELLA-STUFFED CHICKEN

SERVES 4 / SET: FULL

Ingredients

1.5–2 kg/3½–4 lb oven-ready chicken

6 sage leaves

¼–½ cup/25–50 g/1–2 oz mozzarella cheese, sliced

2 tbsp/25 g/1 oz butter

1 onion, chopped

1 cup/50 g/2 oz fresh white breadcrumbs

2 tsp fresh sage, chopped

salt and freshly ground black pepper

⅔ cup/150 ml/¼ pint hot chicken stock (broth)

GLAZE

2 tbsp/25 g/1 oz butter

15 ml/1 tbsp brown sugar

15 ml/1 tbsp sherry

◆ Grasp the flap of skin at the end of the bird and with the other hand, pull the skin away from the flesh as far as you can. Slide in the sage leaves and cheese slices.

◆ Place the butter and onion in a bowl, cover and cook for 3 minutes. Mix in the breadcrumbs, sage, seasoning and stock (broth) to form a moist, doughy consistency. Stuff the chicken and cook 8–10 minutes per 450 g/1 lb.

◆ Halfway through the cooking time, place the butter, sugar and sherry in a small jug. Cook for 1 minute. Remove the bird from the oven and brush with the glaze. Return bird to oven, giving the dish a half turn, and complete cooking. Check to see if the chicken is done by sticking a skewer into it where the leg joins with the breast. The juices should run out clear.

◆ Allow to stand for 15 minutes before serving.

LAMB CHOPS AND CRANBERRY JELLY

*SERVES 2 / SET: HIGH
AND MEDIUM*

Ingredients
4 noisettes of lamb, each 75 g/3 oz,
2.5 cm/1 inch thick

1½ cups/400 g/14 oz canned of consommé

15 ml/1 tbsp gelatine

90 ml/6 tbsp cranberry jelly

5 ml/1 tsp fresh or 2.5 ml/½ tsp dried mint

mint sprigs to garnish

◆ Arrange the chops in a shallow dish. Cook on high for 2 minutes, rearrange, and cook for a further 2 minutes. Cover and set aside.

◆ Place the consommé, cranberry jelly and herbs in a bowl and cook on high for 3 minutes. Do not allow it to boil. Sprinkle on the gelatine and stir until dissolved.

◆ Remove chops from the dish and arrange on a serving plate. Brush with the consommé mixture to glaze and chill.

◆ Pour the consommé mixture into a shallow dish and chill until jellied. Chop roughly and arrange around the chops. Garnish with sprigs of mint and serve with salad.

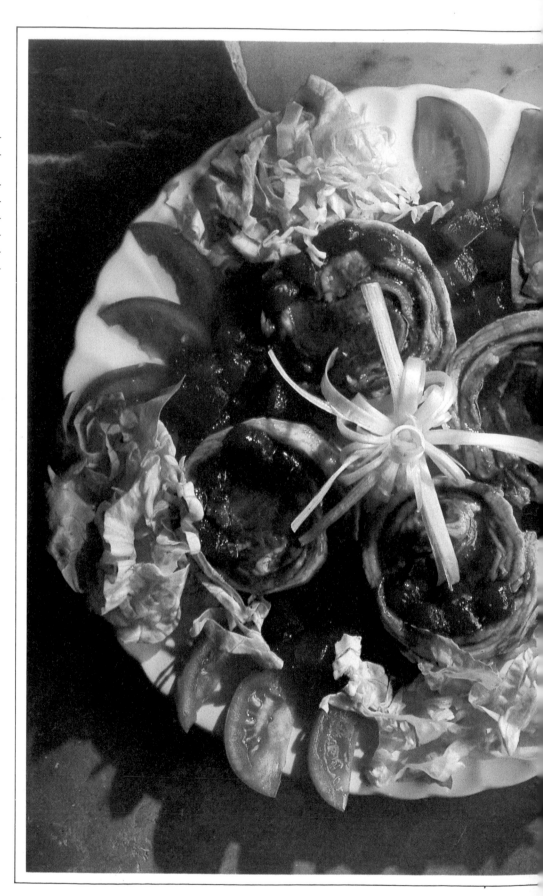

Lamb Chops and Cranberry Jelly

LAMB AND MUSHROOM RISOTTO

SERVES 2 / SET: HIGH

Ingredients

225 g/8 oz cooked lamb, cubed

2 tbsp/25 g/1 oz butter

2/3 cup/100 g/4 oz long grain rice

5 ml/1 tsp garam masala (available at Indian grocery stores)

5 ml/1 tsp curry powder

2 cups/425 ml/15 fl oz chicken stock, (broth)

1½ cups/100 g/4 oz button mushrooms

1 small onion, finely chopped

1 cup/100 g/4 oz mixed frozen vegetables

◆ Place the butter in a large deep dish, cook for 1 minute, add the onion, cover and cook for 1½ minutes.

◆ Stir in the rice, garam masala and curry powder. Pour on the stock (broth) and cook, covered, for 10 minutes.

◆ Stir in the remaining ingredients. Cook for 5 minutes or until the rice is tender but firm. Allow the dish to stand for 5 minutes.

PITTA (PITA) POCKETS

SERVES 4 / SET: LOW, MEDIUM AND HIGH

Ingredients

450 g/1 lb lamb fillet, cubed
1 tbsp/15 g/½ oz butter
30 ml/2 tbsp soy sauce
30 ml/2 tbsp lemon juice
15 ml/1 tbsp honey
4 pitta (pita) breads
30 ml/2 tbsp mayonnaise
12 cucumber slices
12 tomato slices
1 lettuce heart
1 small onion, cut into rings

◆ Mix together the soy sauce, lemon juice and honey. Add the meat cubes and marinate for at least 2 hours.

◆ Heat a browning dish to maximum, according to the manufacturer's instructions. Remove the meat from the marinade, add butter to the browning dish and stir in the meat. Cook on high for 2 minutes, reduce to medium and cook for a further 9 minutes. Cover and reserve.

◆ Place the pitta (pita) breads on 2 layers of kitchen paper (paper towels) and warm on low for 2 minutes. Remove from the oven, cut in half, open up the 'pocket' and spread the inside with mayonnaise. Shred the lettuce and add a little to each pocket with a few slices of tomato, cucumber and onion. Pile in the lamb. Alternatively, thread meat and vegetables onto wooden kebab sticks and serve with the pitta (pita) bread and rice.

LAMB CASSEROLE

SERVES 4 / SET: HIGH AND MEDIUM

Ingredients

700 g/1½ lb boned shoulder of lamb, cubed
2 tbsp/15 g/½ oz flour
1 tbsp/15 g/½ oz butter
2 medium onions, sliced
1 large apple, sliced
100 g/4 oz stoned (pitted) prunes
⅔ cup/150 ml/5 fl oz chicken stock (broth)
⅔ cup/150 ml/5 fl oz red wine
salt and pepper to taste

◆ Toss the lamb in the flour to coat. Place the butter in a casserole dish and cook on high for 1 minute. Add the onions, cover and cook on high for 2 minutes. Add the lamb and cook on high for 5 minutes.

◆ Stir in the apple, prunes, chicken stock and red wine. Cover and cook on medium for 25–30 minutes. Stir twice during the cooking period. Season to taste and serve.

Pitta (Pita) Pockets

ARMENIAN LAMB WITH PILAFF

SERVES 4 / SET: FULL

Ingredients

1 kg/2 lb fillet end leg of lamb

15 ml/1 tbsp oil

2 tbsp/25 g/1 oz butter

2 onions, chopped

1 clove garlic, chopped

4 tbsp/25 g/1 oz flour

5 ml/1 tsp ground cumin

2.5 ml/½ tsp ground allspice

30 ml/2 tbsp tomato paste

1¼ cup/300 ml/½ pint hot chicken stock (broth).

salt and freshly ground black pepper

PILAFF

3 tbsp/40 g/1½ oz butter

1 small onion, chopped

1 cup/225 g/8 oz long-grain rice

2 scant cups/425 ml/¾ pint hot chicken stock (broth)

salt and freshly ground black pepper

½ cup/75 g/3 oz currants

½ cup/75 g/3 oz almonds, blanched and chopped

◆ Remove meat from bone and cut into bite-sized cubes.

◆ Pour oil into a bowl, add butter and cook for 1 minute. Stir in onion and garlic and cook for 3 minutes. Add the meat and cook, covered, for 3 minutes.

◆ Stir in the flour and add remaining ingredients. Cook, covered, for 10 minutes. Allow to stand for 15 minutes then cook for a further 6 minutes.

◆ To make the pilaff, place the butter in a large shallow dish and cook for 1 minute. Stir in onion and rice and cook for 4 minutes.

◆ Add stock (broth) and seasoning and cook for 15 minutes or until rice is fluffy, adding extra liquid if necessary. Check seasoning and stir in currants and almonds before serving with the lamb.

Armenian Lamb with Pilaff

KOFTA MEAT BALLS

SERVES 2 / SET: HIGH

Ingredients

2 cups/450 g/1 lb minced (ground) lamb
2.5 ml/½ tsp garam masala (available at Indian grocery stores)
2.5 ml/½ tsp ground ginger
2 cloves garlic, crushed (minced)
2.5 ml/½ tsp ground cumin
1 egg
salt to taste
15 ml/1 tbsp vegetable oil

◆ Mix together all the ingredients except the oil and roll into small balls.

◆ Meanwhile, preheat a browning dish to maximum as recommended by the manufacturer. Add the oil 30 seconds before the end of this time.

◆ Quickly add the meatballs and cook for 5 minutes, turning once during the cooking time.

MOUSSAKA

SERVES 4 / SET: HIGH

Ingredients

2 cups/450 g/1 lb minced (ground) lamb
2 tbsp/25 g/1 oz butter
1 large onion, finely sliced
4 medium aubergines (eggplants)
1 beef stock (bouillon) cube dissolved in 45 ml/3 tbsp water
60 ml/4 tbsp tomato purée (paste)
salt and pepper to taste

SAUCE

2 tbsp/25 g/1 oz butter
4 tbsp/25 g/1 oz flour
1¼ cups/300 ml/10 fl oz milk
1½ cups/150 g/6 oz cheese, grated

◆ Thinly slice the aubergines (eggplants), sprinkle with salt and leave for 15 minutes. Pour off the bitter juices, rinse and drain.

◆ Meanwhile, place the butter in a dish, cook for 1 minute. Stir in the onions and aubergines (eggplants) when they are ready and cook covered for 5–6 minutes. Add the meat, stock (broth) and tomato purée (paste). Cook covered for 5 minutes.

◆ To make the sauce, cook the butter for 1 minute, add the flour and cook for 2 minutes. Stir in the milk and cook for 3 minutes, stirring every minute until thickened. Add the cheese, stir and keep to one side.

◆ Place half of the meat mixture in a deep casserole, top with half the sauce, then the remaining meat and finally the remainder of the sauce.

◆ Place the dish in the oven and cook for 10 minutes.

◆ Brown under a preheated conventional grill (broiler) and serve.

LAMB CURRY

SERVES 4 / SET: HIGH & LOW

Ingredients

1 kg/2 lb 3 oz shoulder of lamb, cubed
2 tbsp/25 g/1 oz butter
4 cloves garlic, crushed (minced)
1 medium onion, finely sliced
15 g/½ oz freshly grated (green) root ginger
2.5 ml/½ tsp ground mustard seed
2.5 ml/½ tsp ground fenugreek
2.5 ml/½ tsp ground cumin
2.5 ml/½ tsp turmeric
5 ml/1 tsp chilli powder
1½ cups/400 g/14 oz canned tomatoes, finely chopped
60 ml/4 tbsp white wine vinegar
15 ml/1 tbsp sugar

◆ Place half the butter in a dish and cook on high for 1 minute. Add the garlic and onion, cook on high, covered, for 1½ minutes. Add the grated ginger, ground mustard seed, fenugreek, cumin, turmeric and chilli powder and cook for a further 1½ minutes on high. Stir in the tomatoes, vinegar and sugar. Place to one side.

◆ Preheat a browning dish to maximum, according to the manufacturer's instructions. Add the remaining butter and meat and cook on high for 4 minutes, stirring once halfway through the cooking time. Add the curry sauce, cover and cook on low for 25 minutes. Stir every 10 minutes. Let it stand for 5 minutes.

◆ Serve with plain boiled rice.

Lamb Curry

PORK SPARE RIBS IN BARBECUE SAUCE

SERVES 2 / SET: HIGH AND LOW

Ingredients

6 meaty pork spare ribs, total weight approx 675 g/1½ lb

1 small onion, finely sliced

1 tbsp/15 g/½ oz butter

SAUCE

30 ml/2 tbsp honey

30 ml/2 tbsp soy sauce

60 ml/4 tbsp tomato ketchup (catsup)

15 ml/1 tbsp white wine vinegar

spring onions (scallions) to garnish

◆ Place the butter and onion in a shallow casserole. Cover and cook on high for 3 minutes.

◆ Add the ribs to the casserole dish and pour over the sauce, turning the ribs to coat. Cook on high for 4 minutes.

◆ Spoon over the sauce again, cover and cook on low for 25 minutes, rearranging and turning the ribs every 5 minutes. Drain the sauce into a saucepan and boil on the stove top until reduced and of a syrupy consistency, about 10 minutes.

◆ Place the ribs on a serving dish, coat with the sauce and garnish with spring onions (scallions).

◆ Serve with rice or baked potatoes and salad.

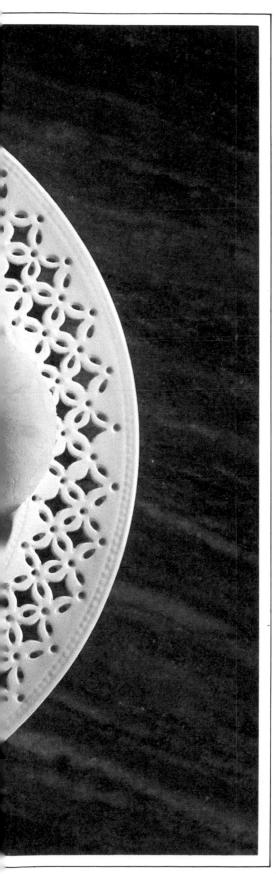

SWEET AND SOUR PORK

SERVES 4 / SET: HIGH AND MEDIUM

Ingredients

450 g/1 lb pork fillet, cut into strips

60 ml/4 tbsp soy sauce

60 ml/4 tbsp dry sherry

15 ml/1 tbsp sesame oil

½ small yellow pepper

½ small red chilli (chili)

1 medium carrot

2 tsp cornflour (cornstarch), dissolved in a little water

2 pineapple rings to garnish

2 spring onions (scallions)

SAUCE

30 ml/2 tbsp vinegar

60 ml/4 tbsp tomato ketchup (catsup)

60 ml/4 tbsp honey

120 ml/8 tbsp pineapple juice

◆ Marinate the pork strips in the soy sauce and sherry for 1 hour. Cut the pepper, chilli (chili) and carrots into julienne strips.

◆ Drain the meat and heat a browning dish to the maximum recommended by the manufacturer. Add the oil and quickly toss the pork strips in the oil. Cover and cook on high for 3 minutes, stirring after 2 minutes. Drain.

◆ Add the vegetables and sauce ingredients, cover and cook on medium for 2 minutes. The vegetables should be crisp. Add the cornflour (cornstarch) and water to the dish and cook on high for 1 minute. Stir well.

◆ Serve with plain boiled rice and garnish with pineapple rings and spring onions (scallions).

TANDOORI PORK CHIPOLATAS

SERVES 4 / SET: MEDIUM

Ingredients

450 g/1 lb pork chipolata sausages

60 ml/4 tbsp tandoori or curry paste

30 ml/2 tbsp cooking oil

◆ Prick the sausages. Combine the tandoori or curry paste and cooking oil and marinate the sausages in the mixture for 1 hour.

◆ Preheat a browning dish to the maximum recommended by the manufacturer. Remove the chipolatas from the marinade and place them in the browning dish. Cook for 3 minutes then turn and cook for a further 4 minutes.

◆ Serve hot or cold as a snack.

PORK KEBABS WITH PEANUT SAUCE

SERVES 4 / SET: HIGH

Ingredients

675 g/1½ lb pork fillet, cut into
2.5-cm/1-inch cubes

1 red pepper, coarsely chopped

1 yellow pepper, coarsely chopped

1 small onion, quartered and layers
separated

2 tbsp/25 g/1 oz butter

SAUCE

1 cup/110 g/4 oz roasted peanuts, ground

30 ml/2 tbsp soy sauce

15 ml/1 tbsp sesame oil

◆ Combine the sauce ingredients and cook covered for 1½ minutes.

◆ Skewer the meat and vegetables onto wooden kebab sticks and brush with the peanut sauce.

◆ Place the kebabs on a plate in a single layer, dot with butter, cover and cook for 4 minutes. Turn and cook for a further 4 minutes.

◆ Serve with extra sauce, plain boiled rice and salad.

CHINESE PANCAKES

SERVES 4 / SET: HIGH

Ingredients

PANCAKES / MAKES 8

scant 1 cup/100 g/4 oz plain flour

1 egg

1¼ cups/300 ml/½ pint milk

pinch salt

cooking fat (shortening) to grease pan

FILLING

150 g/6 oz pork fillet, thinly sliced into strips

1 tbsp/15 g/½ oz butter

1 bunch spring onions (scallions), sliced

1 cup/225 g/8 oz can of water chestnuts, thinly sliced

60 ml/4 tbsp soy sauce

30 ml/2 tbsp dry sherry

1 cup/100 g/4 oz roasted salted cashew nuts

2 spring onions (scallions), to garnish

½ red pepper – thinly sliced, to garnish

◆ To make the pancakes, sift the flour and salt into a bowl. Make a well in the centre. Beat the egg and add it to the flour. Pour in half the milk and mix to a smooth batter. Add the remaining milk and allow to stand for 1 hour.

◆ Melt a little fat in a frying-pan (skillet), add sufficient batter to cover the bottom of the pan thinly and cook on a conventional hob for 1 minute. Turn the pancake over and cook until golden brown. Cover and keep warm. Repeat with the remaining batter.

◆ To make the filling, heat a browning dish to maximum according to the manufacturer's instructions. Add the butter and the pork strips and cook, uncovered, for 3 minutes, stirring once. Add all the remaining ingredients and mix. Cover and cook 4 minutes.

◆ Fold the pancakes in half, then in half again. Open out the edges to make a pocket and stuff with filling.

◆ Garnish with spring onion (scallion) tassels and red pepper.

Chinese Pancakes

CURRIED PORK SLICES

SERVES 4 / SET: HIGH

Ingredients

4 pork slices, 1 cm/$^1/_2$ inch thick
60 ml/4 tbsp curry paste
30 ml/2 tbsp sesame oil

◆ Mix the oil and curry paste together, add the pork slices and coat with the paste. Marinate for 30 minutes.

◆ Heat a browning dish to maximum according to the manufacturer's instructions. Add the slices, cover and cook for 4 minutes. Turn the meat over and cook for a further 4 minutes. Let them stand for 3 minutes.

◆ Serve with baked potatoes and salad.

QUICK COOK'S PATE

SERVES 4 / SET: HIGH

Ingredients

3 rashers (strips) of streaky (fat) bacon
1 small onion, finely chopped
1 clove garlic, crushed (minced)
5 ml/1 tsp dried sage
225 g/8 oz pig's liver, chopped
2 tbsp/25 g/1 oz butter
30 ml/2 tbsp single (light) cream
salt and pepper to taste

◆ Place the bacon, onion, garlic and herbs in a dish and cover with cling film (plastic wrap). Cook on high for 6½ minutes.

◆ Stir in the liver and butter, cover and cook on high for 6½ minutes. Let it stand for 5 minutes.

◆ Stir in the cream and purée the mixture in a blender or food processor until smooth. Season to taste.

◆ Turn into a dish, smooth the top and chill until set.

◆ Serve with hot crusty bread or triangles of toast.

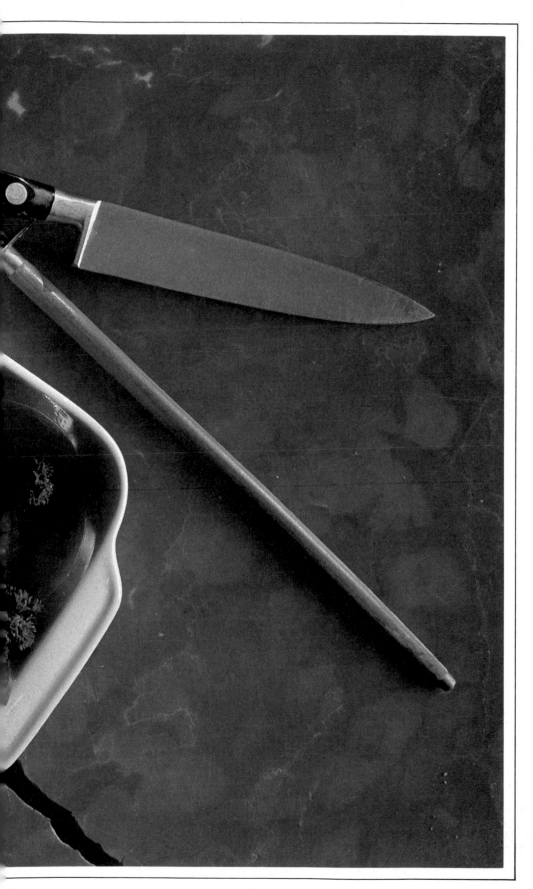

STUFFED PORK CHOPS

SERVES 4 / SET: HIGH AND MEDIUM

Ingredients

4 loin pork chops, 2.5 cm/1 inch thick, 150 g/6 oz each
1 cup/100 g/4 oz Cheddar cheese, grated
S T U F F I N G
3 tbsp/15 g/1½ oz butter
1 small onion, finely sliced
good ½ cup/50 g/2 oz button mushrooms, finely chopped
2 tbsp/50 g/2 oz cooked rice

◆ Slice through the pork chops horizontally from one end, leaving a border on two sides to form a pocket.
◆ Cook the butter on high for 1 minute, add the onion and mushrooms and cook on high for 3 minutes. Stir in the rice.
◆ Spoon the stuffing mixture into the pockets in the pork chops and secure with wooden cocktail sticks.
◆ Arrange the chops in a dish with the thickest parts to the outer edge. Cover and cook on high for 5 minutes. Rearrange and turn the chops, then continue to cook them for a further 9–10 minutes on medium. One minute before the end of the cooking time sprinkle with the grated cheese or brown under a conventional grill (broiler).
◆ Serve with mushrooms and tomatoes.

PORK CHOPS WITH CRANBERRY SAUCE

SERVES 4 / SET: HIGH AND MEDIUM

Ingredients

4 loin pork chops, 150 g/6 oz each
1 cup/100 g/4 oz cranberry sauce
15 ml/1 tbsp cooking oil
⅔ cup/150 ml/¼ pint dry sherry

◆ Preheat a browning dish to the maximum recommended by the manufacturer. Press the chops onto the dish to sear, turn over and cook on high for 5 minutes.

◆ Combine the remaining ingredients and cook on high for 2 minutes. Blend to a smooth sauce and pour over the chops. Cover and cook on medium for 10–12 minutes, turning once.

QUICK HAM AND BEAN HASH

SERVES 4–6 / SET: HIGH
AND MEDIUM

Ingredients

2 tbsp/25 g/1 oz butter
4 rashers (strips) streaky (fat) bacon, diced
1 onion, chopped
2½ cups/400 g/14 oz canned new potatoes, diced
1½ cups/400 g/14 oz canned kidney beans, drained
2 cups/350 g/12 oz canned sweetcorn kernels (corn), drained
225 g/8 oz cooked ham, sliced
1½ cups/400 g/14 oz canned tomatoes, finely chopped
30 ml/2 tbsp tomato purée (paste)
15 ml/1 tbsp Worcestershire sauce
15 ml/1 tbsp soy sauce
Tabasco sauce to taste
salt and pepper to taste

◆ Place the butter, onion and bacon in a casserole, cover and cook on high for 3 minutes. Add all the remaining ingredients, stir well and heat on medium for 10–12 minutes or until piping hot.
◆ Serve with crusty bread.

Quick Ham and Bean Hash

GLAZED BACON (HAM) ROAST

SERVES 6—8 / SET: HIGH AND MEDIUM

Ingredients

1½ kg/3 lb middle gammon joint (ham roast), rind removed, soaked overnight

⅔ cup/150 ml/5 fl oz water

⅔ cup/150 ml/5 fl oz pineapple juice

½ cup/75 g/3 oz brown sugar

1 tbsp/15 g/½ oz butter

◆ Place the joint (roast) in a roasting bag with the water, pierce the bag and close it with a non metallic tie. Stand it in a dish and cook for 6 minutes on high. Reduce to medium and cook for a further 25 minutes, turning over after 12 minutes.

◆ Remove the joint from the bag and wrap it loosely in foil, shiny side inwards. Let it stand for 15 minutes.

◆ Place the pineapple juice, sugar and butter in a bowl. Cook on high for 6 minutes, stirring every 2 minutes, to make a glaze.

◆ Stand the joint in a grill (broiling) pan, brush with the glaze and brown it under a preheated conventional grill (broiler).

GAMMON HAM RISOTTO

SERVES 4 / SET: HIGH

Ingredients

2 cups/350 g/12 oz rice

*2³/4 cups/650 ml/23 fl oz hot chicken stock
(broth)*

*1¹/2 cups/100 g/4 oz button mushrooms,
sliced*

1 small red pepper, chopped

¹/2 cup/100 g/4 oz frozen peas, defrosted

*2 cups/325 g/12 oz canned sweetcorn
kernels (corn)*

*350 g/12 oz gammon steak (ham steak),
diced*

1 clove garlic, crushed (minced)

salt and pepper to taste

◆ Cook the rice in the stock (broth)
for 15 minutes. Let it stand, covered,
for 7 minutes.

◆ Meanwhile, place all the remaining
ingredients in a dish, cover and cook
for 7–9 minutes. Stir twice during the
cooking time.

◆ Mix into the rice and serve.

Gammon Ham Risotto

HAWAIIAN GAMMON HAM

SERVES 4 / SET: HIGH

Ingredients

4 gammon (ham) slices
4 canned pineapple rings, drained
2 tbsp/25 g/1 oz butter
30 ml/2 tbsp sultanas (golden raisins)
4 slices of cheese

◆ Remove the rind from the gammon (ham) and snip the fat with scissors at regular intervals.
◆ Place the butter in a bowl, add the sultanas (golden raisins) and cook for 1½ minutes, or until they are plump and juicy.
◆ Place the gammon steak on a large plate, cover with absorbent kitchen paper (paper towels) and cook for 9 to 10 minutes, turning once.
◆ Remove the paper. Place one pineapple ring on each steak, fill the centre with sultanas (golden raisins) and place a cheese slice on top. Return to the oven and cook for 2–3 minutes. Serve with tomatoes and mushrooms.

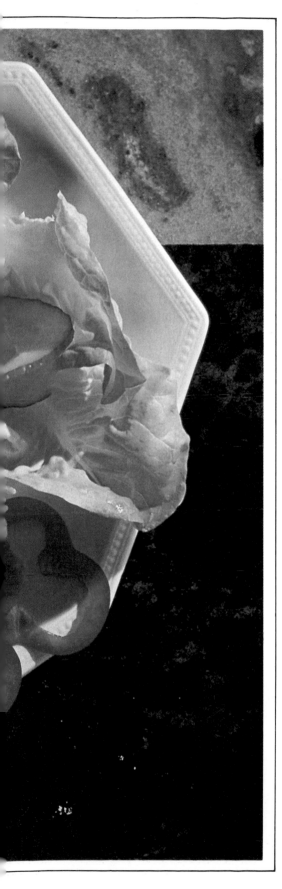

Tandoori Chicken

TANDOORI CHICKEN

*SERVES 4 / SET: HIGH
AND MEDIUM*

Ingredients

4 chicken leg portions, 220 g/8 oz each
45 ml/3 tbsp tandoori or curry paste
²/₃ cup/150 ml/5 fl oz plain yoghurt (yogurt)
lemon wedges and onion rings to garnish

◆ Skin the chicken portions and make 3–4 deep slashes in the flesh. Place in a dish.
◆ Mix together the tandoori or curry paste and yoghurt (yogurt), pour the mixture over the chicken and marinate for at least 2 hours.
◆ Remove the chicken from the marinade, place on a roasting rack, cover with the lid and cook on high for 10 minutes, turning halfway through the cooking time. Reset the oven to medium and cook for a further 15–17 minutes, turning and rearranging twice.
◆ Pierce the chicken at the joint and ensure that the juices run clear. If they are pink, return it to the oven and cook a little longer, checking regularly to see if cooked.
◆ Place on a grill (broiler) rack and char under a preheated conventional grill (broiler) for 5 minutes.
◆ Garnish and serve with salad and rice.

ROAST TURKEY

SERVES 2 / SET: MEDIUM

Ingredients

2 kg/4¹/₂ lb turkey
4 sticks (stacks) of celery, sliced
2 small onions, quartered
2 bay leaves
2 tbsp/25 g/1 oz butter
3 rashers (strips) streaky (fat) bacon

◆ Stuff the turkey with the celery, onion, bay leaves and butter.
◆ Place the turkey, breast down, on a roasting rack and cover with the lid. Cook for 25 minutes.
◆ Turn the bird over, lay the bacon over the breast and cook for a further 25 minutes.
◆ Discard the bacon and wrap the turkey loosely in foil. Let it stand for 10 minutes.
◆ Brown the turkey under a preheated conventional grill (broiler).
◆ Serve with roast potatoes and fresh vegetables.

CHICKEN AND ALMONDS CHINESE-STYLE

SERVES 4 / SET: HIGH

Ingredients

675 g/1½ lb boned chicken breasts, cut into thin strips
1 large onion, quartered and finely sliced
⅓ cup/50 g/2 oz blanched almonds
30 ml/2 tbsp sesame oil
1¼ cups/300 ml/½ pint chicken stock (broth)
15 ml/1 tbsp soy sauce
15 ml/1 tbsp cornflour (cornstarch), mixed with 10 ml/2 tsp water
175 g/6 oz (mung) beansprouts
1 small red pepper cut into julienne strips
1 small green pepper cut into julienne strips

◆ Preheat a browning dish to the maximum recommended by the manufacturer.

◆ Add the oil to the dish with the strips of chicken and cook for 3 minutes.

◆ Add the onion and almonds. Cook for 3 minutes, stirring once during the cooking time.

◆ Blend together the chicken stock (broth), soy sauce and cornflour (cornstarch). Stir into the chicken mixture, cover and cook for 4–5 minutes. Let it stand for 5 minutes.

◆ Place the beansprouts and the red and green peppers in a dish with 15 ml/1 tbsp water, cover with cling film (plastic wrap) and cook for 1 minute.

◆ Place the vegetables in a dish and pile the chicken and almonds on them. Serve with rice.

Chicken and Almonds Chinese-Style

WHOLE ROAST CHICKEN

SERVES 4—6 / SET: MEDIUM

Ingredients

1.5 kg/3 lb roasting chicken
30 ml/2 tbsp clear honey
15 ml/1 tbsp soy sauce
5 ml/1 tsp paprika
2 tbsp/25 g/1 oz melted butter

◆ Mix together the honey, soy sauce and paprika. Brush the chicken with the sauce. Protect the wing tips and drumsticks with foil.

◆ Place the chicken, breast down, on a roasting rack and cover with the lid or a pierced roasting bag closed with a non-metallic tie.

◆ Calculate the cooking time at 9 minutes per pound. Halfway through, turn the chicken, breast up, and brush with butter. Protect the breast bone with a strip of foil. Drain off any accumulated juices from the dish and cook for the remainder of the calculated cooking time.

◆ With a sharp knife, pierce the inside thigh joint and check that the juices run clear. If they are pink, return the chicken to the oven and cook a little longer, checking at regular intervals.

◆ When completely cooked, remove from the roasting rack and cover lightly with foil. Let it stand for 15 minutes.

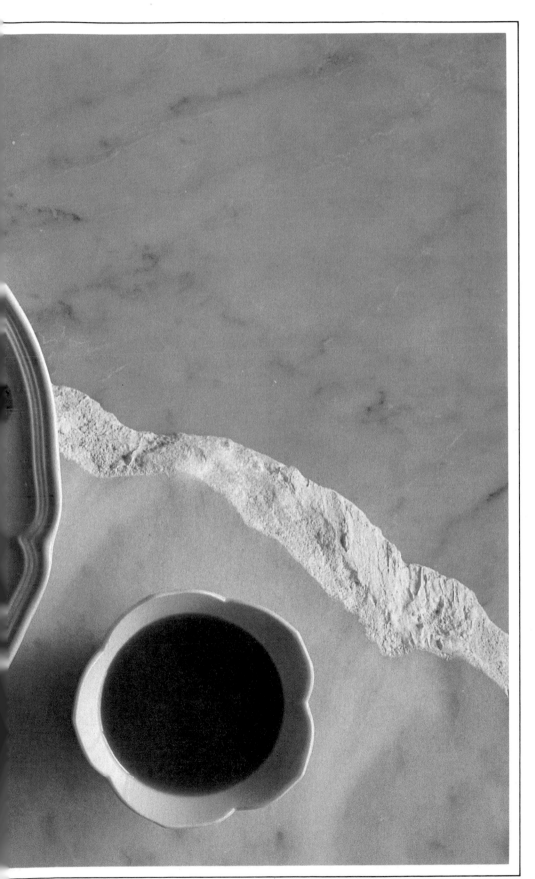

DUCK IN ORANGE SAUCE

SERVES 4 / SET: MEDIUM AND HIGH

Ingredients

4 duck portions, total weight approx 2 kg/4 ½ lb

SAUCE

15 ml/1 tbsp clear marmalade

1 cup/225 ml/8 fl oz orange juice

30 ml/2 tbsp port wine

30 ml/2 tbsp lemon juice

30 ml/2 tbsp honey

10 ml/2 tsp cornflour (cornstarch), mixed with 5 ml/1 tsp water

orange slices and watercress to garnish

◆ Arrange the duck portions on a rack in a large deep dish. Cook covered on medium for 45–60 minutes. Reposition and turn the pieces over several times during the cooking period and drain off the surplus fat. Test to see that they are cooked by piercing with a sharp knife at the joint, the juices should run clear. Brown the cooked duck under a conventional grill (broiler).

◆ For the sauce, place the marmalade jelly in a dish and cook on high for 1 minute. Add the rest of the sauce ingredients and cook for a further 3 minutes or until bubbling. Cool slightly and stir in the cornflour (cornstarch), cook on high for 1 minute and stir well.

◆ Place the duck on a warm serving dish, pour over the sauce and garnish with orange slices and watercress.

QUICK CHICKEN PASTA

SERVES 4 / SET: HIGH

Ingredients

350 g/12 oz green tagliatelle
15 ml/1 tbsp cooking oil
5 ml/1 tsp salt
1 small red pepper, diced
1 small green pepper, diced
1/2 cup/100 g/4 oz frozen peas, defrosted
1 cup/275 g/10 oz canned condensed mushroom soup
2/3 cup/150 ml/5 fl oz water
450 g/1 lb cooked chicken, diced

◆ Place pasta in a deep dish and pour over enough boiling water to cover. Add the oil and salt, cover and cook for 6 minutes. Let it stand for 6 minutes.

◆ Place the peppers in a dish, cover and cook for 3 minutes. Add the peas and cook for a further 3 minutes.

◆ Combine the mushroom soup and water, and add it with the chicken to the vegetables. Cook uncovered for 6–8 minutes, stirring once halfway through the cooking time.

◆ Drain the pasta and place in a warm serving dish. Arrange the chicken mixture on top and serve.

TURKEY BREASTS CORDON BLEU

SERVES 4 / SET: HIGH & LOW

Ingredients

4 turkey breasts, approx 175 g/6 oz each
1/4 cup/50 g/2 oz butter, diced
4 slices of ham
4 slices of mozzarella cheese
pinch of paprika

◆ Place the turkey breasts in a shallow dish and dot with the butter. Cover and cook on high for 4 minutes. Rearrange and turn the breasts over, cover and cook on low for 5–6 minutes, turning them again half way through the cooking time.

◆ Transfer the pieces to a microwave proof serving dish. Place a slice of ham and a slice of cheese on top of each breast and cook on high, uncovered, for 3 minutes.

◆ Sprinkle with paprika and serve.

Turkey Breasts Cordon Bleu

ROAST POUSSINS

SERVES 2 / SET: MEDIUM

Ingredients

2 oven ready poussins (young chickens), 450 g/1 lb each

STUFFING

½ cup/150 g/5 oz redcurrant jelly

3 tbsp/40 g/1½ oz butter

¼ cup/3 tbsp/50 g/2 oz cooked rice

30 ml/2 tbsp sultanas (golden raisins)

salt and pepper to taste

GLAZE

30 ml/2 tbsp soy sauce

15 ml/1 tbsp honey

◆ Combine the stuffing ingredients in a bowl, cover and cook for 1½ minutes.

◆ Stuff the poussins and lay them on a roasting rack, breast down.

◆ Mix the soy sauce and honey in a bowl, and cook for 1 minute. Brush the poussins with half the glaze, cover with a lid and cook for 15 minutes.

◆ Drain, then turn the poussins breast up. Coat with the remainder of the glaze, cover and cook for a further 15 minutes. Remove from rack, cover in foil and allow to stand for 10 minutes.

Roast Poussins

LIVER AND BACON KEBABS

SERVES 2 / SET: HIGH

Ingredients

225 g/8 oz chicken livers

8 rashers (strips) streaky (fat) bacon

1½ cups/100 g/4 oz button mushrooms

Worcestershire sauce to taste

◆ Cut each bacon rasher (strip) into 2 or 3 pieces and wrap the pieces around the livers.

◆ Thread onto wooden kebab sticks, alternating with the mushrooms. Sprinkle with Worcestershire sauce to taste.

◆ Place the kebabs on a plate in an even layer. Cover with absorbent kitchen paper (paper towels) and cook for 6–7 minutes, turning once during the cooking time.

VEAL ITALIENNE

SERVES 4 / SET: HIGH AND MEDIUM

Ingredients

350 g/12 oz tagliatelle
5 ml/1 tsp oil
5 ml/1 tsp salt
450 g/1 lb diced fillet of veal
225 g/8 oz diced gammon (ham) steak
1 tbsp/14 g/½ oz butter
1 large onion, thinly sliced
1½ cups/100 g/4 oz button mushrooms, halved
2 gherkins (pickles), chopped

S A U C E

2 tbsp/25 g/1 oz butter
4 tbsp/25 g/1 oz flour
1¼ cups/300 ml/½ pint milk
salt and pepper to taste
julienne strips of red pepper to garnish

◆ Place the pasta in a deep dish, pour over enough boiling water to cover, add the salt and oil. Cook on high for 6 minutes. Cover and keep to one side.

◆ Place the veal, gammon (ham) and butter in a dish. Cover and cook on high for 3 minutes, stirring once. Add the onion and mushrooms. Cook on high for 2 minutes and place to one side.

◆ For the sauce, melt the butter on high for 1 minute then stir in the flour and cook for a further minute. Add the milk and cook on high for 3 minutes, stirring every minute. Add this to the meat mixture and cook on medium for 15 minutes. Stir in the chopped gherkins (pickles) and season to taste.

◆ Drain the pasta, arrange in a serving dish and top with the meat sauce. Garnish and serve.

VEAL ROULADE AND MUSHROOM SAUCE

SERVES 4 / SET: HIGH AND MEDIUM

Ingredients

4 veal escalopes (fillets) beaten thin

2 large carrots cut into long sticks

30 ml/2 tbsp water

8 frozen French (green) beans

4 tbsp/50 g/2 oz butter

SAUCE

1 cup/275 g/10 oz canned condensed mushroom soup

2/3 cup/150 ml/5 fl oz water

salt and pepper to taste

◆ Cook the carrots in 2 tbsp of water in a covered dish for 3 minutes on high. Add the French (green) beans and cook for 1 minute.

◆ Lay the veal escalopes (fillets) on a board and place a carrot stick and 2 beans at the shortest end. Roll up neatly and secure each roll with a wooden cocktail stick.

◆ Arrange the veal in a shallow dish, dot with butter, cover and cook for 5 minutes on high. Rearrange and continue to cook for a further 9 minutes on medium. Add salt and pepper to taste, cover and reserve.

◆ Blend the soup with the water and cook on high for 5 minutes or until hot. Transfer to a warm sauceboat.

◆ Remove cocktail sticks from roulades and slice into even-sized rings. Serve with the sauce, new potatoes, French (green) beans and carrots.

MEAT AND FRUIT PILAFF

SERVES 4 / SET: HIGH AND MEDIUM

Ingredients

2 cups/350 g/12 oz brown rice

2³⁄4 cups/650 ml/12 fl oz hot chicken stock (broth)

225 g/8 oz diced cooked meat

1 banana, sliced

1 red apple, diced

1 green apple, diced

1 peach, peeled and diced

15 ml/1 tbsp lemon juice

³⁄4 cup/100 g/4 oz cashew nuts

¹⁄3 cup/50 g/2 oz sultanas (golden raisins)

salt and pepper to taste

◆ Place the rice in a deep dish, add the hot stock (broth), cover and cook on high for 30–35 minutes. Let it stand, covered, for 10 minutes.

◆ Toss the apples and banana in the lemon juice. Combine with the rest of the ingredients. Cover and cook on medium for 5 minutes. Mix into the cooked rice and serve.

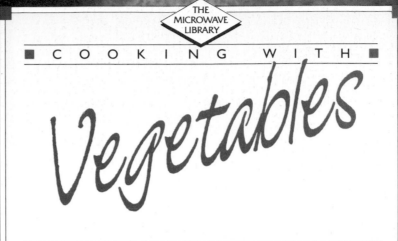

THE
MICROWAVE
LIBRARY

■ C O O K I N G W I T H ■

Vegetables

■ ELIZABETH CORNISH ■

VEGETABLES

VEGETABLES prepared in the microwave are cooked to perfection. They are both tender and crisp and full of flavour and freshness. The vegetables look as if they have been harvested only moments before, because they keep their shape and their colour. They keep their goodness too – research has shown that microwave cooking destroys fewer nutrients than any other method.

These advantages are due to the speed of the microwave, and to the fact that the moisture content of vegetables is high, so that they literally cook in their own juices.

Gone are the days of soggy sprouts and cabbage, when their crisp leaves were boiled until they had collapsed, lost all their colour and flavour and become virtually worthless as a source of nutrient. Now you can cook these and other vegetables in just a few minutes without getting a kitchen full of steam and unpleasant smells that linger in the house for days. What you will get is a vegetable looking and tasting like nature intended it to – delicious.

Microwaved vegetables are good for slimmers as well as the generally health-conscious, because they retain their fibre content and even if you are cooking in fat, very little is needed. For the most part, fat can be avoided altogether.

Bearing in mind that the taste and appearance of the vegetable will not be altered by microwave cooking, you should select only the best specimens. Buy fresh vegetables in season, or frozen vegetables, which are picked and then frozen at their best. This book will give you plenty of ideas for all kinds of vegetable dishes. Many are meals in themselves; others can be served as light suppers, starters, or as part of a vegetarian meal or an accompaniment to meat and fish.

CONTENTS

PUREE OF ROOT VEGETABLES

SERVES 4 / SET: FULL

Ingredients

2½ *cups/350 g/12 oz carrots, sliced*

2½ *cups/350 g/12 oz swede (rutabaga), sliced*

45 *ml/3 tbsp water*

butter to taste

salt and freshly ground black pepper

⅔ *cup/150 ml/5 fl oz single (light) cream*

chopped chives

◆ Peel the vegetables and slice them thinly. Reserve some of the carrot slices and cut them into star shapes for the garnish.

◆ Put the vegetables in a dish with the water. Cover with vented cling film (plastic wrap) and cook for 6–8 minutes, until soft.

◆ Drain the vegetables and purée in a blender or food processor with butter to taste. Season the purée and reheat for 1 minute.

◆ To serve, spoon a thin pool of cream onto each of 4 heated plates. Make a small mound of purée on each plate and garnish the surrounding cream with shooting stars made of carrot and snipped chives.

VARIATION You can make this purée with any of the winter root vegetables, such as turnip, parsnip and sweet potato.

Artichoke Hearts, Kidney Beans and Mushrooms with Vegetable Puree

SERVES 4 / SET: FULL

Ingredients

1 onion, sliced

1 clove garlic, crushed (minced)

15 ml/1 tbsp sunflower oil

3 good cups/225 g/8 oz mushrooms, wiped and sliced

1½ cups/400 g/14 oz canned kidney beans

good cup/200 g/7 oz canned artichoke hearts, drained

salt and freshly ground black pepper

fresh coriander (cilantro) or parsley

¾ cup/175 g/6 oz Puree of Root Vegetables (see recipe)

This delicious and rather unusual mixture of flavours is enhanced even further by the tang of fresh coriander (cilantro) leaves.

◆ Put the onion and garlic in a casserole with the oil, cover and cook for 3 minutes. Stir in the mushrooms, kidney beans – with a little of the liquid from the can – and artichoke hearts and cook, covered, for about 5 minutes, stirring once, until the mushrooms are done and the beans cooked through.

◆ Season to taste with salt and pepper and sprinkle with coriander (cilantro) or parsley leaves.

◆ Serve with vegetable purée.

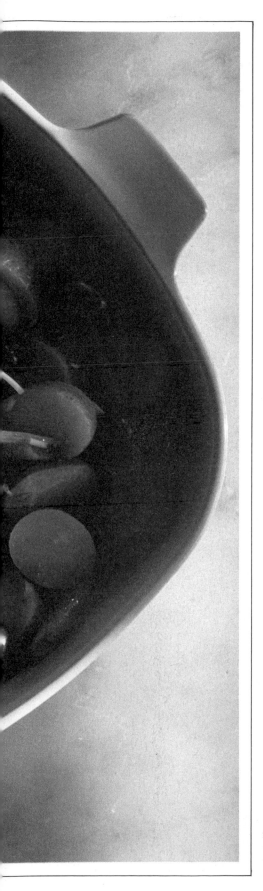

HOT POTATO SALAD

SERVES 4 / SET: FULL

Ingredients

700 g/1½ lb new potatoes, washed but not peeled
60 ml/4 tbsp water
30 ml/2 tbsp virgin olive oil
15 ml/1 tbsp lemon juice or white wine vinegar
salt and freshly ground black pepper
5 ml/1 tsp dry mustard
1 bunch spring onions (scallions)
1 bunch radishes
about 12 black olives, stoned (pitted)
1 good cup/200 g/7 oz canned green beans, drained (use cooked fresh beans if in season)
chopped chives (optional)

Mix the salad with mayonnaise dressing if you prefer. For less cholesterol, use half and half mayonnaise and yoghurt (yogurt).

◆ Put the potatoes in a dish with the water, cover and cook for about 8 minutes, shaking twice, until done. Do not overcook the potatoes, or they will be spongy.

◆ Drain the potatoes, slice them and return to the dish.

◆ Make a dressing by combining the olive oil, vinegar or lemon juice, salt, pepper and mustard in a screw-topped jar and shaking well. Pour this over the hot potatoes and keep covered.

◆ Trim the spring onions (scallions) and slice down the stalk, making 2 cuts at right angles to each other. Put the onions in iced water for a couple of minutes. The stalks will curl up to make tassels.

◆ Trim and slice the radishes.

◆ Mix the spring onion (scallion) tassels, radishes, olives, green beans and chives, if liked, into the salad and serve at once.

Hot Potato Salad

GREEN BEAN AND MUSHROOM CURRY

SERVES 2—4 / SET: FULL

Ingredients

4 tbsp/50 g/2 oz butter or ghee
1 large onion, chopped
2 cloves garlic, chopped
1 cup/100 g/4 oz green beans, trimmed and cut into 2-cm/1-in lengths
1½ cups/100 g/4 oz mushrooms, sliced
3 tomatoes, peeled and chopped
15 ml/1 tbsp lemon juice
2 slices fresh (green) ginger
2.5 ml/½ tsp turmeric
2.5 ml/½ tsp ground coriander
2.5 ml/½ tsp garam masala
fresh coriander (cilantro) or parsley

◆ Place the butter or ghee in a bowl and cook for 1 minute. Add the onion and garlic and cook for 3 minutes.

◆ Stir in the rest of the ingredients except the fresh coriander (cilantro) or parsley. Cover and cook for 8–10 minutes, stirring twice.

◆ Garnish with fresh coriander or parsley and serve with rice.

STUFFED PEPPERS WITH TOMATO SAUCE

SERVES 4
SET: FULL AND MEDIUM

Ingredients

4 baby peppers, red, green or yellow

60 ml/4 tbsp water

TOMATO SAUCE

15 ml/1 tbsp oil

1 large onion, chopped

1 clove garlic, chopped

1 carrot, chopped

1 stick (stalk) celery, chopped

1½ cups/400 g/14 oz canned tomatoes, with juice

15 ml/1 tbsp tomato purée (paste)

a few sprigs of basil

salt and freshly ground black pepper

STUFFING

1 scant cup/175 g/6 oz cooked rice

⅓ cup/50 g/2 oz cooked bacon, chopped

⅓ cup/50 g/2 oz salami, chopped

30 ml/2 tbsp chopped parsley

15 ml/1 tbsp tomato purée (paste), diluted with 15 ml/1 tbsp water

salt and freshly ground black pepper

Use baby peppers for this dish. They look much more tempting – and less daunting – than the large ones.

◆ Cut the tops off the peppers and reserve. Scoop out the pith and seeds. Put the peppers and their lids in a deep dish with the water, cover and cook on full for about 7 minutes, rearranging twice. Drain and keep warm.

◆ To make the sauce, put the oil in a pot and cook for 30 seconds. Add the onion, garlic, carrot, and celery and cook on full, covered with vented cling film (plastic wrap) for 4 minutes.

◆ Stir in the tomatoes, tomato purée (paste) and basil. Cover and cook on full power for 8 minutes, stirring twice. Put the sauce in a blender or food processor and blend until smooth. Season to taste.

◆ For the stuffing, mix together the rice, bacon, salami and parsley. Stir in the tomato purée (paste), diluted with water, and season to taste with salt and pepper.

◆ Stuff the peppers with this mixture and put on their lids. Stand the peppers upright in a deep dish, cover with vented cling film (plastic wrap) or a lid and cook on medium power for 8–10 minutes, turning the dish 3 times, until the peppers are cooked through and the filling hot.

◆ Remove the lids and serve each pepper in a pool of the reheated sauce.

PARSNIPS AND MUSHROOMS IN A CHEESE SAUCE

SERVES 4 / SET: FULL

Ingredients

450 g/1 lb parsnips
45 ml/3 tbsp water
15 ml/1 tbsp lemon juice
3 good cups/225 g/8 oz mushrooms, wiped and sliced
SAUCE
3 tbsp/40 g/1½ oz butter
⅓ cup/40 g/1½ oz flour
1¼ cups/300 ml/½ pt milk
½ cup/50 g/2 oz grated cheese
salt and freshly ground black pepper
nutmeg

◆ Peel the parsnips, trim them and cut into eighths. Cut away any very woody cores. Put them in a dish with the water and lemon juice. Cover with vented cling film (plastic film) and cook for 7 minutes, stirring twice.

◆ Stir in the mushrooms. Cover again and cook for a further 3–4 minutes, until the vegetables are done. Keep hot.

◆ Make the sauce. Put the butter in a dish and cook for 30 seconds. Stir in the flour. Pour on the milk and cook for 3 minutes, whisking after each minute. Stir in the cheese. Cook for a further minute, then whisk again. Season to taste with salt, pepper and nutmeg.

◆ Drain the vegetables and pour the sauce over them. Reheat for a minute if necessary.

NEW POTATOES WITH PEAS AND BACON

SERVES 4 / SET: FULL

Ingredients

450 g/1 lb new potatoes, washed and scrubbed

1 kg/2 lb fresh peas (about 3 cups/450 g/ 1 lb peas shelled weight)

60 ml/4 tbsp water

2 rashers (strips) bacon

²⁄₃ cup/150 ml/¼ pt cream

paprika

mint leaves or chopped chives (optional)

◆ Put the potatoes and peas in a dish with the water, cover and cook for about 8 minutes, shaking the dish twice. Test the potatoes before the cooking time is up. You should not overcook them, or they will go spongy.

◆ Put the bacon rashers (strips) on a grilling (browning) dish, cover with a sheet of kitchen paper to stop them splattering and cook for 1½ minutes. Chop up the bacon and mix it with the vegetables.

◆ Heat the cream in a jug for 1–2 minutes, pour over the vegetables and sprinkle with paprika.

◆ Serve garnished with mint leaves, or chopped chives if available.

New Potatoes with Peas and Bacon

BLACK-EYED BEANS (PEAS) WITH MUSHROOMS AND CORIANDER (CILANTRO)

S E R V E S   4   /   S E T :   F U L L

Ingredients

2 tbsp/25 g/1 oz butter

1 large onion, chopped

2 cloves garlic, chopped

2¼ cups/450 g/1 lb cooked black-eyed beans (peas)

1½ cups/400 g/14 oz canned tomatoes, drained and mashed

1 slice fresh (green) ginger

salt and freshly ground black pepper

garam masala

fresh coriander (cilantro)

◆ Put the butter in a dish and cook for 45 seconds. Add the onion and garlic and cook, covered, for 3 minutes.

◆ Add the black-eyed beans (peas), tomatoes and ginger and cook, covered, for 4–5 minutes until heated through, stirring once.

◆ Season to taste with salt, pepper and garam masala and stir in plenty of chopped coriander (cilantro) leaves. Eat hot with rice.

◆ This dish is also delicious cold.

BRUSSELS SPROUTS WITH WATER CHESTNUTS, GARLIC AND MUSHROOMS

S E R V E S   4   /   S E T :   F U L L

Ingredients

1 tbsp/15 g/½ oz butter or margarine

1 clove garlic, crushed (minced)

5 cups (approx.)/400 g/14 oz baby Brussels sprouts, trimmed

1½ cups/100 g/4 oz mushrooms, sliced

1 scant cup/200 g/7 oz canned water chestnuts, drained

soy sauce

◆ Put the butter in a dish and cook for 30 seconds. Add the garlic and cook for 1 minute.

◆ Add the sprouts, mushrooms and water chestnuts, with 15 ml/1 tbsp of the chestnut liquid. Cover and cook for 3–4 minutes, until hot through.

◆ Season with soy sauce and serve.

VARIATION This recipe can also be cooked as for Mixed Vegetable Sauté (see recipe).

Brussels Sprouts with Water Chestnuts, Garlic and Mushrooms

LASAGNE WITH RATATOUILLE

SERVES 4 / SET: FULL

Ingredients

Ratatouille (see Ratatouille Alla Mozzarella)
6 sheets spinach lasagne
boiling water
salt
oil
1¼ cups/250 g/8 oz fromage frais (or ricotta)
60 ml/4 tbsp Parmesan cheese

◆ Make the Ratatouille according to the instructions (omitting the Mozzarella) and keep warm.

◆ Put the lasagne in a deep dish and cover with boiling water. Add a pinch of salt and a few drops of oil, cover with vented cling film (plastic wrap) and cook for 15 minutes. Leave to stand for 3 minutes, then drain and rinse thoroughly under cold running water. Lay the lasagne on a tea (dish) towel to dry. Do not use kitchen paper (paper towels) – it will stick.

◆ To assemble, put a layer of lasagne in the bottom of an oblong dish, cover with pasta, then spread with fromage frais (or ricotta) and sprinkle with Parmesan cheese. Continue until all the ingredients are used up, finishing with a sprinkling of Parmesan cheese.

◆ Heat through in the microwave or, if you want the top to brown, under the grill (broiler) or in a conventional oven.

MIXED VEGETABLE SAUTE

SERVES 4 / SET: FULL

Ingredients

2 tbsp/25 g/1 oz butter or margarine
1 yellow pepper, seeded and chopped
1¾ cups/100 g/4 oz broccoli florets
½ cup/75 g/3 oz mangetout (snow peas)
1 cup/75 g/3 oz mushrooms, sliced
½ cup/50 g/2 oz spring onions (scallions)
soy sauce (optional)

The good thing about using the microwave to cook vegetables together is that they retain their individual flavours.

◆ Heat a browning dish to maximum, according to manufacturer's instructions. Add the butter or margarine and, using oven gloves, tilt the dish so that it is coated with the hot fat.

◆ Put the vegetables in the dish and cook for 2 minutes, stirring once.

◆ Serve with soy sauce and rice.

Mixed Vegetables Sauté

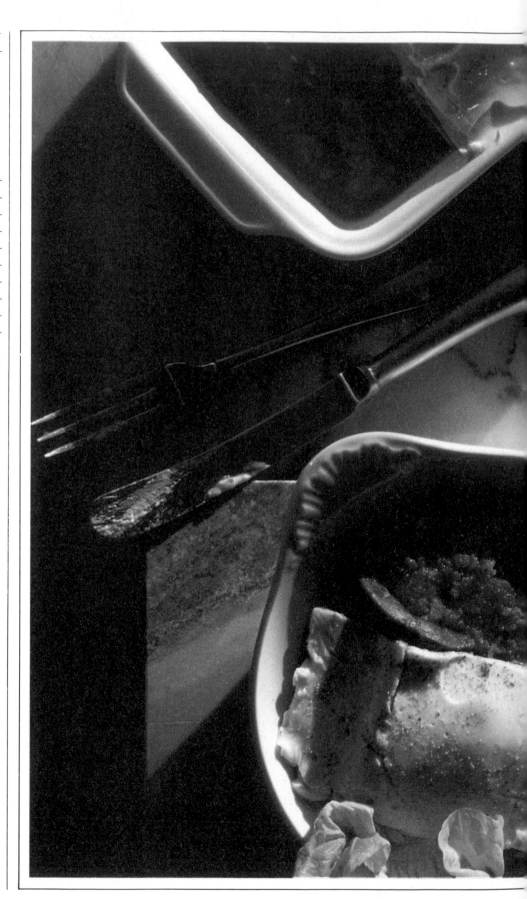

CHICORY (BELGIAN ENDIVE) IN HAM AND CHEESE SAUCE

SERVES 4 / SET: FULL

Ingredients

4 heads chicory (Belgian endive)
45 ml/3 tbsp water
3 tbsp/40 g/1 1/2 oz butter
1/3 cup/40 g/1 1/2 oz flour
1 1/4 cups/300 ml/1/2 pt milk
1/3 cup/50 g/2 oz Parmesan cheese
1/3 cup/50 g/2 oz cooked ham, chopped
salt and freshly ground black pepper

◆ Trim the chicory (Belgian endive) and cut in half lengthways. Lay in a dish and add the water. Cover with vented cling film (plastic wrap) and cook for 4–6 minutes, until tender, turning the dish twice.

◆ Make the sauce. Put the butter in a dish and cook for 1 minute. Stir in the flour. Pour on the milk and cook for 3 minutes, whisking after each minute. Stir in the cheese, cook for a further minute and whisk again. Stir in the ham and season to taste.

◆ Drain the chicory, pour over the sauce and heat through for 1 minute.

AUBERGINE (EGGPLANT) LASAGNE

SERVES 4 / SET: FULL

Ingredients

2 medium aubergines (eggplant)
30–45 ml/2–3 tbsp water
6 sheets spinach lasagne
salt
oil
Tomato Sauce (see Stuffed Peppers with Tomato Sauce)

CHEESE SAUCE

3 tbsp/40 g/1½ oz butter or margarine
⅓ cup/40 g/1½ oz flour
1¼ cups/300 ml/½ pt milk
½ cup/50 g/2 oz Edam cheese, grated
salt and freshly ground black pepper

◆ Slice the aubergines (eggplant). Arrange them in a deep oblong dish, in which you will cook the finished lasagne. Add the water, cover with vented cling film (plastic wrap) and cook for 7 minutes, rearranging once, until tender. Drain and set aside.

◆ Put the lasagne in a large deep pot and pour over enough boiling water to cover. Add salt and a few drops of oil to stop the pieces sticking together. Cover and cook for 12–15 minutes, until done.

◆ Drain the lasagne, rinse thoroughly under running cold water and drain again. If you omit this step you are liable to be left with a soggy mass of unmanageable pasta. Lay the sheets to dry on a tea (dish) towel. (Don't use kitchen paper (paper towels) – they will stick.)

◆ To make the cheese sauce, put the butter or margarine in a bowl and cook for 1 minute. Stir in the flour and pour on the milk. Cook for 3 minutes, whisking after each minute. Stir in the cheese. Cook for a further minute and whisk again. Season to taste with salt and pepper.

◆ To assemble the dish start with a layer of aubergines, then cover with tomato sauce, a layer of pasta and a layer of cheese sauce. Continue until all the ingredients are used up, finishing with a layer of cheese sauce.

◆ Heat through in the microwave, or in a conventional oven or under the grill (broiler) if you want the top to brown.

◆ Serve hot.

VARIATION Omit the pasta for an Aubergine (Eggplant) Layer Bake.

Aubergine (Eggplant) Lasagne

LEEK PARCELS

S E R V E S   4 / S E T :   F U L L

Ingredients

3 tbsp/40 g/1½ oz polyunsaturated vegetable margarine or butter
⅓ cup/40 g/1½ oz flour
1¼ cups/300 ml/½ pt milk
½ cup/50 g/2 oz Edam cheese, grated
5–10 ml/1–2 tsp mustard (optional)
salt and pepper
4 leeks
30 ml/2 tbsp water
4 slices ham

◆ First make the sauce. Put the margarine or butter in a bowl and cook for 1 minute. Stir in the flour. Pour on the milk. Cook for 3 minutes, whisking after each minute. Stir in the cheese and mustard, if used. Cook for a further minute and whisk again. Season to taste with salt and pepper. Keep the sauce warm while you cook the leeks.

◆ Trim the leeks and wash thoroughly. Put them in a dish with the water, cover with vented cling wrap (plastic wrap) and cook for about 8 minutes, rearranging once, until done.

◆ Drain the leeks and cut off a few rings for the garnish. Wrap each in a slice of ham, lay side by side in the dish and pour the sauce over. Cover and cook for 2–3 minutes until hot through.

◆ Garnish with leek rings and serve at once.

FRENCH BEAN SALAD

SERVES 4 / SET: FULL

Ingredients

4 cups approx./450 g/1 lb French beans, trimmed and left whole

60 ml/4 tbsp water

3 cups/450 g/1 lb tomatoes, peeled, seeded and cut into strips

22½ ml/1½ tbsp olive oil

22½ ml/1½ tbsp lemon juice

salt and freshly ground black pepper

2 hardboiled (hard-cooked) eggs

chives (optional)

◆ Put the beans in a dish, add the water, cover with vented cling film (plastic wrap) and cook for 6 minutes, rearranging twice. The beans should be done but still crisp. Set aside, covered, while you make the dressing.

◆ Mix the oil, lemon juice and seasoning. (Shake them together in a screw-topped jar if you have one handy.)

◆ Drain the beans, mix them with the tomatoes and toss in the dressing.

◆ Separate the whites from the yolks of the eggs. Chop both. Garnish the salad with the egg.

VARIATION If you are feeling artistic, tie the beans into bundles with the chives instead of mixing them together with the tomatoes.

BROCCOLI WITH ALMONDS AND BLUE CHEESE SAUCE

SERVES 4 / SET: FULL

Ingredients

450 g/1 lb broccoli

45 ml/3 tbsp water

⅔ cup/150 ml/¼ pt cream

6 tbsp/40 g/1½ oz Danish blue cheese

salt and white pepper

scant ⅓ cup/40 g/1½ oz flaked (slivered), toasted almonds

diamonds of red pepper

◆ Wash the broccoli and remove the outer leaves and tough stalks. Make slits up the stalks to speed up cooking.

◆ Put the broccoli in a dish with the water. Cover with vented cling film (plastic wrap) and cook for 10 minutes, rearranging once, until tender. Drain and keep hot.

◆ Mash the cream into the cheese until smooth. Cook for 1–2 minutes. Season with salt and pepper and pour over the broccoli.

◆ Serve garnished with flaked (slivered) almonds, or with the broccoli florets in a pool of sauce, as shown, and decorate with diamonds of red pepper.

Broccoli with Almonds and Blue Cheese Sauce

ARTICHOKE HEARTS WITH SPINACH

SERVES 4 / SET: FULL

Ingredients

1 kg/2 lb fresh spinach
2 tbsp/25 g/1 oz butter
1 large onion, chopped
8 artichoke hearts, fresh or canned
1/2 cup/75 g/3 oz Parma ham, cut into strips
SAUCE
3 tbsp/40 g/1 1/2 oz butter
1/3 cup/40 g/1 1/2 oz flour
1 1/4 cups/300 ml/1/2 pt milk
1/3 cup/50 g/2 oz grated Parmesan cheese
nutmeg
salt and freshly ground black pepper

◆ Wash the spinach and discard tough stalks and discoloured leaves. Put it in a boiling or roasting bag and tie loosely. Cook for about 6 minutes, shaking the bag once, until the spinach has collapsed. Let it stand for a while, then chop coarsely.

◆ Put the butter in a dish and cook for 30 seconds. Add the onion and the artichoke hearts and cook for 3 minutes. (If using canned artichoke hearts, however, arrange them on top of the onion when cooked.)

◆ Lay strips of Parma ham in between the artichokes and put the chopped spinach in a layer on top of that.

◆ To make the sauce, put the butter in a bowl and cook for 30 seconds to 1 minute to melt it. Stir in the flour. Pour on the milk and cook for 3 minutes, whisking after each minute. Add the cheese. Cook for a further minute and whisk again. Season to taste with nutmeg, salt and pepper.

◆ Pour the sauce over the vegetables and heat through in the microwave, or brown in a conventional oven or under the grill (broiler).

AUBERGINE (EGGPLANT) WITH TWO SAUCES

SERVES 4 / SET: FULL

Ingredients

2 medium aubergines (eggplant), sliced
60 ml/4 tbsp water
flour
beaten egg
fresh breadcrumbs
a little butter
Tomato Sauce (see Stuffed Peppers with Tomato Sauce)
Cheese Sauce (see Aubergine (Eggplant) Lasagne)

◆ Put the aubergines (eggplant) in a dish, add the water, cover with vented cling film (plastic wrap) and cook for 7 minutes, rearranging once, until tender.

◆ Dust the drained aubergine (eggplant) slices with flour, then dip in the beaten egg and breadcrumbs. Push the breadcrumbs on well with your fingers.

◆ Heat a browning dish to maximum, according to the manufacturer's instructions. Add a little butter and, holding the dish with oven gloves, tilt it to cover with the hot fat.

◆ Fry the aubergine (eggplant) slices in batches for 30 seconds on each side, until golden. Keep warm.

◆ Serve with the Tomato Sauce and Cheese Sauce.

Aubergine (Eggplant) with Two Sauces

CAULIFLOWER IN ORANGE SAUCE

SERVES 4 / SET: FULL

Ingredients

1 cauliflower
45 ml/3 tbsp water
2 tbsp/25 g/1 oz butter
3 tbsp/25 g/1 oz cornflour (cornstarch)
1¼ cups/300 ml/½ pt unsweetened orange juice
finely grated rind of ½ orange
orange bows

This makes a welcome change from cauliflower cheese.

◆ Trim the cauliflower and break into florets. Put them in a dish, add the water, cover with vented cling film (plastic wrap) and cook for 8–10 minutes, depending on size, until tender but not soft. Drain and keep warm.

◆ Put the butter in a jug and cook for 30 seconds. Stir in the cornflour (cornstarch) and cook for 1 minute. Stir in the orange juice and cook for 3 minutes, whisking after each minute. Stir in the orange rind.

◆ Serve the cauliflower on pools of sauce, garnished with the orange bows.

PEPPERS AND FRIED EGGS

SERVES 4 / SET: FULL

Ingredients

1 red pepper, cut into julienne strips
1 green pepper, cut into julienne strips
1 yellow pepper, cut into julienne strips
2 large tomatoes, peeled, seeded and cut into strips
1 bunch spring onions (scallions), trimmed
45 ml/3 tbsp water
a knob of butter
4 eggs
salt and pepper

◆ Put the vegetables into a dish with the water, cover with vented cling film (plastic wrap) and cook for 4–5 minutes, stirring once, until tender but not soft. Keep warm.
◆ Heat a browning dish for 3–4 minutes. Add the butter and, using oven gloves, tilt the dish to coat with the hot fat. Break an egg into each corner of the dish and pierce the yolks with a cocktail stick (toothpick). Cook until nearly set (about 2½ minutes, but this will depend on the size of the eggs). Allow to stand for 30 seconds.
◆ Divide the vegetables between 4 heated plates and lay an egg on each.
◆ Offer salt and pepper at the table.

VARIATION You can add garlic to the ingredients if you like and, for a touch of style, make the spring onions (scallions) into tassels.

Peppers and Fried Eggs

PERFECT ASPARAGUS

SERVES 4 / SET: FULL

Ingredients

3 cups/350 g/12 oz asparagus spears
45 ml/3 tbsp water
3 tbsp/40 g/1½ oz butter
30 ml/2 tbsp Parmesan cheese

If you have too little asparagus to go round, serve it with fried eggs, or scrambled eggs and triangles of toast.

◆ Trim the woody ends from the asparagus spears so that they are all the same length. Lay them in a dish arranged top to tail and pour on the water. Cover with vented cling film (plastic wrap) and cook for 5–7 minutes, depending on the size of the spears.
◆ Drain the asparagus and keep warm.
◆ Put the butter and Parmesan in a jug and cook for 1 minute
◆ Serve the sauce separately.

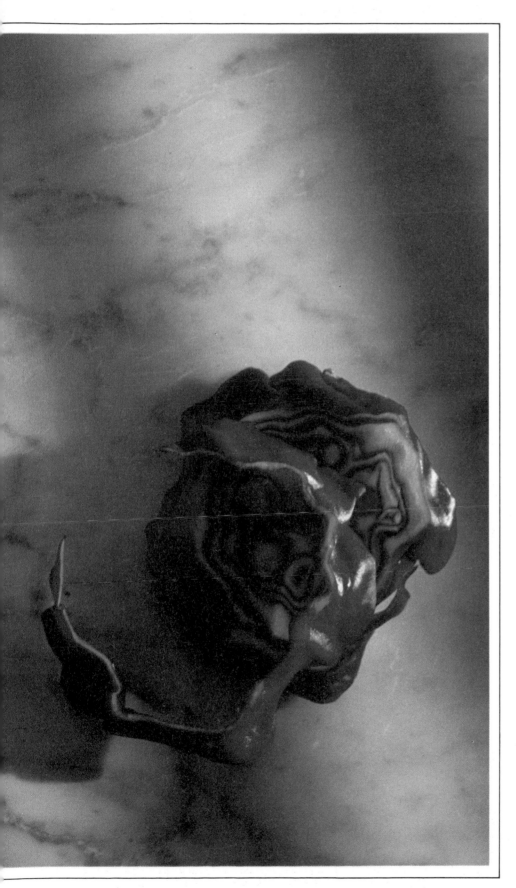

RED CABBAGE AND APPLE

SERVES 4 / SET: FULL

Ingredients

6 cups/450 g/1 lb red cabbage, finely shredded

1⅓ cups/225 g/8 oz cooking apples, peeled, cored and sliced

60 ml/4 tbsp red wine vinegar

30 ml/2 tbsp brown sugar

a pinch of mixed spice (sweet baking spice)

salt and freshly ground black pepper

Cooked conventionally, red cabbage turns blue. Microwave it if you want it to keep its crunch and stay red. This combination is very good with pork chops and baked potatoes.

◆ Mix all the ingredients together in a large dish.

◆ Cover and cook for 15 minutes, stirring twice, until tender but still crunchy.

ITALIAN STYLE COURGETTES (ZUCCHINI)

SERVES 4 / SET: FULL

Ingredients

3½ cups/400 g/14 oz courgettes (zucchini), sliced

1 small onion, chopped

1 clove garlic, crushed (minced)

45 ml/3 tbsp water

1½ cups/400 g/14 oz canned tomatoes, drained and sieved (strained) or blended

salt and freshly ground black pepper

45 ml/3 tbsp grated Parmesan cheese

◆ Put the courgettes (zucchini) in a dish with the onion and garlic. Add the water. Cover with vented cling film (plastic wrap) and cook for about 7 minutes, until nearly done.

◆ Stir in the sieved (strained) tomato and season with salt and pepper. Cover and cook for 2–3 minutes, until hot through.

◆ Sprinkle with grated Parmesan cheese and serve.

VARIATION You can layer the courgettes with sliced mozzarella cheese and tomato sauce instead of serving them with Parmesan.

BAKED POTATOES WITH . . .

SET: FULL

◆ Wash the potatoes, 1 per person, and prick with a fork to stop the skins bursting. Put them in the oven on a sheet of absorbent kitchen paper (paper towel). Arrange in a circle if you are cooking several.

◆ Cook for 4 minutes (1 potato weighing about 175 g/6 oz); 6–8 minutes (2 potatoes); or 12–14 minutes (4 potatoes). Turn them over half-way through cooking time.

SUGGESTED FILLINGS

Chilli (Chili) Beans (see recipe)
Blue cheese mashed with cream
Cottage cheese and chives
Grated Cheddar and crispy bacon pieces
Butter melted with garlic and herbs
Broad (lima) beans and sweetcorn (corn).

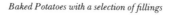

Baked Potatoes with a selection of fillings

CHILLI (CHILI) BEANS

SERVES 4 / SET: FULL

Ingredients

1 large onion, chopped
1–2 cloves garlic, chopped
15 ml/1 tbsp sunflower oil
1 fresh green chilli (chili), chopped and seeded
chilli (chili) powder to taste
½ red pepper, seeded and chopped
½ green pepper, seeded and chopped
1½ cups/400 g/14 oz canned tomatoes, drained and mashed, juice reserved
4 cups/800 g/28 oz canned kidney beans, drained
salt
red and green pepper cut into julienne strips
sliced green chillies (chilis), (optional)
triangles of toast

Use as much or as little chilli (chili) powder as you like.

◆ Put the onion and garlic in a casserole with the oil, cover and cook for 3 minutes. Stir in the chilli (chili), chilli (chili) powder, chopped red and green peppers and 60 ml/4 tbsp reserved tomato juice. Cover and cook for 5 minutes.

◆ Stir in the tomatoes and kidney beans, cover and cook for 5 minutes, or until the mixture is heated through, stirring once. Season with salt to taste.

◆ Garnish with julienne strips of red and green pepper and sliced chillies (chilis) if liked (remember to warn your guests!).

◆ Serve with triangles of toast. This is also good with rice or baked potatoes.

GLAZED ONIONS

SERVES 4 / SET: FULL

Ingredients

8 small onions, peeled but left whole

30 ml/2 tbsp honey

2 tbsp/25 g/1 oz butter

30 ml/2 tbsp hot water

◆ Put the onions in a dish.

◆ Cream the honey and butter with the water and pour over the onions. Cover with vented cling film (plastic wrap) and cook for 8–10 minutes, until the onions are tender, shaking or stirring the dish once.

◆ Serve hot. This is particularly good with pork chops and mashed potatoes.

CRUDITES WITH HOT ANCHOVY DIP

SET: FULL

Ingredients

A selection of crisp raw vegetables, cut into manageable pieces, such as: carrots, celery, green, red and yellow peppers, cucumber, cauliflower and broccoli florets, radishes, mushrooms.

DIP

¹/2 cup/100 g/4 oz butter, diced

2 cloves garlic, crushed (minced)

8 anchovy fillets, pounded

1¹/4 cups/300 ml/¹/2 pt double (heavy) cream

◆ To make the dip, put the butter in a pot and cook for 1 minute until melted. Add the garlic and cook for 30 seconds.

◆ Put the anchovy fillets with the cream in a blender or food processor and blend until smooth.

◆ Pour the anchovy cream onto the garlic butter, stir well and cook for 1–2 minutes, until hot.

◆ Put the pot with the anchovy dip on a large platter and arrange the crudités around it.

Crudités with Hot Anchovy Dip

COUSCOUS WITH VEGETABLES

SERVES 4 / SET: FULL

Ingredients

½ cauliflower, cut into florets
1½ cups/225 g/8 oz carrots, diced
1 large parsnip, diced
45 ml/3 tbsp water
2 cups/400 g/14 oz canned chick peas (garbanzos), drained
good cup/200 g/7 oz canned peas, drained
Tomato Sauce (see Stuffed Peppers with Tomato Sauce) made with chilli (chili) powder to taste instead of basil
2 cups/350 g/12 oz couscous
2 cups/450 ml/¾ pt boiling water
salt
2 tbsp/25 g/1 oz butter

◆ First prepare the vegetable topping. Put the cauliflower, carrots and parsnip into a dish with the water, cover with vented cling film (plastic wrap) and cook for 5 minutes, stirring once.

◆ Stir in the chick peas (garbanzos) and peas and cook for a further 4 minutes, stirring once. Drain and keep hot.

◆ For the couscous, put the grain in a deep pot, cover with the boiling water, add a pinch of salt and cook for 4 minutes. Stir in the butter.

◆ Reheat the tomato sauce for 3 minutes in a sauce boat.

◆ Serve the couscous topped with the spicy vegetable mixture and allow guests to serve themselves with the sauce.

POTATO OMELETTE (OMELET)

SERVES 2
SET: FULL AND LOW

Ingredients
1 cup/100 g/4 oz cooked potato, sliced
a little butter
4 eggs
salt and freshly ground black pepper
freshly chopped herbs or chives (optional)

This is a good way of using leftover potatoes. Add other vegetables, if you like.

◆ Put the potato in 1 or 2 layers in a buttered dish. Use a shallow dish or a pie plate. Cover and cook on full for 45 seconds.

◆ Beat together the eggs, seasoning and chives or herbs if used and pour them over the vegetables. Cook on low power for 8 minutes, or until almost set.

◆ Leave to stand for 1–2 minutes before serving, then cut in two.

◆ Left until cold, then cut into wedges, this makes a good picnic dish, especially if served with salad.

NOTE Quite often quiches and omelettes (omelets) won't cook in the 'cold spot' in the middle of the microwave. To correct this place under a hot grill (broiler) for 2–3 minutes.

LASAGNE AND LEEK ROLLS

SERVES 4 / SET: FULL

Ingredients

4 young leeks
boiling water
30 ml/2 tbsp water
4 sheets spinach lasagne
salt
oil
boiling water
2/3 cup/100 g/4 oz ricotta cheese

Use only very young leeks to make this elegant-looking dish.

◆ Trim the leeks and blanch the discarded tops by pouring boiling water over them and leave to stand for 2 minutes. Put to one side. Put the leeks in a dish with 30 ml/2 tbsp water, cover with vented cling film (plastic wrap) and cook for 4 minutes, until tender. Drain and allow to cool.

◆ Put the pasta in a deep dish with a pinch of salt and a few drops of oil. Cover with boiling water. Cook for 10 minutes. Let the pasta stand for 2 minutes, then drain and rinse thoroughly under cold running water. Lay the pasta on a tea (dish) towel to dry. (Do not use kitchen paper (paper towels)– it will stick.)

◆ When the pasta has cooled, spread each sheet with 1½ tbsp/25 g/1 oz ricotta cheese. Lay a leek at the end of each sheet and roll up tightly.

◆ Trim away any excess leek, and cut the rolls into slices.

◆ Trim the blanched leek tops and arrange on individual plates as shown. Place the slices in the middle and serve cold.

Lasagne and Leek Rolls

ARTICHOKE RISOTTO

SERVES 4 / SET: FULL

Ingredients

3 tbsp/40 g/1½ oz butter
1 onion, chopped
2 cups/350 g/12 oz long-grain Italian rice
3 cups/700 ml/1¼ pt boiling water
1 chicken stock (bouillon) cube
4 very small globe artichokes
salt and freshly ground black pepper
30 ml/2 tbsp Parmesan cheese

To make this risotto you will need very young, very tender artichokes. If these are not available, use tinned (canned) artichoke hearts.

◆ Put half the butter in a deep pot and cook for 30 seconds. Add the onion, cover and cook for 1 minute.

◆ Stir in the rice. Pour over the boiling water and crumble on the stock (bouillon) cube. Cover and cook for 8 minutes.

◆ Meanwhile, prepare the artichokes. Trim off the stalks and remove any tough outer leaves. Slice the artichokes vertically. Stir them into the rice and cook for a further 4 minutes. Let the pot stand, covered, for 7 minutes.

◆ Stir in the remaining butter, season with salt and pepper and stir in the Parmesan cheese.

◆ Serve at once.

TURNIP AND POTATO BAKE

SERVES 4 / SET: FULL

Ingredients

2½ cups/450 g/1 lb turnips, peeled and thinly sliced

3 cups/450 g/1 lb potatoes, peeled and thinly sliced

butter

salt and freshly ground black pepper

60 ml/4 tbsp single (light) cream

chopped chives

◆ Layer the turnips and potatoes in a round dish, dotting each layer with butter and seasoning with salt and pepper. Cover with waxed paper and press well down.

◆ Stand the dish on an inverted plate. Cover and cook for 9 minutes, turning once.

◆ Slowly pour over cream so that it seeps between the layers. Brown slightly under the grill (broiler), garnish with chives and serve.

OKRA WITH TOMATOES

SERVES 4 / SET: FULL

Ingredients

approx. 4 cups/450 g/1 lb okra

vinegar

2 tbsp/25 g/1 oz butter

15 ml/1 tbsp olive oil

15 ml/1 tbsp lemon juice

1 onion, chopped

1 clove garlic, chopped

3 cups/450 g/1 lb fresh tomatoes, skinned, seeded and cut into strips

salt and freshly ground black pepper

plenty of chopped flat-leaved parsley or fresh coriander (cilantro)

lemon wedges

Canned okra are a perfectly acceptable alternative to the fresh variety, should these be unavailable. Serve this dish with rice.

◆ Cut off the okra stalks without damaging the seed cavity inside. Soak them for 30 minutes in cold water acidulated with a little vinegar. This is to combat the stickiness of the vegetable. Rinse in fresh water and pat dry.

◆ Put the butter, olive oil and lemon juice in a dish, add the onion and garlic and cook, covered, for 3 minutes. Add the okra and tomatoes, cover and cook for 4–5 minutes, until tender.

◆ Season to taste with salt and freshly ground black pepper and sprinkle with parsley or coriander.

◆ Serve with lemon wedges.

Okra with Tomatoes

ROMAN SPINACH

SERVES 4 / SET: FULL

Ingredients

1 kg/2 lb fresh spinach
7 ml/½ tbsp oil
7 ml/½ tbsp butter (approx.)
⅓ cup/50 g/2 oz pine nuts
⅓ cup/50 g/2 oz sultanas (golden raisins)
2 rashers (strips) bacon, derinded and diced
1 clove garlic, crushed (minced)
salt and freshly ground black pepper

◆ Wash the spinach and discard tough stalks and discoloured leaves. Put it in a roasting or boiling bag and tie loosely. Cook for about 6 minutes, shaking the bag once, until the spinach has collapsed.

◆ Put the oil and butter in a dish (use more if you want a richer taste), and add the pine nuts, sultanas (golden raisins), diced bacon and garlic. Cook for 1 minute.

◆ Meanwhile, shred the spinach, add it to the dish and toss well. Season with salt and pepper to taste.

◆ Cook for a further minute, covered with vented cling film (plastic wrap), to heat through.

DAL

SERVES 4 / SET: FULL

Ingredients

1⅓ cups/250 g/8 oz red lentils
2 cups/425 ml/¾ pt boiling water (approx.)
2 slices fresh (green) ginger
a pinch of turmeric
a pinch of salt
15–30 ml/1–2 tbsp sunflower oil
5 ml/1 tsp mustard seeds
1 clove garlic, crushed (minced)
1 green chilli (chili), chopped
a pinch of garam masala
pitta (pita) bread

◆ Put the lentils in a pot and pour on the boiling water. Add the ginger, turmeric and salt, cover and cook for 12–15 minutes, stirring twice, and adding more boiling water if it becomes dry. (Cooking time and the amount of water needed depend on age of lentils.)

◆ Leave the pot to stand, covered, while you prepare the dressing.

◆ Put the oil in a jug and cook for 1 minute. Add the mustard seeds, garlic and chilli (chili), cover with vented cling film(plastic wrap), (the seeds might shoot out, as they start to pop when very hot), and cook for 2 minutes. Stir into the dal. Stir in the garam masala and serve hot with pitta (pita) bread.

◆ If you have any left over, add a little water to thin it down before reheating.

Dal

BEETROOT (BEETS) WITH CREAM AND MUSHROOMS

SERVES 4 / SET: FULL

Ingredients

2 tbsp/25 g/1 oz butter
1 clove garlic, crushed (minced)
3 good cups/225 g/8 oz mushrooms, sliced (or whole button mushrooms)
3 cups/450 g/1 lb beetroot (beets), cooked and chopped
2/3 cup/150 ml/1/4 pt cream
30 ml/2 tbsp grated Parmesan cheese
30 ml/2 tbsp breadcrumbs

◆ Put the butter in a dish and cook for 1 minute to melt it. Add the garlic and mushrooms, cover with vented cling film (plastic wrap) and cook for 3–4 minutes, stirring once.

◆ Mix in the beetroot (beets).

◆ Stir the cream and cheese together and pour over the vegetables.

◆ Sprinkle on the breadcrumbs and cover and cook for 4–5 minutes, until hot through.

MARINATED MUSHROOMS

SERVES 4 / SET: FULL

Ingredients

6 cups/500 g/1 lb button mushrooms, wiped

60 ml/4 tbsp olive oil

60 ml/4 tbsp lemon juice

15 ml/1 tbsp coriander seeds

salt and freshly ground black pepper

parsley or coriander (cilantro) leaves

chopped chives (optional)

toast

◆ Put the mushrooms in a dish with the oil, lemon juice and coriander seeds. Let them marinate for an hour or two or in the fridge overnight.

◆ Remove the mushrooms from the marinade with a slotted spoon and place in a shallow dish. Brush with the marinade and cook for 3 minutes, stirring every minute.

◆ Season to taste, sprinkle with parsley or coriander (cilantro), and chives, if liked, and serve with triangles of toast.

Marinated Mushrooms

RUSSIAN BEETROOT (BEETS)

SERVES 4 / SET: FULL

Ingredients

6 tbsp/75 g/3 oz butter
5 medium uncooked beetroots (beets), diced
30 ml/2 tbsp red wine vinegar
2.5 ml/½ tsp dried dill
2.5 ml/½ tsp dried fennel
salt and freshly ground black pepper
3 tbsp/25 g/1 oz cornflour (cornstarch)
30 ml/2 tbsp milk
fresh dill or fennel
sour cream

◆ Place butter in a bowl and cook for 1 minute. Stir in beetroot (beets), vinegar, herbs and seasoning. Cover and cook for 8 minutes or until beetroots are tender.

◆ Place cornflour (cornstarch) and milk in a small bowl and mix until smooth. Stir mixture into beets and cook, covered, for about 4 minutes until thickened.

◆ Allow to stand, covered, for 2 minutes. Garnish with fresh dill or fennel and serve hot or cold, with sour cream, to accompany cold meats.

CABBAGE WITH BACON AND POTATOES

SERVES 4 / SET: FULL

Ingredients

1 curly cabbage, shredded
2 rashers (strips) bacon, chopped
½ cup/75 g/3 oz spicy sausage, diced
2 cups/225 g/8 oz baby onions, peeled but left whole
⅔ cup/150 ml/¼ pt chicken stock (broth)
2 cups/450 g/1 lb potatoes, cooked and mashed
2 egg yolks
butter
milk
salt and freshly ground black pepper

◆ Put the cabbage, bacon, sausage and onions in a dish and pour over the stock (broth). Cover with vented cling film (plastic wrap) and cook for about 8 minutes, stirring once, until done.

◆ Purée the potatoes with the egg yolks in a blender or food processor, adding enough butter and milk to make them smooth and creamy. Season to taste with salt and pepper.

◆ Put the potato purée on top of the cabbage, cover and cook for 3 minutes, or until hot through. If preferred, brown in a conventional oven or under the grill (broiler).

Cabbage with Bacon and Potatoes

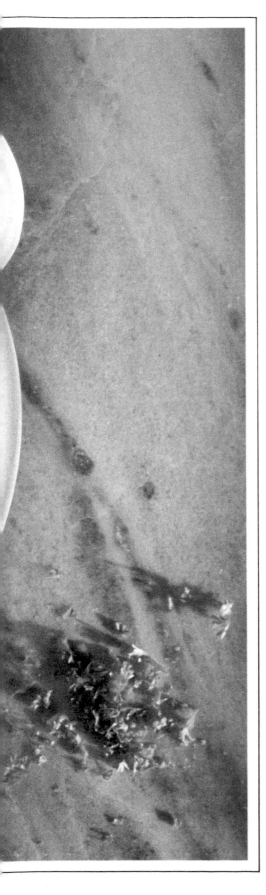

Rice with Peppers and Cheese

RICE WITH PEPPERS AND CHEESE

SERVES 4 / SET: FULL

Ingredients

2 cups/350 g/12 oz rice
3 cups/700 ml/1¼ pt boiling water
1 beef stock (bouillon) cube
1 small red pepper, seeded and chopped
1 small yellow pepper, seeded and chopped
1 small green pepper, seeded and chopped
1 cup/100 g/4 oz Edam cheese, grated
salt and freshly ground black pepper
1 bunch parsley, chopped

◆ Put the rice in a deep pot, pour over the boiling water and crumble on the stock (bouillon) cube. Cover and cook for 8 minutes.
◆ Stir in the green, yellow and red peppers. Cover and cook for 4 minutes.
◆ Stir in the cheese. Check the seasoning and add salt and pepper if necessary (depending on the saltiness of the stock (bouillon) cube). Cover and leave to stand for 5 minutes.
◆ If the cheese has not melted heat through again for 2 minutes.
◆ Stir in the parsley and serve.

ARTICHOKES WITH HOLLANDAISE SAUCE

SERVES 2 / SET: FULL AND MEDIUM OR DEFROST

Ingredients

2 globe artichokes
30 ml/2 tbsp lemon juice
90 ml/6 tbsp water
HOLLANDAISE SAUCE
¼ cup/50 g/2 oz butter, diced
15 ml/1 tbsp lemon juice
2 small egg yolks
salt and white pepper

◆ Soak the artichokes for an hour or so in a bowl of water, acidulated with half of the lemon juice, to loosen any soil or grit that may be stuck between the leaves. Rinse thoroughly in clean water and set upside down to drain. Trim off the stalk close to the vegetable so that it stands upright. Remove any damaged outer leaves and rub the cut surfaces with lemon juice. Do not bother to cut the points off the leaves – this is unnecessary and ruins the look of the vegetable.
◆ Put the artichokes upright in a dish, add the water and the remaining lemon juice, cover and cook for 7–8 minutes on full. Tug at one of the lower leaves to see if done. If it promises to come away in your fingers, the artichokes are ready. Leave them to stand for 3 minutes while you make the sauce.
◆ Put the butter in a bowl and cook on medium or defrost for 2 minutes until melted. Add the lemon juice and egg yolks and whisk lightly.
◆ Cook on medium or defrost for 1 minute, whisk again and season.
◆ Drain and serve with the sauce.
◆ To eat the artichoke, pull away the leaves and suck off the tender fleshy part, dipped in the sauce. When you come to the "choke", cut it away and discard it. Eat the heart with a knife and fork – and more sauce.

RATATOUILLE ALLA MOZZARELLA

SERVES 4 / SET: FULL

Ingredients

1 large aubergine (eggplant), sliced
3 courgettes (zucchini), sliced
60 ml/4 tbsp olive oil
1 large onion, sliced
2 cloves garlic, chopped
1 small red pepper, seeded and chopped
1 small green pepper, seeded and chopped
1½ cups/100 g/4 oz mushrooms, sliced
1½ cups/400 g/14 oz canned tomatoes, mashed
15 ml/1 tbsp tomato purée (paste)
10 ml/2 tsp fresh mixed herbs, chopped
1 bayleaf
salt and freshly ground black pepper
1 cup/100 g/4 oz mozzarella cheese, cubed

◆ Place aubergine (eggplant) and courgettes (zucchini) on a plate, sprinkle with salt and allow to stand for 30 minutes. Rinse in cold water and pat dry. Cut the aubergine (eggplant) into bite-sized pieces.

◆ Pour the oil into a casserole and cook for 1 minute. Add onion and garlic and cook for 1 minute. Stir in peppers, aubergine (eggplant) and courgettes (zucchini) and cook for 5 minutes, stirring once.

◆ Stir in remaining ingredients, cover and cook for 15 minutes, stirring twice. Stir in mozzarella. Cover and cook for 5 minutes until cheese has melted or brown under the grill (broiler) if preferred. Serve with crusty French bread to mop up the juices.

BABY ONIONS ESCOFFIER

SERVES 4 / SET: FULL

Ingredients

4 cups/450 g/1 lb baby onions
15 ml/1 tbsp oil
1 bay leaf
a sprig of thyme
5 ml/1 tsp fennel seeds
1/3 cup/50 g/2 oz sultanas (golden raisins), soaked
45 ml/3 tbsp dry white wine
15 ml/1 tbsp brandy

◆ Peel the onions, but leave them whole. Put them in a dish with the remaining ingredients, cover with vented cling film (plastic wrap) and cook for about 10 minutes, shaking the dish twice.

◆ Serve with lamb, beef or game.

FENNEL WITH PARMESAN

SERVES 4 / SET: FULL

Ingredients

2 bulbs fennel
1/4 cup/50 g/2 oz butter
15 ml/1 tbsp lemon juice
salt and freshly ground black pepper
30 ml/2 tbsp Parmesan cheese
30 ml/2 tbsp chopped fresh herbs (optional)

◆ Remove the tough outer leaves of the fennel. Trim and slice the bulbs, reserving the feathery fronds.

◆ Put the butter in a dish and cook for 1 minute. Add the fennel and turn in the butter to coat. Cover with vented cling film (plastic wrap) and cook for about 10 minutes, stirring the dish a couple of times, until the fennel is tender.

◆ Sprinkle on the lemon juice, season with salt and pepper and spoon over the Parmesan cheese.

◆ Garnish with the chopped fennel fronds or fresh herbs.

Fennel with Parmesan

BROAD (LIMA) BEANS WITH SWEETCORN (CORN) IN A SPICY CREAM SAUCE

SERVES 4 / SET: FULL

Ingredients

2 tbsp/25 g/1 oz butter

2 cups/200 g/14 oz broad (lima) beans, shelled

2 cups/200 g/14 oz sweetcorn kernels (corn)

30 ml/2 tbsp water

2/3 cup/150 ml/1/4 pt cream

a pinch of ginger

a pinch of cayenne pepper

◆ Put the butter in a dish and cook for 1 minute. Add the broad (lima) beans and sweetcorn (corn) with the water, stir, cover with vented cling film (plastic wrap) and cook for 3–4 minutes, until nearly done, stirring once.

◆ Mix in the cream, with ginger and cayenne pepper to taste. Cover and cook for 1 minute.

◆ Serve hot.

NOTE If you want to make an attractive starter of this dish, arrange on individual dishes as shown and pour on the butter. Cover with cling film (plastic wrap) and cook for 1½ minutes. Serve the sauce separately.

BUTTERED CARROTS WITH ORANGE

SERVES 4 / SET: FULL

Ingredients

*3 1/2 cups/400 g/14 oz baby carrots,
scrubbed, with a little bit of leaf, if possible*

3 tbsp/40 g/1 1/2 oz butter

30 ml/2 tbsp orange juice

salt and white pepper

*orange peel, cut into julienne strips and
blanched in water for 1 minute*

orange slices

*Tiny carrots look and taste much nicer than
their large relations, but if you can only get
the bigger ones, trim them, peel them and
cut into slices. If you manage to find small
ones, wash them well, but leave on a few
fronds, as they look very pretty.*

◆ Put the carrots in a dish with the
butter and orange juice, cover and
cook for about 10 minutes, until
tender. Stir or shake a couple of times
during cooking.

◆ Season the carrots lightly with salt
and white pepper to taste.

◆ Serve decorated with the orange
peel and slices.

CELERY IN STILTON SAUCE

SERVES 4 / SET: FULL

Ingredients

1 head celery, trimmed and cut into pieces
about 5 cm/2 in long (reserve the leaves)

60 ml/4 tbsp water

1 cup/100 g/4 oz ripe Stilton

2/3 cup/150 ml/¼ pt double (heavy) cream

salt and white pepper

hot toast

◆ Put the celery in a dish and add the water. Cover with vented cling film (plastic wrap) and cook for about 10 minutes, until tender. Drain and keep hot.

◆ Crumble the Stilton into the cream. Mash with a fork or blend until smooth in a food processor or blender. Season with salt and white pepper. Pour over the celery. Reheat for 1–2 minutes, covered.

◆ Garnish with the celery leaves and serve with hot toast.

Celery in Stilton Sauce

CURRIED RICE

SERVES 4 / SET: FULL

Ingredients

2 tbsp/25 g/1 oz butter
1 onion, chopped
1 good cup/225 g/8 oz long-grain rice
2½ cups/575 ml/1 pt boiling water
a pinch of salt
5 ml/1 tsp turmeric
2 slices pineapple, chopped
⅓ cup/50 g/2 oz sultanas (golden raisins)
⅓ cup/50 g/2 oz dry-roasted peanuts
a pinch of garam masala
30 ml/2 tbsp desiccated (shredded) coconut

◆ Put the butter in a pot and cook for 30 seconds. Add the onion, cover and cook for 3 minutes.

◆ Stir in the rice, pour over the boiling water and add the salt and turmeric. Cover and cook for 10 minutes.

◆ Stir in the pineapple, sultanas (golden raisins) and peanuts. Stir in the garam masala and leave, covered, for 5 minutes.

◆ Stir in the desiccated (shredded) coconut and serve.

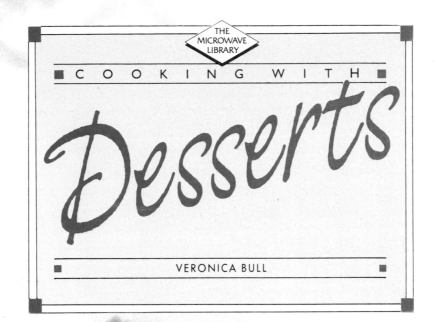

THE
MICROWAVE
LIBRARY

COOKING WITH

Desserts

VERONICA BULL

DESSERTS

WHETHER cooking for one or planning a special dinner party, a delicious dessert completes the meal perfectly. There are limitless desserts based upon the enormous variety of fruit grown throughout the world. Fruit cooked in the microwave oven retains its shape, colour and natural fresh flavour. Fruit can be poached or made into delicious sauces, jellies and jams to accompany a dessert.

The microwave oven can also help in many ways in the preparation of a dessert, offering you a quick, foolproof method of dissolving gelatine, melting chocolate, making caramel, sauces and small amounts of jam. Indeed, it is unlikely that you will ever return to conventional methods once you have used your microwave in this way.

The microwave oven offers the best method of reheating, which is a big advantage for the busy housewife. Many desserts can be prepared ahead of time and reheated without losing their fresh flavour and appearance.

A mouthwatering selection of cakes, flans, pastry, cheesecakes and confectionery are featured in the following recipes to serve for all occasions.

CONTENTS

FRUIT FONDUE

SERVES 4 / SET: MEDIUM

Ingredients

3¹/₂ cups/450 g/1 lb fresh raspberries or other berries
1¹/₄ cups/300 ml/10 fl oz double (heavy) cream, whipped
30 ml/2 tbsp sugar
60 ml/4 tbsp brandy
selection of fresh fruit

◆ Mash the raspberries in a glass bowl. Stir in the sugar and fold in the cream.

◆ Place in the oven and cook for 3–4 minutes until warm. Do not let the mixture boil.

◆ Stir in the brandy, fill 4 individual dishes with the sauce and serve with the fruit.

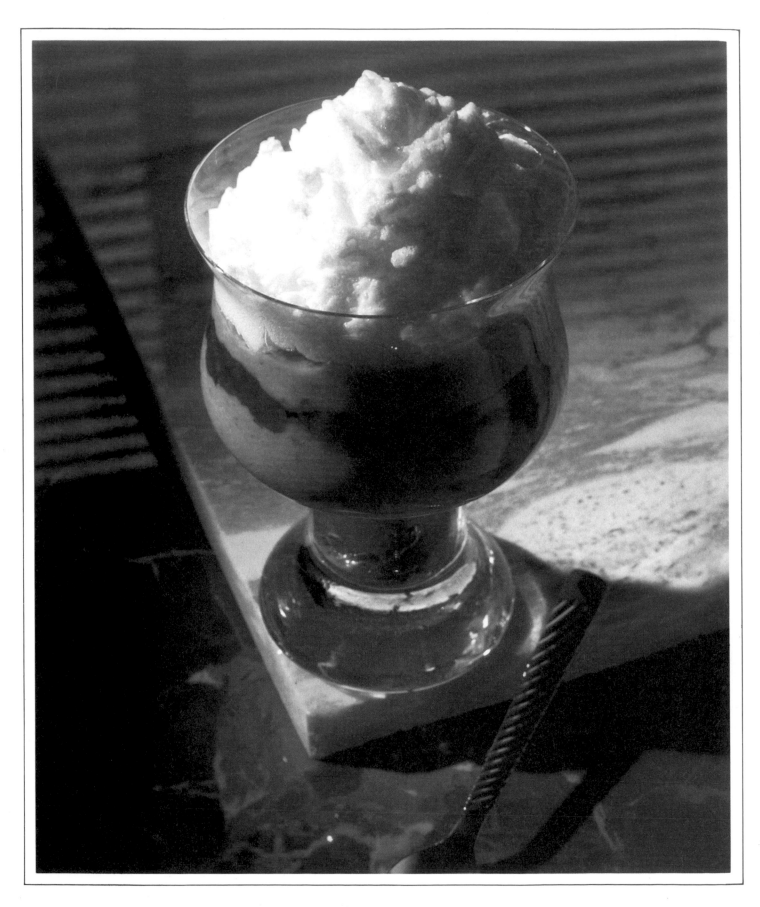

BLACKBERRY SURPRISE

SERVES 4 / SET: HIGH & LOW

Ingredients
2½ cups/575 ml/1 pt milk
4 tbsp/60 g/2 oz ground rice
30 ml/2 tbsp sugar
2 eggs, separated
3⅓ cups/800 g/1 lb 12 oz canned
blackberries, drained
2½ tbsp/30 g/1 oz caster (superfine) sugar

◆ Pour the milk into a bowl, add the rice and 30 ml/2 tbsp of sugar. Cook on high for 8 minutes.
◆ Beat the egg yolks and stir them in. Smooth out any lumps and then cook on low for 9 minutes until all the milk is absorbed. Fold in half the drained blackberries. Layer the rice and the remaining blackberries in 4 individual dishes.
◆ Whisk the egg whites until stiff, fold in the caster sugar and spoon them on top of the dessert. Cook on high for 2–3 minutes and serve.

LEMON MERINGUE PIE

SERVES 4–6 / SET: HIGH AND MEDIUM

Ingredients
1 Basic Shortcrust Pastry Case (see recipe)
LEMON CURD
grated rind and juice of 2 lemons
30 ml/2 tbsp cornflour (cornstarch)
½ cup/75 g/3 oz caster (superfine) sugar
¼ cup/50 g/2 oz butter
3 egg yolks
MERINGUE
3 egg whites
⅓ cup/50 g/2 oz caster (superfine) sugar

◆ Make the Basic Shortcrust Pastry Case as shown in recipe.
◆ For the lemon curd, add to the lemon juice enough water to make 300 ml/½ pt. Blend in the cornflour (cornstarch). Add the sugar, grated rind and butter. Cook for 3 minutes on high. Stir and return to the oven for 2 minutes.
◆ Remove from the oven, stir well and cool slightly. Add the egg yolks, mix well and cook on medium for 1–1½ minutes. Pour into the pastry case.
◆ For the meringue beat the egg whites until stiff, fold in the sugar and pile it on the lemon mix. Cook on high for 1 minute.
◆ Place under a conventional grill (broiler) to brown. Serve hot or cold.

MANGO MERINGUE DESSERT

SERVES 4 / SET: HIGH

Ingredients
1 can of sliced mangoes, chopped
2 egg whites
1 scant cup/100 g/4 oz sifted icing
(confectioners') sugar
3 tbsp/25 g/1 oz chopped nuts

◆ Divide the mangoes between 4 glasses or bowls.
◆ Beat the egg whites until stiff, beat in the sugar until the mixture becomes stiff again.
◆ Pile the meringue mixture on the mangoes to 2cm/¾ inch below the rim of the glass or bowl.
◆ Place the 4 dishes in a circle in the oven and cook for 2 minutes. Turn the glasses and cook for a further 1 minute or until the meringue puffs up.
◆ Sprinkle with the chopped nuts and serve immediately.

Blackberry Surprise

CARAMEL ORANGES

SERVES 4 / SET: HIGH

Ingredients

4 large oranges, seedless if available
scant ¹/₂ cup/75 g/3 oz sugar
1 cup/285 ml/¹/₂ pint water
1 pinch ground ginger
orange zest and ginger snaps to decorate

◆ Peel away the rind and pith from the oranges and cut the fruit into horizontal slices. Arrange them in 4 individual dishes either in slices or reshape the orange, and secure it with a cocktail stick through the centre.

◆ Place the sugar in a bowl with 45 ml/3 tbsp water and cook for approx 4½ minutes until the colour is pale caramel. Add the ground ginger and the remaining water, stir and heat for 2 minutes.

◆ Pour the mixture over the oranges and decorate with ginger snaps and orange zest, or Caramel Cotton (see recipe).

POACHED BRANDIED PEACHES

SERVES 4 / SET: HIGH

Ingredients

4 fresh peaches
60 ml/4 tbsp brandy
30 ml/2 tbsp orange juice
15 ml/1 tbsp caster (superfine) sugar
45 ml/3 tbsp mincemeat
brandy butter or whipped cream

◆ Skin the peaches by placing them in boiling water for a few seconds, then into cold. Peel away the skins.
◆ Cut the peaches in half and remove the stones (pits). Cut a thin slice from the round side of the peach so that it will stand, hollow side up, when served.
◆ Place the peaches hollow side down, in a large round shallow dish. The peaches in the centre must be moved to the outside halfway through the cooking time.
◆ Mix together the brandy, orange juice and sugar and pour the mixture over the peaches. Cover and poach for 3 minutes. Remove from the oven and turn peaches hollow side up. Add 1 tsp of mincemeat to each peach. Return to the oven and cook for 1½ minutes.
◆ Arrange the peaches on individual plates with some of the syrup and serve with brandy butter or whipped cream.

APRICOT LAYER DESSERT

*SERVES 4 / SET: HIGH
AND MEDIUM*

Ingredients

2 scant cups/225 g/8 oz self-raising (self-rising) flour

½ cup/100 g/4 oz cooking fat (shortening)

milk to mix

3 good cups/800 g/1 lb 12 oz unsweetened canned apricots, juice reserved

⅔ cup/150 g/5 oz sugar

APRICOT SAUCE

½ cup/150 g/5 oz apricot jam

⅔ cup/150 ml/5 fl oz apricot juice

juice of ½ lemon

15 ml/1 tbsp sherry

◆ Sift the flour and mix in the suet. Sprinkle the milk on gradually and mix until you have a soft but not sticky dough. Grease a 1.1 lt/2 pt pudding (flat-bottom) bowl.

◆ Reserve one apricot half for decoration and roughly chop the remainder.

◆ Roll out the dough to 5 mm/¼ in thickness. Cut it into 4 circles to fit your bowl. Place one pastry circle in the bottom of the bowl, top with ⅓ of the apricots, sprinkle with sugar to taste and continue to layer the pastry, fruit and sugar, ending with a circle of pastry. Seal the top layer and cover with cling film (plastic wrap). Cook on high for 8 minutes. Let it stand for 5 minutes.

◆ For the apricot sauce, place the jam with some of the apricot juice and lemon juice in a bowl and cook on medium for 3 minutes. Work the mixture through a sieve or purée it in a blender or food processor. Add sufficient apricot juice to bring the sauce to the correct consistency. Cook on high for 3 minutes and stir in the sherry.

◆ Turn out the apricot layer dessert. Top with the reserved apricot and serve with the hot sauce.

Apricot Layer Dessert

CHRISTMAS PUDDING

SERVES 10−12 / SET: HIGH AND MEDIUM

Ingredients

1 good cup/175 g/6 oz currants
³/₄ cup/100 g/4 oz sultanas (golden raisins)
2 cups/275 g/10 oz raisins
³/₄ cup/100 g/4 oz mixed dried fruit peel
60 ml/4 tbsp brandy or rum
15 ml/1 tbsp black treacle (black-strap molasses)
3 large eggs
²/₃ cup/150 ml/5 fl oz ale (beer)
5 ml/1 tsp gravy browning or brown colouring
³/₄ cup/100 g/4 oz moist brown sugar
³/₄ cup/175 g/6 oz shredded suet or leaf lard
³/₄ cup/75 g/3 oz fresh brown breadcrumbs
³/₄ cup/75 g/3 oz chopped mixed nuts
2.5 ml/¹/₂ tsp each ground allspice, ginger, nutmeg and cinnamon
grated rind of half a lemon
grated rind of half an orange
1¹/₄ cups/175 g/6 oz self-raising (self-rising) flour

◆ The mixture will fill two 1.1 l/2 pt basins (flat-bottom bowls).

◆ Place the dried peel, sultanas (golden raisins), raisins and currants in a large bowl and cover with boiling water. Cook on high for 4 minutes. Let it stand for 1 hour.

◆ Strain and replace the fruit in the bowl, then add brandy or rum. Let it stand overnight.

◆ Stir in all the other liquids and mix in the remaining ingredients. The flavour is improved if you can leave it to stand overnight.

◆ Line the two basins (bowls) with cling film (plastic wrap). Divide the mixture between the basins (bowls) and cover with cling film.

◆ Cook the Christmas pudding on medium for 7 minutes. Let it stand for 4 minutes. Cook for a further 6 minutes. Repeat with the second pudding.

APPLE AND COCONUT RINGS

SERVES 4 / SET: HIGH

Ingredients

6 dessert apples, approx 150 g/6 oz each

30 ml/2 tbsp lemon juice

60 ml/4 tbsp brown sugar

2 good cups/175 g/6 oz desiccated (shredded) coconut

30 ml/2 tbsp blackberry jam (jelly)

⅔ cup/150 ml/5 fl oz double (heavy) cream, whipped

glacé (candied) cherries, to decorate

◆ Peel the apples and cut them horizontally into 0.6-cm/¼-in thick slices. Cut out a circle removing the core, to make the apple rings. Sprinkle with lemon juice.

◆ Mix together the brown sugar and coconut.

◆ Place the jam (jelly) and 15 ml/1 tbsp of water in a bowl and heat for 2 minutes. Stir.

◆ Brush the hot jam (jelly) over the apple rings. Transfer them to a plate and cook for 2–3 minutes. Do not overcook the apples; they should stay firm.

◆ Sprinkle the apples with the coconut mixture, transfer them to 4 individual plates, decorate with glacé (candied) cherries. Serve with the whipped cream.

Apple and Coconut Rings

BAKED SHERRY APPLES

SERVES 4 / SET: MEDIUM

Ingredients

4 dessert apples

15 ml/1 tbsp lemon juice

¾ cup/100 g/4 oz sultanas (golden raisins)

30 ml/2 tbsp honey

60 ml/4 tbsp sweet sherry

⅔ cup/150 ml/5 fl oz double (heavy) cream, whipped

◆ Peel and slice the apples and arrange them attractively in 4 individual dishes. Sprinkle with lemon juice.

◆ Mix together the sultanas (golden raisins), honey and sherry and spoon them over the apples. Cover and cook for 3 minutes (1 dish), 4½ minutes (2 dishes) or 6–7 minutes (4 dishes) or until the apples are tender and the sultanas (golden raisins) plump. Cooking time will vary depending on the type of apple.

◆ Serve with whipped cream.

ORANGE ICE CREAM CRUNCH

SERVES 4—6 / SET: MEDIUM

Ingredients
1 Chocolate Crunch Flan Case (see recipe)

FILLING

½ lt/1 pt vanilla ice cream

30 ml/2 tbsp orange liqueur

5 mandarin orange segments – to decorate

◆ Make the Chocolate Crunch Flan Case as shown in recipe.

◆ Allow the ice cream to soften slightly. Place it in a bowl, add the liqueur and blend together. Spoon it into the flan case.

◆ Cover the case with foil and place in the freezer until solid.

◆ Just before serving decorate it with the mandarin segments.

FRUIT SOUFFLE

SERVES 4 / SET: HIGH

Ingredients

30 ml/2 tbsp orange liqueur
60 ml/4 tbsp water
30 ml/2 tbsp powdered gelatine
1¼ cups/300 ml/10 fl oz liquidized orange pulp (puréed in a blender or food processor)
good ½ cup/100 g/4 oz sugar
1¼ cups/300 ml/10 fl oz double (heavy) cream, whipped
6 egg whites, stiffly beaten
mandarin orange segments to decorate

◆ Place the liqueur and water in a bowl and sprinkle on the gelatine. Cook for 30 seconds or until gelatine has dissolved. Stir well.

◆ Stir in the orange purée and sugar, then cool. Stir occasionally. Fold in the cream and then the egg whites.

◆ Place a collar of greaseproof (wax) paper around the outside of a soufflé dish to extend 2.5 cm/1 inch above the rim. Secure it with tape.

◆ Spoon the mixture into the soufflé dish to reach the edge of the paper. Chill until set.

◆ Decorate with mandarin orange segments.

Fruit Soufflé

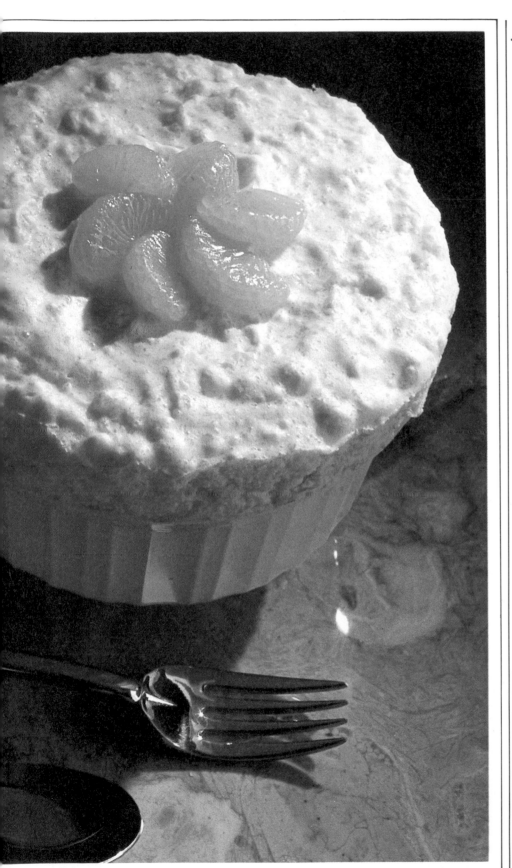

JAMAICAN DESSERT

S E R V E S   4 — 5   /   S E T :   H I G H

Ingredients

1 scant cup/100 g/4 oz self-raising (self-rising) flour
¹/₂ cup/100 g/4 oz semolina
¹/₃ cup/50 g/2 oz brown sugar
¹/₄ cup/50 g/2 oz cooking fat (shortening)
2.5 ml/¹/₂ tsp bicarbonate of soda (baking soda)
15 ml/1 tbsp milk
15 ml/1 tbsp golden (dark corn) syrup
15 ml/1 tbsp rum
S A U C E
60 ml/4 tbsp golden (dark corn) syrup
5 tbsp/75 ml/3 fl oz water
³/₄ cup/100 g/4 oz sultanas (golden raisins)
45 ml/3 tbsp rum
cream

◆ Mix together the flour, semolina, sugar and fat.

◆ Dissolve the bicarbonate of soda (baking soda) in the milk and stir in the syrup and rum. Add this to the dry ingredients. The mixture should be soft enough to drop off a spoon easily. Add more milk if necessary to obtain the correct consistency.

◆ Grease a 1 1/2 pt pudding basin (flat-bottom bowl) and pour in the mixture. Cover and cook for 6 minutes. Let it stand for 3 minutes.

◆ To make the sauce, place all the sauce ingredients in a bowl and cook, covered, for 4 minutes until the sultanas (golden raisins) plump up.

◆ Turn the pudding out onto a serving plate and serve with the sauce and cream.

BASIC CRUMB CASE

SERVES 4 / SET: HIGH

Ingredients

6 tbsp/75 g/3 oz butter

225 g/8 oz digestive biscuits (plain tea or sugar cookies or graham crackers), crushed

3 tbsp/40 g/1½ oz brown sugar

3 tbsp/25 g/1 oz chopped nuts

◆ Melt the butter in a 23-cm/9-in pie dish and cook for 40–45 seconds. Add the crumbs, sugar, and nuts and mix well. Press the mixture firmly against the base and sides of the dish, using a spoon.

◆ Stand the dish on an inverted plate and cook for 30 seconds, rotate the dish and cook for a further 45 seconds. Cool before filling.

◆ VARIATIONS:

1. Use ginger biscuits (cookies).
2. Add chopped raisins to the crumb mix.
3. Add mixed spice (sweet baking spice) to the mix.

JAMAICAN BANANAS

SERVES 4 / SET: MEDIUM

Ingredients

4 large firm bananas

15 ml/1 tbsp lemon juice

2 tbsp/25 g/1 oz butter

30 ml/2 tbsp orange juice

60 ml/4 tbsp rum

15 ml/1 tbsp clear honey

2.5 ml/½ tsp cinnamon

8 ginger biscuits (cookies), crushed into crumbs

⅔ cup/150 ml/5 fl oz double (heavy) cream, whipped

◆ Peel the bananas, cut them in half lengthways and then in half again. Sprinkle them with the lemon juice and dot with the butter.

◆ Stir all the remaining ingredients together and add them to the dish. Cover and cook for 5–6 minutes. Arrange the bananas in 4 individual dishes and sprinkle with the biscuit crumbs.

◆ Serve with whipped cream.

CHOCOLATE BLANCMANGE

SERVES 4 / SET: HIGH

Ingredients

60 ml/4 tbsp cornflour (cornstarch)

30 ml/2 tbsp cocoa powder

10 ml/2 tsp caster (superfine) sugar

2½ cups/575 ml/1 pt milk

5 ml/1 tsp vanilla essence (extract)

½ cup/100 g/4 oz butter

12 mini chocolate Swiss rolls or devil's food cake, sliced

400 g/14 oz canned pears, drained

⅔ cup/150 ml/5 fl oz double (heavy) cream, whipped

◆ In a large bowl blend together the cornflour (cornstarch), cocoa powder and sugar. Gradually stir in the milk with the vanilla essence (extract). Cook uncovered for 3 minutes, then stir and cook for a further 3 minutes or until thickened. Stir in the butter. Cool slightly.

◆ Press the sliced Swiss roll or devil's food cake against the sides of four individual glass dishes. Chop the drained pears and spoon them into the centre. Pour on the blancmange and cover with cling film (plastic wrap) to prevent a skin forming.

◆ Place the dish in the refrigerator to set. Remove the cling film and decorate with the whipped cream.

Chocolate Blancmange

CHERRY CHEESECAKE

SERVES 4 / SET: HIGH

Ingredients

1 Basic Crumb Case (see recipe)
2 scant cups/450 g/1 lb cream cheese
2 eggs
⅔ cup/100 g/4 oz caster (superfine) sugar
30 ml/2 tbsp lemon juice
1¼ cups/300 ml/½ pint sour cream
2.5 ml/½ tsp vanilla essence (extract)
1½ cups/400g/14 oz can of cherry pie filling
⅔ cup/150 ml/5 fl oz double (heavy) cream, whipped

◆ Make the Basic Crumb Case (see recipe).

◆ Beat the cheese until smooth. Whisk the eggs and ½ cup/75 g/3 oz of sugar together until thick. Add to the cheese with the lemon juice. Pour the mixture into the crumb case and cook for 6 minutes.

◆ Mix together the sour cream, remaining sugar and vanilla essence and pour it over the cheese mixture.

◆ Cook for a further 6 minutes. Gently spread the topping after 3 minutes to ensure that it cooks evenly.

◆ Cool the cake in the refrigerator. Remove it 1 hour before serving, top it with the cherry pie filling and decorate it with whipped cream.

DESSERTS

COCONUT ICE

MAKES 1LB / SET: HIGH

Ingredients

2¼ cups/450 g/1 lb sugar

⅔ cup/150 ml/¼ pt milk

1½ cups/125 g/4 oz desiccated (shredded) coconut

15 ml/1 tbsp double (heavy) cream

few drops red colouring

◆ Stir together the sugar and milk in a large bowl until the sugar has dissolved. Cook for 6–8 minutes. The mixture should reach the soft ball stage. To test, drop a little of the mixture in cold water, it should form a soft ball when rolled between the fingers. Check for this stage after 5 minutes and then every minute until ready. Stir occasionally.

◆ Stir in the coconut and cream, beat briskly until the mixture is thick and creamy. Pour half of it into a buttered 20 cm/8 in square tin.

◆ Colour the remaining half pink with the red colouring and spread it over the white layer. Cool until firm and set. Mark into squares and cut into pieces when cold.

DESSERTS

GINGERED PEARS

SERVES 4 / SET: HIGH

Ingredients

4 pears, peeled, halved and cored

⅔ cup/150 ml/5 fl oz lemonade

⅓ cup/85 ml/3 fl oz ginger wine or ginger ale

15 ml/1 tbsp brown sugar

whipped cream (optional)

◆ Place all the ingredients in a dish, cover and cook for 3–4 minutes or until tender.

◆ Serve with whipped cream if desired.

◆ Variation: Leave the pears whole with the stalk intact.

PEACH CRUMBLE

SERVES 4 / SET: HIGH

Ingredients

5 fresh peaches

15 ml/1 tbsp sweet sherry

30 ml/2 tbsp orange juice

30 ml/2 tbsp sugar

TOPPING

150 g/6 oz digestive biscuits, (plain tea or sugar cookies) crushed

2 tbsp/25 g/1 oz butter

3 tbsp/25 g/1 oz sultanas (golden raisins)

⅓ cup/50 g/2 oz chopped almonds

2 tbsp/25 g/1 oz brown sugar

◆ Skin the peaches by placing them in boiling water for a few seconds, then plunge them into cold. Peel away the skins, cut them in half and remove the stones (pits). Chop them roughly.

◆ Place the peaches, sherry, orange juice and sugar in a shallow dish. Cover and cook for 3 minutes. Keep to one side.

◆ Place the butter and sultanas (golden raisins) in a dish, cook for 1½ minutes, add the biscuit (cookie) crumbs, almonds and sugar. Mix well.

◆ Pile the topping on the peaches, cook for 2 minutes and then brown under a conventional grill (broiler). Serve with cream or custard.

VARIATION: Replace the peaches with any fruit of your choice.

Peach Crumble

GINGER UPSIDE DOWN PUDDING

SERVES 4 / SET: HIGH

Ingredients

6 tbsp/75 g/3 oz butter

3 tbsp/75 g/3 oz black treacle (black-strap molasses)

3½ tbsp/75 g/3 oz golden (dark corn) syrup

⅔ cup/150 ml/¼ pt milk

1 large egg

2 scant cups/225 g/8 oz self-raising (self-rising) flour, sifted

5 ml/1 tsp ground ginger

2 tbsp/30 g/1 oz brown sugar

400 g/14 oz canned pineapple rings, juice reserved

4 glacé (candied) cherries, halved

SAUCE

reserved pineapple juice

lemon juice

10 ml/2 tsp cornflour (cornstarch), mixed with a little water

syrup to taste

◆ Heat the butter, treacle (molasses) and syrup in a bowl for 3 minutes. Add the milk, stir and cool.

◆ Add the egg and beat well. Pour the mixture onto the sieved flour. Add the remaining ingredients, with the exception of the pineapple rings, and continue to beat.

◆ Line a 1.1 lt/2 pt bowl with the pineapple slices and glacé (candied) cherries, pour the gingerbread mixture into the bowl, cover and cook for 7–8 minutes or until it is firm to the touch. Let it stand for 5 minutes, then turn it out onto a dish.

◆ Decorate with extra pineapple slices and glacé (candied) cherries if desired.

◆ To make the sauce, add the lemon juice to the reserved pineapple juice to make ⅔ cup/150 ml/5 fl oz. Cook for 2 minutes, stir in the cornflour (cornstarch) and cook for 1 minute or until thickened and clear. Taste and add syrup if required. Stir well. Pour the sauce over the pudding and serve.

PINEAPPLE CUSTARD

SERVES 4 / SET: HIGH AND MEDIUM

Ingredients

60 ml/4 tbsp caster (superfine) sugar
4 eggs, beaten
10 ml/2 tsp cornflour (cornstarch)
2 scant cups/425 ml/15 fl oz milk
2 drops vanilla essence (extract)
ground cinnamon for dusting
400 g/15 oz canned pineapple rings, drained
1 kiwi fruit (Chinese gooseberry), sliced

◆ Beat the sugar and eggs together in a 1.7 l/3 pt bowl. Blend the cornflour (cornstarch) with 45 ml/3 tbsp of milk and stir it into the egg mixture.

◆ Place the remaining milk in a bowl and cook it on high for 2 minutes. The milk must not boil. Pour the egg mixture into the milk and add the vanilla essence (extract). Cook on medium for 4–5 minutes, whisking every minute. Do not allow the mixture to boil as the eggs will scramble.

◆ Arrange the pineapple rings in a dish and pour the custard over them. Do not overfill the dish. Place the dish on an inverted saucer and cook on medium for 10–12 minutes. Turn the dish 4 or 5 times during the cooking period.

◆ The filling should be almost firm in the centre. Let it stand for 10 minutes to cool and set.

◆ Serve the custard **cold**, dusted with cinnamon and **decorated** with the kiwi fruit (Chinese gooseberry).

Pineapple Custard

CHOCOLATE SEMOLINA PUDDING

*SERVES 2—3 / SET: HIGH
AND LOW*

Ingredients

2½ cups/575 ml/1 pint milk
¼ cup/40 g/1½ oz semolina
2½ tbsp/25 g/1 oz sugar
¼ cup/25 g/1 oz plain (semi-sweet) chocolate, grated

◆ Place all the ingredients in a 2 l/3½ pt glass bowl. Cook on high for 3 minutes. Stir well, and continue to cook on high for a further 3—4 minutes or until the milk boils. Stir.

◆ Cover and cook on high to return to the boil. Reduce to and cook for 10—15 minutes. Stir every 5 minutes. Let the pudding stand, covered, for 5 minutes. Stir before serving.

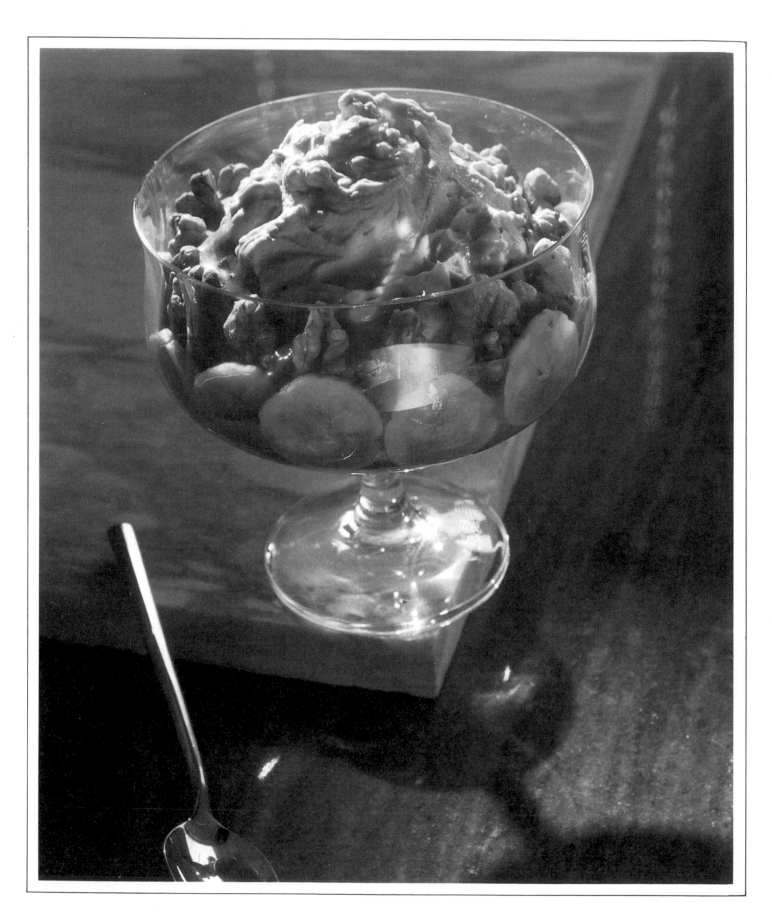

COFFEE AND WALNUT DESSERT

SERVES 4–6 / SET: MEDIUM

Ingredients

¾ cup/150 ml/5 fl oz strong black coffee
1 cup/175 g/6 oz marshmallows
4 bananas, 2 chopped, 2 sliced
⅔ cup/150 ml/5 fl oz double (heavy) cream, lightly whipped
1 cup 100 g/4 oz walnut halves, whole or chopped, to decorate

◆ Place the coffee and marshmallows in a bowl. Cook for 1–1½ minutes or until dissolved. Let it stand until cold. Stir the chopped bananas and the whipped cream into the coffee mixture.

◆ Spoon half the mixture into 4 glasses. Press the banana slices and walnut halves down the sides of the glasses. Add the remaining coffee mixture and serve.

GRAPEFRUIT AND CAMPARI SORBET (SHERBET)

SERVES 4 / SET: HIGH

Ingredients

⅓ cup/50 g/2 oz sugar
⅓ cup/85 ml/3 fl oz Campari
2 cups/480 ml/17 fl oz grapefruit juice
15 ml/1 tbsp gelatine
2 egg whites
mint leaves to decorate

◆ In a medium size bowl, stir the sugar into the Campari. Heat for 2 minutes. Stir halfway through the cooking time.

◆ Add the gelatine to a few tbsp of grapefruit juice. Stir into the Campari and sugar mixture and continue stirring until dissolved. Cool and add the remainder of the grapefruit juice.

◆ Place the mixture in the freezer until lightly frozen.

◆ Whisk the egg whites until stiff and beat them into the lightly frozen grapefruit mixture. Spoon into a container and freeze until required.

◆ To serve, let the sorbet (sherbet) stand at room temperature for approx 30 minutes. Decorate with mint leaves.

BLACKBERRY MALLOW

SERVES 4 / SET: HIGH

Ingredients

3 cups/450 g/1 lb blackberries
⅔ cup/100 g/4 oz marshmallows
good ½ cup/100 g/4 oz sugar

◆ Place the blackberries and sugar in a bowl, cover and cook for 2–3 minutes. Stir and mash lightly.

◆ Top with the marshmallows and cook for a further 1½–2 minutes until they have melted. Mix thoroughly into the blackberries.

◆ Let it cool a little, then pour into 4 sundae glasses. Cool for several hours or overnight. Serve with whipped cream.

Coffee and Walnut Dessert

CHOCOLATE RUM TRUFFLES

SERVES 12—16 / SET: HIGH

Ingredients

150 g/5 oz plain (semi-sweet) chocolate

1 tbsp/15 g/½ oz butter

5 ml/1 tsp rum

1 egg yolk

2 tbsp/25 g/1 oz ground almonds

chocolate vermicelli, chopped walnuts and cocoa powder to decorate

◆ Break the chocolate into pieces in a bowl and cook them for 2 minutes or until the chocolate has melted.

◆ Beat in the butter, egg yolk and rum. Mix in and add the ground almonds.

◆ Set the mixture aside in the refrigerator to thicken. Shape it into small balls and roll half in the chocolate vermicelli and the remainder in the chopped nuts and cocoa powder.

◆ Place in paper cases and serve as petit fours with coffee.

RASPBERRY PINWHEELS

SERVES 4 / SET: HIGH

Ingredients

225 g/8 oz Swiss roll (jelly roll), sliced
1 package raspberry jelly (jello)
3½ cups/450 g/1 lb fresh raspberries
water

◆ Place the raspberries in a bowl. Cover and cook for 2–3 minutes. Drain off any juice and add water to make 575 ml/1 pt.

◆ Place the jelly (jello) in 300 ml/½ pt of the liquid and cook for 4–5 minutes or until melted. Stir halfway through the cooking time. Allow to cool slightly, then add the remaining liquid stirring vigorously as you pour.

◆ Press the Swiss roll (jelly roll) slices onto the base and sides of a 850 ml/1½ pt pudding (flat bottom) bowl.

◆ Stir the raspberries into the liquid and pour the mixture into the lined bowl.

◆ Leave the bowl in the refrigerator to set, then turn out the pinwheels and serve with cream or custard.

TOFFEE (CANDY) APPLE TREAT

SERVES 4 / SET: HIGH

Ingredients

4 dessert apples
450 g/1 lb treacle toffee (taffy)
15 ml/1 tbsp water
⅓ cup/50 g/2 oz chopped nuts

◆ Peel and core the apples, cut into approx 8 pieces each, keep to one side.

◆ Place the treacle toffee (taffy) and water in a large bowl and cook for 3–4 minutes or until melted. Stir after 2 minutes.

◆ Spear the apple pieces on wooden cocktail sticks, dip and coat them in the toffee (taffy). Sprinkle them with the chopped nuts, stand them on greaseproof (waxed) paper and refrigerate for 1 hour.

Toffee Apple Treat

SNOWDEN PUDDING

SERVES 4 / SET: HIGH

Ingredients

25 g/1 oz glacé (candied) cherries, halved
¾ cup/100 g/4 oz raisins
½ cup/100 g/4 oz cooking fat (shortening)
1 cup/100 g/4 oz fresh breadcrumbs
2 tbsp/25 g/1 oz ground rice
finely grated rind of 1 lemon
90 ml/6 tbsp lemon marmalade
2 eggs, beaten
30 ml/2 tbsp milk

SAUCE

60 ml/4 tbsp lemon marmalade
⅔ cup/150 ml/¼ pt hot water
5 ml/1 tsp cornflour (cornstarch)
30 ml/2 tbsp cold water

◆ Butter a 1.1 l/2 pt bowl, press half the raisins and cherries, cut side down, against the bottom and sides of the bowl.

◆ Place the remaining raisins, cooking fat (shortening), breadcrumbs, ground rice, lemon rind and marmalade in a mixing bowl. Mix well. Add the eggs and sufficient milk to make a soft dropping consistency.

◆ Spoon the mixture into the bowl and press it down firmly. Cover and cook for 9 minutes. Let it stand for 5 minutes.

◆ For the sauce, place the marmalade and hot water in a bowl and cook for 3 minutes. Mix the cornflour (cornstarch) with the cold water, blend into the marmalade mixture and cook for 2 minutes.

◆ Turn out the pudding and serve with the sauce.

Snowden Pudding

SUMMER FRUITS DESSERT

S E R V E S   4 – 6 / S E T :   H I G H

Ingredients

1¼ cups/225 g/8 oz peaches, peeled, stoned (pitted) and chopped
1½ cups/225 g/8 oz apricots, peeled, stoned (pitted) and chopped
scant cup/100 g/4 oz rhubarb, sliced
45 ml/3 tbsp apricot brandy
5 ml/1 tsp ground ginger
15 ml/1 tbsp arrowroot
good ½ cup/100 g/4 oz sugar
30 ml/2 tbsp water
ice cream and brandy snaps (or ginger cookies)

◆ Place the fruit in a deep bowl together with the apricot brandy and ground ginger. Cover and cook for 6 minutes or until mushy. Rub through a sieve or purée in a blender or food processor.

◆ Measure the puréed fruit and allow 15 ml/1 tbsp arrowroot per 2½ cups/575 ml/1 pt of purée. Mix the arrowroot to a smooth paste with 30ml/2 tbsp of water. Place to one side.

◆ Add the sugar to the fruit. The dish should be deep enough so that the mixture fills it only one third. Cover and cook for 7–8 minutes or until boiling, stirring every 2 minutes. The sugar should be completely dissolved. Stir in the arrowroot and return it to the boil for 2–3 minutes until clear.

◆ Allow the fruit to cool and pour it into sundae glasses. Chill and serve with the ice cream and brandy snaps.

QUICK LEMON PUFFS

SERVES 6—8 / SET: HIGH

Ingredients
370 g/13 oz package of frozen puff pastry
120 ml/8 tbsp Lemon Curd (see Lemon Meringue Pie)
⅔ cup/150 ml/5 fl oz whipping cream
icing (confectioners') sugar for dusting

◆ Defrost the pastry at room temperature.

◆ Sprinkle a board with icing (confectioners') sugar and roll out the pastry as thinly as possible. Cut into 10-cm/4-in squares.

◆ Preheat a microwave griddle for 4 minutes. Place three squares of pastry at a time on the griddle and cook for approx 5–7 minutes, turning once. The pastry is ready when it no longer deflates when the oven door is opened.

◆ Slice horizontally through the puffs and spread the bottom layer with lemon curd and whipped cream. Replace the top layer of pastry and dust with icing sugar.

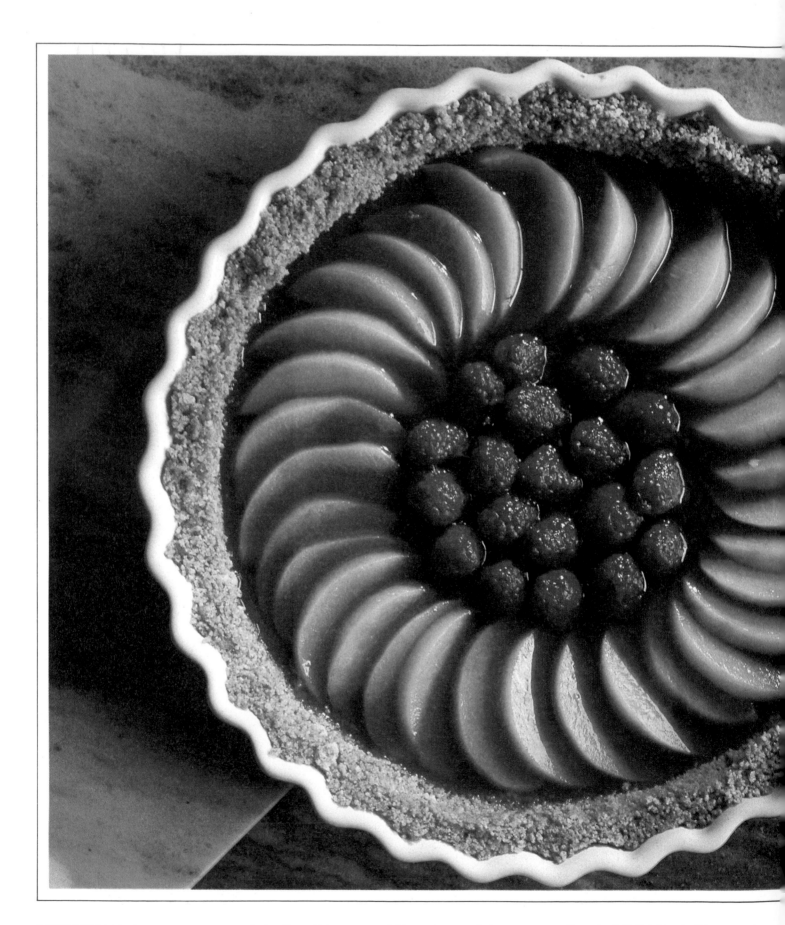

RASPBERRY AND PEACH FLAN

SERVES 4—6 / SET: HIGH

Ingredients
1 Basic Crumb Case (see recipe)
3 good cups/875g/1 lb 12 oz fresh or canned peach slices, drained
2½ good cups/325g/12 oz fresh or thawed frozen raspberries
⅓ cup/50 g/2 oz sugar
1½ tbsp/15 g/½ oz cornflour (cornstarch)
⅔ cup/150 ml/5 fl oz double (heavy) cream, whipped

◆ Make the Basic Crumb Case as shown in the recipe.
◆ If using fresh peaches, peel and slice them. Place them in a dish, cover and cook for 3 minutes.
◆ Reserve ⅓ cup/100 g/4 oz well-shaped raspberries for decoration and place the remainder and their juice in a small basin (bowl) with the sugar and cornflour (cornstarch). Stir, cover and cook for 3—4 minutes or until thickened and clear. Stir once every minute during the cooking period.
◆ Spoon the pulp over the base of the flan case, arrange the peaches on top with the reserved raspberries in the centre. Spoon the remaining juice over the top, cool to set.
◆ Serve with the whipped cream.

Raspberry and Peach Flan

BASIC VICTORIA SANDWICH CAKE

SERVES 4—6 / SET: HIGH

Ingredients
¾ cup/175 g/6 oz butter
¾ cup/175 g/6 oz caster (superfine) sugar
3 eggs, beaten
1¼ cups/175 g/6 oz self-raising (self-rising) flour
30 ml/2 tbsp milk
2.5 ml/½ tsp baking powder
⅔ cup/150 ml/5 fl oz double (heavy) cream, whipped
30 ml/2 tbsp jam (jelly)

◆ Grease a round 19-cm/7½-in soufflé dish and line the base with greased greaseproof (baking) paper.
◆ Cream the butter until soft, add the sugar and beat well until light and fluffy. Add the eggs gradually, beating all the time. Sift the flour and baking powder and fold into the mixture. Add the milk and fold in carefully. Add more milk if necessary to obtain a soft dropping consistency.
◆ Place the mixture in the prepared dish and cook for 4—5 minutes. Let it stand for 5 minutes.
◆ Turn it out onto a cooling rack. When cold, cut it in half horizontally and sandwich it back together with whipped cream and jam of your choice.
◆ Omit the whipped cream and jam if using the Basic Sandwich for another recipe in this book.

CHOCOLATE GATEAU

SERVES 4–6 / SET: MEDIUM

Ingredients

1 Basic Victoria Sandwich (see recipe) replacing 4 tbsp/25 g/1 oz self-raising (self-rising) flour with ⅓ cup/25 g/1 oz cocoa powder
¾ cup/175 g/6 oz butter, softened
2 cups/275 g/10 oz icing (confectioners') sugar
15 ml/1 tbsp rum
50 g/2 oz plain (semi-sweet) chocolate
400 g/14 oz canned sliced peaches, drained
⅔ cup/150 ml/5 fl oz double (heavy) cream, whipped
good ½ cup/75 g/3 oz chocolate, grated

◆ Make the Basic Victoria Sandwich Cake (see recipe), replacing some of the self-raising flour with the cocoa or chocolate powder.

◆ Place the 50 g/2 oz chocolate in a bowl. Cook for 3 minutes and cool.

◆ Cream the butter until soft, add the sugar and rum and beat well. Stir in the melted chocolate until well blended.

◆ Cut the chocolate sponge (cake) in half horizontally. Spread the bottom layer with the whipped cream. Roughly chop half the drained peaches and put them on top of the cream. Replace the top layer and coat the whole cake with the chocolate butter cream.

◆ Press the grated chocolate onto the sides of the cake and serve.

STRAWBERRY DELIGHT

SERVES 4–6 / SET: LOW AND HIGH

Ingredients

4½ cups/675 g/1½ lb fresh strawberries, hulled

1¼ cup/200 g/7 oz caster (superfine) sugar

15 ml/1 tbsp lemon juice

2.5 ml/½ tsp butter

1 large meringue nest or 4–6 individual nests

◆ Mix 1½ cups/225 g/8 oz strawberries, the sugar and lemon juice in a large 2.75 l/5 pt mixing bowl.

◆ Three quarters cover the bowl with cling film (plastic wrap). Cook on low for 10–12 minutes, stirring every 3 minutes. Mash and stir until the sugar is dissolved.

◆ Cook uncovered on high for 5 minutes, stir in the butter, then add the remaining strawberries and stir gently.

◆ Cool slightly and pile the strawberry mixture into the meringue nest(s) and serve.

◆ Alternatively place a thin layer of the cooled 'jam' mixture in the meringue nests, slice selected strawberries and arrange them as shown. Brush with a little of the 'jam' to glaze.

Strawberry Delight

CHOCOLATE CRUNCH FLAN CASE

SERVES 4—6 / SET: MEDIUM

Ingredients

225 g/8 oz plain (semi-sweet) chocolate

1/4 cup/50 g/2 oz butter

2 cups/75 g/3 oz Rice Krispies

◆ Place the butter and chocolate in a large bowl. Cook for 3 minutes.

◆ Stir in the Rice Krispies. Place the mixture in a 20-cm/8-inch flan dish and press the mixture into the base and up the sides. Put it in the freezer until firm.

CHOCOLATE CHEESECAKE CRUNCH

SERVES 4 — 6 / SET: HIGH

Ingredients

1 Chocolate Crunch Flan Case (see recipe)
FILLING
2 scant cups/450 g/1 lb cream cheese
3 eggs, separated
good ½ cup/100 g/4 oz sugar
⅔ cup/150 ml/¼ pt sour cream
1 tsp/15 g/½ oz gelatine
60 ml/4 tbsp warm water
1¼ cups/175 g/6 oz plain (semi-sweet) chocolate, grated

◆ Make the Chocolate Crunch Flan Case (see recipe).

◆ Place the cheese and egg yolks in a bowl, add half the sugar and beat vigorously. Stir in the sour cream.

◆ Place the water and gelatine in a cup, cook for 30 seconds, stir until dissolved and then cool.

◆ Whisk the egg whites until stiff. Whisk in the remaining sugar.

◆ Stir the gelatine into the cheese mixture. Fold in the egg whites and chopped chocolate.

◆ Pour the mixture into the prepared case, swirl the top with a fork and chill it until set.

◆ Decorate with grated chocolate.

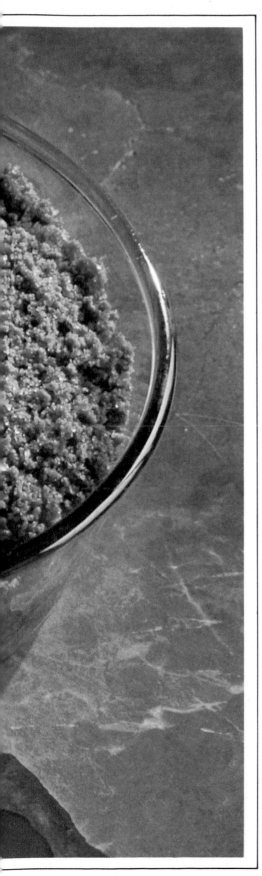

APPLE LAYER DESSERT

SERVES 4 / SET: HIGH

Ingredients

900 g/2 lb dessert apples
30 ml/2 tbsp lemon juice
75 g/3 oz ginger biscuits (cookies)
⅓ cup/50 g/2 oz moist brown sugar
⅓ cup/50 g/2 oz sultanas (golden raisins)
5 ml/1 tsp ground cinnamon
custard or whipped cream

◆ Peel, core and thinly slice the apples. Sprinkle them with lemon juice.

◆ Crush the ginger biscuits (cookies) in a polythene bag with a rolling pin. Add the crumbs to the sugar, sultanas (golden raisins) and ground cinnamon. Mix well.

◆ In a large soufflé dish, alternate layers of apple and biscuit mixture, ending with a biscuit layer on top.

◆ Cook uncovered for 10 minutes. Serve hot or cold with custard or whipped cream.

Apple Layer Dessert

BASIC SHORTCRUST PASTRY CASE

SERVES 6 / SET: HIGH

Ingredients

¼ cup/50 g/2 oz butter
2 tbsp/25 g/1 oz lard
1¼ cups/175 g/6 oz plain (all-purpose) flour
2.5 ml/½ tsp salt
45 ml/3 tbsp cold milk

◆ Rub the butter and lard into the flour and salt in a bowl until the mixture resembles fine breadcrumbs. Sprinkle the milk over it, a little at a time, as you may not need it all. Stir lightly until the mixture forms a soft ball.

◆ Roll out the pastry on a lightly floured surface to 3 mm/⅛ in thickness and 5 cm/2 in larger than the top of your dish.

◆ Transfer the pastry to a 20-cm/8-in flan dish. Pat out any air pockets. Do not stretch the pastry as it will shrink during the cooking. Stand the pastry in a cool place for 15 minutes.

◆ Trim the pastry overhang and thoroughly prick the sides and base with a fork to ensure even cooking. Cover the sides with foil as they will cook faster than the base. Cover the base with a double thickness of absorbent kitchen paper (paper towels). Place the flan dish on an inverted plate in the oven and cook for 3–4 minutes.

◆ Remove the foil and paper and cook for a further 2–3 minutes, then let it stand for 5 minutes.

◆ Fill the case when it is cool and reheat it if necessary. Do not cook the case with a filling in it as it will become soggy.

LEMON SPONGE SANDWICH

SERVES 5 / SET: MEDIUM

Ingredients

1 Basic Victoria Sandwich (see recipe),
replacing milk with 30 ml/2 tbsp lemon
juice

LEMON CURD

$1^1/_3$ cups/225 g/8 oz caster (superfine)
sugar

2 eggs, beaten

grated rind and juice of 1 large lemon

$^1/_4$ cup/50 g/2 oz butter

$1^1/_4$ cups/300 ml/10 fl oz double (heavy)
cream, whipped

$^3/_4$ cup/100 g/4 oz mixed chopped nuts and
lemon-shaped sweets (candies) to decorate

◆ Make the Basic Victoria Sandwich
as shown in the recipe, replacing the
milk with the lemon juice.

◆ To make the lemon curd, put the
sugar, butter, juice and rind of the
lemon in a bowl and cook for 10–12
minutes. The sugar should have
dissolved and the mixture come to
boiling point. Add the eggs, return it
to the oven and cook for 6–8 minutes,
until the mixture thickens. Stir
frequently. This will make 450 g/1 lb
of lemon curd. Bottle it in the usual
way.

◆ Cut the Victoria Sandwich in half
horizontally. Coat the base of the cake
thickly with lemon curd. Pile on
whipped cream to the desired
thickness.

◆ Coat the sides and top of the
sponge with a layer of whipped cream.
Press the chopped nuts onto the sides.

◆ Place the remaining whipped
cream into an icing bag and decorate
the cake as desired.

CHOCOLATE SPONGE DESSERT

SERVES 4 / SET: HIGH

Ingredients

½ cup/100 g/4 oz butter

¾ cup/100 g/4 oz caster (superfine) sugar

2 large eggs

¾ cup/75 g/3 oz self-raising (self-rising) flour

⅓ cup/25 g/1 oz cocoa powder

60 ml/4 tbsp milk

SAUCE

100 g/4 oz plain (semi-sweet) chocolate, broken into pieces

30 ml/2 tbsp golden (dark corn) syrup

1 small can evaporated milk

◆ Cream together the butter and sugar until soft and light. Beat in the eggs. Sift the flour and fold it into the creamed mixture.

◆ Grease a 1.1 l/2 pt basin (flat-bottomed bowl). Put in the sponge mixture. Cover and cook for 5–6 minutes. Allow it to stand for 5 minutes.

◆ Place all the sauce ingredients in a bowl and cook for 4–5 minutes, stirring after 3 minutes. The chocolate should be melted and smooth.

◆ Turn the sponge out onto a plate and serve with the sauce.

COFFEE AND BANANA CREAM

SERVES 6 / SET: HIGH

Ingredients

15 ml/1 tbsp plain (all-purpose) flour

⅓ cup/50 g/2 oz brown sugar

30 ml/2 tbsp cornflour (cornstarch)

2¼ cups/500 ml/18 fl oz milk

3–4 egg yolks

2 tbsp/25 g/1 oz butter

10 ml/2 tsp instant coffee

3 tbsp/25 g/1 oz chopped walnuts

2 chopped bananas

banana slices and walnuts to serve

◆ Blend together the flour, sugar, cornflour and milk in a 1.7 l/3 pt bowl. Whisk well and cook for 7–7½ minutes until thick. Whisk vigorously every 2 minutes.

◆ Lightly beat the egg yolks and add 90 ml/6 tbsp of the custard mixture. Blend it well and add it to the remaining custard. Cook it for 1–2 minutes until thick.

◆ Beat in the butter and coffee. Stir in the walnuts and chopped bananas. Cover with cling film (plastic wrap) and cool.

◆ Serve in individual dishes topped with banana slices and chopped walnuts.

CHOCOLATE MOUSSE

SERVES 6 / SET: HIGH

Ingredients

225 g/8 oz plain (semi-sweet) chocolate, in pieces

45 ml/3 tbsp water

1 tbsp/15 g/½ oz butter

4 large eggs, separated

15 ml/1 tbsp brandy

TOPPING

⅔ cup/150 ml/5 fl oz double (heavy) cream

3 tbsp/25 g/1 oz icing (confectioners') sugar

3 tbsp/15 g/½ oz cocoa powder

5 ml/1 tsp instant coffee

1 drop vanilla essence

chocolate (candy) sticks to decorate

◆ Place the chocolate and water in a 2 l/3½ pt (microwave) bowl. Cook for 1½ minutes or until the chocolate has melted. Beat vigorously until smooth. Return to the oven and cook for 30 seconds. Beat again.

◆ Beat in the butter and the egg yolks, one by one. Stir in the brandy.

◆ Whip the egg whites into stiff peaks, stir one tbsp into the chocolate mixture and fold in the remainder. Pour into 6 individual dishes and set aside in the refrigerator for 3–4 hours.

◆ Just before serving, whisk together all the topping ingredients until thick. Top the mousse with the mixture.

◆ Decorate with the chocolate (candy) sticks and serve.

Chocolate Mousse

CARAMEL COTTON

SET: HIGH

Ingredients

½ cup/75 g/3 oz caster (superfine) sugar
45 ml/3 tbsp water

◆ Place the sugar and water in a deep bowl and, cook for 4–5 minutes or until golden.

◆ Remove from the oven using gloves as the dish will be very hot.

◆ Let it cool until the liquid thickens slightly.

◆ Scoop a small amount of caramel into a spoon and pour it slowly back into the bowl. The mixture will stiffen and you will be able to draw it into threads to decorate various desserts. See the photograph of Caramel Oranges.

◆ Decorate just before serving as the sugar dissolves if left standing too long.

Orange Rice Pudding

ORANGE RICE PUDDING

SERVES 2 / SET: HIGH AND MEDIUM

Ingredients

¼ *cup/50 g/2 oz pudding (Italian) rice*
⅓ *cup/50 g/2 oz sugar*
2½ *cups/575 ml/1 pt milk*
5 *ml/1 tsp grated orange rind*
⅓ *cup/50 g/2 oz sultanas (golden raisins)*

◆ Place all the ingredients in a 2¼ l/ 4 pt glass bowl. Cook on high for 7–8 minutes or until the mixture is just boiling. Stir thoroughly.

◆ Reduce to medium and cook for 20–25 minutes. Stir several times during the cooking period to prevent lumps forming.

◆ Remove the pudding from the oven and allow it to stand and thicken for 7–8 minutes before serving.

FUDGE CAKE

S E R V E S   6 — 8   /   S E T :   M E D I U M

Ingredients

⅔ cup/150 g/5 oz butter

30 ml/2 tbsp golden (dark corn) syrup

150 g/5 oz plain (semi-sweet) chocolate, cut into pieces

175 g/6 oz digestive biscuits (plain tea or sugar cookies or graham crackers), crushed

3 tbsp/25 g/1 oz sultanas (golden raisins)

25 g/2 tbsp chopped glacé (candied) cherries

⅓ cup/50 g/2 oz chopped nuts

T O P P I N G

50 g/2 oz chocolate in small pieces

⅓ cup/75 g/3 oz butter

15 ml/1 tbsp rum

1 good cup/150 g/5 oz icing (confectioners') sugar

glacé (candied) cherries and chopped nuts to decorate

◆ Place the butter, syrup and chocolate in a bowl and cook for 3 minutes. Stir in the biscuit (cookie) crumbs, sultanas (golden raisins), glacé (candied) cherries and chopped nuts. Mix well.

◆ Spoon this into a ½ kg/1 lb springform loaf tin (pan). Chill in the refrigerator for approx 30 minutes until set. Remove the sides of the tin and transfer the cake to a plate.

◆ For the topping, cream together the butter and rum. Add the icing (confectioners') sugar little by little until the mixture is a thick spreading consistency.

◆ Pipe the top of the cake with the topping and decorate it with chopped nuts and glacé (candied) cherries.

◆ Serve it sliced, with whipped cream.

FONDANT FANCIES

MAKES 1LB / SET: HIGH

Ingredients

²/₃ cup/150 ml/¼ pt milk

2¼ cups/450 g/1 lb sugar

15 ml/1 tbsp double (heavy) cream

2.5 ml/½ tsp cocoa powder

◆ Stir the milk and sugar together in a large bowl until the sugar is dissolved. Cook for 6–8 minutes. The mixture should reach the soft ball stage. To test, drop a little of the mixture in cold water, it should form a soft ball when rolled between the fingers. Check for this stage after 5 minutes and then every minute until ready. Stir occasionally.

◆ Stir in the cream and beat until the mixture is thick and creamy. Spoon half the mixture into small paper moulds until they are half full.

◆ Beat the cocoa powder into the other half of the mixture and spoon it into the moulds.

PINEAPPLE CUPS

SERVES 4 / SET: HIGH

Ingredients

2 medium pineapples, trimmed and halved

4 kiwi fruit (Chinese gooseberries), sliced

3 peaches, peeled and sliced

¾ cup/100 g/4 oz black grapes, halved, deseeded

30 ml/2 tbsp orange liqueur

30 ml/2 tbsp clear honey

30 ml/2 tbsp orange juice

◆ Scoop the flesh from the pineapples, leaving the skin intact. Dice the flesh and place in a dish. Add the peaches, kiwi fruit (Chinese gooseberries) and grapes.

◆ Heat the orange liqueur, honey and orange juice for 2 minutes, stir well and pour it over the mixed fruit. Leave it to marinate until ready to serve.

◆ Cover the fruit mixture and cook it for 4 minutes. Pile it into the pineapple cups with a little of the syrup and serve.

Pineapple Cups

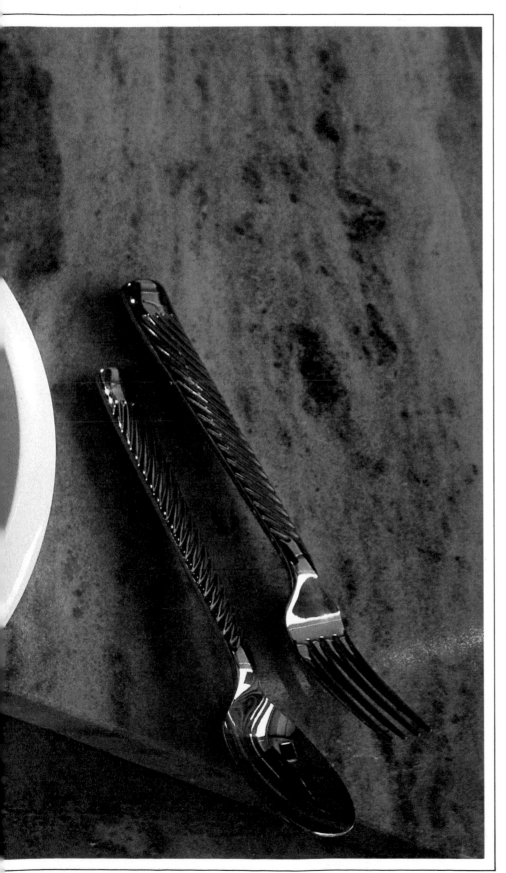

PINEAPPLE DESSERT

SERVES 4 / SET: HIGH

Ingredients

100 g/4 oz pineapple rings, canned or fresh, chopped

1 scant cup/100 g/4 oz self-raising (self-rising) flour

pinch of baking powder (baking soda)

⅓ cup/50 g/2 oz sugar

¼ cup/50 g/2 oz cooking fat (shortening)

½ cup/75 g/3 oz sultanas (golden raisins)

1 egg

30 ml/2 tbsp milk

pineapple rings and glacé (candied) cherries to decorate

S A U C E

125 g/5 oz pineapple jam (jelly)

⅔ cup/150 ml/5 fl oz pineapple juice

45 ml/3 tbsp lemon juice

◆ Mix all the ingredients together in a bowl.

◆ Line an 825 ml–1 l/1½–1¾ pt basin with cling film (plastic wrap). Place the mixture in the basin and cover with cling film.

◆ Cook for 7 minutes on high. Let it stand for 3 minutes, then turn out onto a serving dish and decorate with the pineapple rings and cherries.

◆ For the sauce, place the jam with some of the pineapple and lemon juice in a bowl and cook for 1½–2 minutes. Work it through a sieve or pureé it in a blender or food processor. Add sufficient pineapple juice to bring the sauce to the correct consistency. Cook for 2 minutes, pour over the pudding and serve.

FRESH VEGETABLES COOKING GUIDE

vegetables	quantity	minutes on full
globe artichokes	4	10 – 20
asparagus spears	1½ cups/225 g/8 oz	6 – 7
aubergines (eggplant), diced	2 cups/450 g/1 lb	5 – 6
beans, broad (fava, lima), French (green) or runner	2½ cups/450 g/1 lb	8 – 10
beetroot (beets), sliced	4 cups/450 g/1 lb	7 – 8
broccoli florets	6 cups/450 g/1 lb	4 – 5
Brussels sprouts	6 cups/450 g/1 lb	8 – 10
cabbage, shredded	6 cups/450 g/1 lb	7 – 10
carrots, sliced	2 cups/225 g/8 oz	7 – 10
cauliflower florets	6 cups/450 g/1 lb	10 – 11
celery	1 head	10 – 13
corn on the cob	1	3 – 5
courgettes (zucchini), sliced	4	7 – 10
Kohlraki	4 cups/450 g/1 lb	7 – 8
leeks, sliced	4 cups/450 g/1 lb	7 – 10
marrow (squash), sliced	4 cups/450 g/1 lb	8 – 10
mushrooms, whole	2½ cups/225 g/8 oz	5 – 6
okra	4 cups/450 g/1 lb	8 – 10
onions, sliced	2 cups/225 g/8 oz	5 – 7
parsnips, sliced	2 cups/225 g/8 oz	8 – 10
peas	4 cups/450 g/1 lb	7
potatoes, new	6 cups/450 g/1 lb	8 – 10
potatoes, jacket (baked)	2 large	8
potatoes, boiled	4 cups/450 g/1 lb	6 – 7
spinach	2 cups/450 g/1 lb	5
greens, chopped	6 cups/450 g/1 lb	7 – 9
swedes (rutabaga), sliced	3 cups/450 g/1 lb	6 – 7
tomatoes, sliced	1½ cups/450 g/1 lb	2 – 3
turnips, sliced	1½ cups/225 g/8 oz	6 – 7

FROZEN VEGETABLES COOKING GUIDE

vegetables	quantity	minutes on full
asparagus spears	1½ cups/225 g/8 oz	6 – 7
beans, broad (fava), French (green) or runner	1½ cups/225 g/8 oz	7
broccoli spears	4 cups/225 g/8 oz	6 – 8
cabbage, chopped	3 cups/225 g/8 oz	6 – 7
carrots, sliced	2 cups/225 g/8 oz	6 – 7
cauliflower florets	4 cups/225 g/8 oz	4 – 6
sweetcorn (corn)	2 cups/225 g/8 oz	4 – 6
corn on the cob	1	4 – 5
courgettes (zucchini), sliced	2 cups/225 g/8 oz	4
peas	2 cups/225 g/8 oz	4
spinach, chopped	3 cups/225 g/8 oz	5
swedes (rutabaga), cubed	2 cups/225 g/8 oz	7
turnips, sliced	1½ cups/225 g/8 oz	8
vegetables, mixed	2 cups/225 g/8 oz	4 – 6

FRESH MEAT COOKING GUIDE

meat	minutes on full per 450 g/1 lb	standing minutes
bacon (ham) roast	12 – 14	10
bacon, rashers (slices) 4	4½	—
beef, boned roasts, rare	5 – 6	15 – 20
beef, boneless roast, medium	7 – 8	15 – 20
beef, boneless roast, well-done	8 – 9	15 – 20
beef, roasts with bone, rare	5 – 6	15 – 20
beef, roasts with bone, medium	6 – 7	15 – 20
beef, roasts with bone, well-done	8 – 9	15 – 20
beef, ground, 4 patties	10	5
chicken, whole roast	8 – 10	10 – 15
chicken, portions	6 – 8	10
lamb, boned roast	7 – 8	20
lamb, boned and rolled roast	9	20
lamb, roast with bone	6 – 7	20
lamb, crown roast	9 – 10	20
lamb chops	2	10
liver, ox (beef)	8	5
liver, lamb, calves'	7	5
pork, boned rolled roast	8 – 10	15
pork, roast with bone	8 – 9	15
poussin (Cornish rock hen), pigeon, pheasant, quail	5 – 7	5
sausages (links), 4	4	—
portions	15	10
turkey, whole roast	11	10 – 15

FROZEN MEAT DEFROSTING GUIDE

meat	minutes on low per 450 g/1 lb	standing minutes
beef, boned roasts	8 – 10	30
beef, roasts on bone	8 – 10	30
beef, minced (ground)	8 – 10	2
beef steak, cubed	6 – 8	5
hamburgers, two	2	2
hamburgers, four	4	2
chicken, whole	6 – 8	30
chicken portions	5	30
duck and duckling	5 – 7	30
kidney	6 – 9	5
lamb, boned roasts	5 – 6	30 – 45
lamb, with bone	8 – 10	30 – 45
lamb chops	8 – 10	15
liver	8 – 10	5
pork, boned roasts	7 – 8	30
pork roast with bone	7 – 8	45
poussin (Cornish rock hen), grouse, pigeon, pheasant	5 – 7	10
sausages (links)	5 – 6	5
turkey, whole	10 – 12	60
veal, boned rolled roast	5 – 6	30
veal, with bone	8 – 10	45
veal chops	8 – 10	30
veal, minced (ground)	8 – 10	5

FISH
Defrost and Cooking Guide

fish	weight	defrost minutes	standing minutes	cooking in minutes on full
bass	225 g/8 oz	5–6	15	5–6
bonito tuna steaks,	225 g/8 oz	10	15	—
bream, sea-bream	225 g/8 oz	—	15	10–12
cod fillets	225 g/8 oz	4–5	5	4–6
cod steaks	225 g/8 oz	5	5	6
crab claws	100 g/4 oz	5	5	2–3
crab, dressed (crab cakes)	100 g/4 oz	2	10	—
haddock fillets	100 g/4 oz	4–5	5	5–7
haddock steaks	100 g/4 oz	4–5	5	4–7
halibut steaks	100 g/4 oz	4–5	5	4–5
hake steaks	100 g/4 oz	4–5	5	4–6
kipper (kippered herrings)	100 g/4 oz	—	—	1–2
kipper (kippered herrings) fillets (boil-in-the-bag)	200 g/7 oz	3	5	3
mackerel	225 g/8 oz	6–8	8–10	4–5
mahi-mahi	225 g/8 oz	6–8	—	4–6
red and grey mullet	225 g/8 oz	6–8	8–10	4–6
mussels	225 g/8 oz	5	5	—
plaice (flounder) fillets	225 g/8 oz	4–5	5	4
prawns (small shrimp), cooked	225 g/8 oz	5	5	—
red salmon steaks	225 g/8 oz	5	5	4–5
scrod fillets	225 g/8 oz	4–5	30	4–5
scampi (king prawns), raw		5	5	4–6
scallops	225 g/8 oz	5	5	5–7
snapper	225 g/8 oz	6–8	8–10	5–7
sole	225 g/8 oz	5–6	8–10	4
trout	225 g/8 oz	6–8	8–10	7
yellowtail	225 g/8 oz	6–8	8–10	7

TIME AND SETTINGS FOR PASTA AND GRAINS

Although there are no real time savings in cooking rice and pasta in the microwave, it may be a more foolproof way of cooking as there is no risk of sticking to the pan. Standing is usually necessary to complete cooking.

Cooking times will vary according to the type of pasta. Fresh pasta needs microwaving for only 1 minute. It requires no standing time, but should just be drained and served immediately. Times for dried pasta and rice are given below.

PASTA AND GRAINS COOKING GUIDE
PER 225 G/8 OZ

food	boiling salted water to add	cooking in minutes on full	standing minutes
long grain rice (1 generous cup)	3 cups/725 ml/1¼ pt	14	5
pudding (Carolina) rice (1 generous cup)	2½ cups/600 ml/1 pt		
American (converted) rice (2½ cups)	2½ cups/600 ml/ 1 pint	12	5
brown rice	3½ cups/900 ml/ 1½ pt	30	5
egg noodles & tagliatelle (fettucini) (6 cups)	4 cups/1 litre/1¾ pt with 2 tsp oil	6–8	2–3
spaghetti	4 cups/1 litre/1¾ pt with 2 tsp oil	12	5–10
pasta shells (2 cups) & shapes	4 cups/1 litre/1¾ pt with 2 tsp oil	12–14	5–10
macaroni (2 cups)	4 cups/1 litre/1¾ pt with 2 tsp oil	12–15	2–3
lasagne (6 cups)	4 cups/1 litre/1¾ pt with 2 tsp oil	9	2

CAKES, BREAD AND DESSERTS DEFROSTING GUIDE

product	quantity	minutes on low	standing minutes
bread, whole loaf	1 large	6–8	5–15
bread, whole loaf	1 small	4–6	10
bread, sliced loaf	1 large	6–8	10
bread, sliced loaf	1 small	4–6	5
bread slice	25 g/1 oz	10–15 secs	1–2
bread rolls, crumpets,	2	15–20 secs	1–2
scones (biscuits), etc	4	25–35	1–2
cakes, cream	2	45–60	10
	4	1¼	10
cakes, small	2	30–60	5
cupcakes	4	1¼–1¾	5
cakes, large:			
sponge (yellow) cake	450 g/1 lb	4	10
cheesecake	23 cm/9 in	3–4	20
dough, pizza and bread	450 g/1 lb	4	10
dough, shortcrust and puff	227 g/8 oz	4	20
dough, shortcrust and puff	397 g/14 oz	6	20
mousse (soufflé), small	1	30 secs	15
pie, fruit or cream	650 g/26 oz	5	10
trifle	1	1	15